'...is exemplary account ... an almost thrillerish sense of ¦ loses sight of how the Falcon¦ the wider workings of both the Mafia and the police.'

Sunday Times

'A compelling narrative ... From the "walking corpses" to " 'stinguished cadavers", bomb plots and dissolving dead bodies in acid baths, Follain's work is testimony not only to the determination and bravery of the forces of law and order but also of the arrogance and contempt shown by the Mafia.'

Press Association

'A cool, lucid, always vivid reconstruction ... A gripping chronicle ... A book which reads like a novel but is in fact a true story.'

La Repubblica, Rome

'A book which causes deep anger because you see Italy once again lose its best men, like Falcone and Borsellino, who were exposed to slander even before they were hit by Mafia explosives.'

Roberto Olla, *TG1 News*, Rome

'John Follain, who interviewed Judge Falcone seven months before his death ... relates the assassinations and the incredible race against time of Judge Borsellino, who died 57 days after Falcone, to discover who killed his friend and colleague.'

La Gazzetta del Sud, Bari

John Follain has covered Italy for the *Sunday Times* and the *Sunday Times Magazine* for the past thirteen years. His previous books include DEATH IN PERUGIA, THE LAST GODFATHERS, which was translated into 10 languages, MUSSOLINI'S ISLAND and the international bestseller ZOYA'S STORY. He was voted runner-up for the 2006 Paul Foot Award for Campaigning Journalism, and nominated for the 2008 Magazine Journalism Awards for his interview with the Knox family.

Vendetta

The Mafia, Judge Falcone, and the
Quest for Justice

JOHN FOLLAIN

HODDER

First ~~published~~ ~~in~~ ~~2012~~ ~~by~~ ~~Hodder & Stoug~~hton
An Hachette UK company

First published in paperback in 2012

1

Copyright © John Follain 2012

Map © Neil Gower

The right of John Follain to be identified as the Author of the Work has
been asserted by him in accordance with the Copyright, Designs and
Patents Act 1988.

A CIP catalogue record for this title is available from the British Library

ISBN 978 1 444 71414 2
Ebook ISBN 978 1 444 71413 5

Printed and bound by CPI Group (UK) Ltd, Croydon, CR0 4YY

Hodder & Stoughton policy is to use papers that are natural, renewable
and recyclable products and made from wood grown in sustainable forests.
The logging and manufacturing processes are expected to conform to the
environmental regulations of the country of origin.

Hodder & Stoughton Ltd
338 Euston Road
London NW1 3BH

www.hodder.co.uk

To Giovanni Falcone, Francesca Morvillo, Rocco Dicillo,
Antonio Montinaro and Vito Schifani

And to Paolo Borsellino, Agostino Catalano, Walter Cosina,
Vincenzo Li Muli, Emanuela Loi and Claudio Traina

I believe that each of us must be judged for what he or she has done. What matters are actions, not words.

Giovanni Falcone

It is beautiful to die for something you believe in.

Paolo Borsellino

Contents

MESSINA

Mount
Etna

ENNA

CALTANISSETTA

CATANIA

LENTINI

GELA

SIRACUSA

Principal characters

Investigators

Giovanni Falcone, Palermo prosecutor, Italy's leading anti-Mafia fighter

Paolo Borsellino, ex-Palermo prosecutor, a close friend of Falcone's

Giuseppe Ayala, ex-Palermo prosecutor, also a close friend of Falcone's

Alfonso Sabella, Palermo prosecutor

Gianni De Gennaro, deputy-head of the DIA agency, the Italian FBI

Corleonesi family

Salvatore 'The Beast' Riina, godfather of Cosa Nostra, head of the Corleonesi family

Bernardo 'The Tractor' Provenzano, Riina's closest lieutenant

Leoluca Bagarella, boss from Corleone and Riina's brother-in-law

Antonino 'Little Hand' Giuffrè, boss of the Caccamo clan near Palermo

San Giuseppe Jato family

Giovanni 'The Executioner' Brusca, boss
Mario Santo 'Half Nose' Di Matteo, soldier
Baldassare Di Maggio, soldier

San Lorenzo family, Palermo

Salvatore Biondino, boss, Riina's driver
Giovan Battista Ferrante, soldier
Salvatore Biondo, Ferrante's cousin, soldier

Plotters

Raffaele Ganci, butcher, boss of Palermo's Noce family
Pietro 'The Artificer' Rampulla, buffalo breeder, explosives
    expert
Antonino Gioè, soldier from Altofonte
Gioacchino 'The Industrialist' La Barbera, owner of an
    earthmoving business, boss of the Altofonte family
Salvatore Cancemi, butcher, boss of Palermo's Porta Nuova
    family

Negotiators

Vito Ciancimino, better known as 'Don Vito', ex-mayor of
    Palermo
Massimo Ciancimino, Don Vito's son
Captain Giuseppe De Donno, Special Operations Group
    (ROS), *carabinieri* police
Colonel Mario Mori, Special Operations Group

Collaborators

Tommaso Buscetta, 'The Godfather of Two Worlds', senior
  member of Palermo's Porta Nuova family
Gaspare 'Mr Champagne' Mutolo, car mechanic, soldier
  from Palermo's Partanna-Mondello family
Giuseppe Marchese, car mechanic, a soldier affiliated to the
  Corleonesi, a relative of Riina
Gaspare 'Baldy' Spatuzza, whitewasher, soldier from
  Palermo's Brancaccio family

Prologue:
March 1992

The godfather's beady, deep-set eyes flashed with anger. 'It's time we got moving . . .' Salvatore 'The Beast' Riina whispered.

Sitting behind a rough wooden table, the 'boss of bosses' stared at the four lieutenants standing silently before him. That evening in March 1992, Riina had summoned them to a hilltop farmhouse of yellow tufa stone built like a fortress among bare, treeless brown fields in eastern Sicily. Riina was the only one sitting, perhaps because he hated to be dwarfed by other Mafiosi – the heavily built godfather was also nicknamed 'Shorty' because he was only five feet three inches tall.

After twenty-two years on the run, 'The Beast' was feeling caged. The semi-literate son of poor peasant labourers from the dismal town of Corleone, he had killed his first victim at the age of eighteen in a brawl with other young peasants over a woman. After that, he had bludgeoned his way to the top of Cosa Nostra – or 'Our Affair', as the Mafia is known – turning it into a totalitarian state. One supergrass described him as 'incredibly ignorant' but blessed with intuition and intelligence. 'And at the same time he was like a beast,' the supergrass added. 'His philosophy was that if someone's finger hurt, it was best to cut his arm off – it's safer that way.'

Another collaborator praised Riina's good manners and his 'gentle expression' before adding in the same breath: 'He was the first person to invent the method, before killing someone, of inviting him for a meal, making him eat and relax and making him enjoy himself. After eating, you would strangle him and that would be the end of it . . . You eat, you have fun and then you kill.'

Italian police had given Riina top billing on its list of 16,000 wanted outlaws, and put a price of £500,000 on his head, but the only photograph they had of Riina was from the 1960s and he stayed on the run. Time and time again, the Mafiosi he commanded had kept out of prison by threatening or killing judges and jurors.

But that January the Supreme Court, Italy's highest court, had inflicted nineteen life sentences on Riina and other Mafiosi, locking up another 338 of them for more than twenty-six centuries. The case – the maxi-trial – was postwar Italy's biggest judicial assault on the Mafia. The secret society could no longer consider itself invincible.

Riina had failed the Mafia. That realisation tormented the godfather so much that, according to one of his closest henchmen, he became 'unrecognisable . . . There was a ferocity in his eyes which was frightening. Until then, he had kept everything on a tight rein. But now he started to lose control.'

Riina wasn't used to 'losing control' of anything. But if he did nothing, he feared, the Italian state would go on to lock up hundreds of Mafiosi – for hundreds of years. At stake was the very survival of Cosa Nostra. It was time to act against the prosecutor who had masterminded the maxi-trial – Italy's bravest investigator, whom newspapers labelled the Mafia's 'Number One Enemy': the Sicilian-born Judge Giovanni Falcone.

That day in the farmhouse, one of the four bosses facing Riina dared to break the silence. 'Falcone's gone and done it.'

Riina lifted his hand to shut him up – he was going to do all the talking. 'This year's been terrible,' he said. 'The gentlemen in Rome aren't listening to us; they don't want to listen to us,'

– a reference to obliging politicians the Mafia could usually count on for favours in exchange for votes.

Riina singled out Salvo Lima, a former mayor of Palermo who was now a member of the European parliament, and whom he said had promised to ensure the Supreme Court would not convict the Mafiosi: 'We were supposed to have guarantees at the Supreme Court ... we told Lima that if he didn't respect the deal we'd kill him and all his family ... Nothing, nothing ... even the friend in Rome stopped listening to us ... but what do they think, what the f— are they thinking? Don't they know who we are? Don't they know who the Corleonesi are?'

Cosa Nostra had backed the conservative Christian Democrat party since the end of the Second World War in exchange for virtual impunity. But now the party faction led by the prime minister Giulio Andreotti, which Lima belonged to, could no longer be trusted. 'It gave Falcone a free hand, and it didn't lift a finger to help us in the Supreme Court. We've got to break the horns of all those who didn't keep their promises,' Riina said.

But the brunt of the godfather's anger was directed at Judge Falcone. The judge had moved from the Sicilian capital Palermo to Rome and was setting up an unprecedented agency headed by a 'super-prosecutor' to co-ordinate anti-Mafia investigations nationwide – and, Riina said, Falcone wanted the job for himself.

'We need to eliminate Falcone,' the godfather went on. 'He knows too much, he understands too much, he scares our possible friends. In Rome, Falcone has shown himself much more dangerous than in Palermo. He created the national prosecutor's office so he could head it and not give us a moment's rest.'

Riina interrupted his monologue for a moment, giving the four bosses another withering look. His gaze could strike fear into anyone; as one Mafioso explained, 'a strange light would appear in his eyes which silenced everybody near him ... Everybody was struck dumb, and felt uncomfortable – you could feel death in the air.'

Now Riina's tone changed abruptly, his anger gone. He had made up his mind, and there was work to be done. 'In a few days' time ... tell the *picciotti* [soldiers] that things are going to get hot,' he said.

Cosa Nostra, the godfather added, 'must wage war to make peace.'

Part 1

Plot:

1939–1992

Judge Falcone:
Learning to live and think like Mafiosi

Giovanni Falcone had dedicated most of his career to fighting the Mafia, but he always prided himself on having grown up among Mafiosi. The Kalsa, the Palermo neighbourhood near the harbour where Falcone was born, was once one of the most aristocratic areas of the Sicilian capital but in more recent times had become a place where, as one Mafioso put it, 'more thieves and robbers lived than honest people' and cigarette smugglers became millionaires by switching to heroin trafficking.

As a boy, Falcone played with the children of Mafia bosses in the streets, and went to school with them. A girl he courted without success as a fourteen-year-old crossed paths with him more than two decades later, when her husband was arrested with ten kilos of heroin. Falcone refused to prosecute the case. In a separate affair, a boy he used to play ping-pong with was given a thirty-year prison sentence for drug trafficking.

Falcone had a privileged insight into the organisation. 'I know the Sicilian spirit well,' he explained. 'From an inflexion in the voice, a wink of the eye, I can understand much more than from a long statement. My collaborators know that I know that the Mafia is nothing more than a distortion, an exaggeration, an extreme and aberrant version of the traditional Sicilian way of life.'

In his daily dealings with the Mafia, Falcone always asked himself: 'If I were a Mafioso, what would I do now?' To fight the Mafia, he said, 'you have to learn to live and think like the Mafiosi.'

Nothing predestined Falcone for taking on Cosa Nostra. He was born to a Catholic family on 20 May 1939, his father the head of a provincial chemistry laboratory in Palermo. The city has been the hub of Sicily since the ninth century, and is home to the majority of today's five million Sicilians. Enclosed by mountains, modern-day Palermo is a teeming maze of bygone splendour and romantic decay.

Falcone had been alive only a few moments when something happened that left a lasting impression on his family. 'Just after Giovanni's birth, a white dove flew into the flat. It came in through the open window of a room. It stayed in the room and we fed it; it never flew away, even though the window stayed open,' his sister Maria recalled. She told the story even though she worried that she might be ridiculed for doing so.

Falcone's strict father taught him to work hard and keep his promises. 'He was proud of the fact that he had never drunk a cup of coffee in a bar. There were no trips to the seaside, no holidays,' Falcone remembered. His mother was very energetic, and authoritarian; she rarely showed him any affection. 'Both of them were very demanding parents who expected the maximum from me,' he said.

His mother taught him to be brave from a very young age. When he was a couple of years old, a big stone fell on his foot as he played in a garden; the boy said nothing. When his mother realised what had happened, she took him to hospital. The doctor expressed surprise at his self-control. 'Men don't cry. That's the way I brought up my son,' his mother explained.

The boy would often put his courage to the test. At the age of four or five years old, he had to go down a dark corridor to get to his room. The light switch was too high for him to reach, and he was very scared of the dark, but he didn't want to ask for anyone's help, so he used to run down the corridor instead. At school, he would often get into fights with other children – even with bigger ones, if he thought one of his classmates was being picked on.

For his parents, bravery was an ideal to aim at throughout one's life. His mother encouraged him and his two sisters to lead what she called 'a heroic life'. She had lost a brother in the First World War, who died at the age of eighteen, and spoke with passion of ideals such as 'love for the fatherland', 'heroism' and 'sacrifice'. Falcone's father was himself a wounded veteran – doctors found thirty-three bone fragments in his head but decided not to operate and he was plagued by difficulty walking. From an early age, the children were taught that they should serve their country, whatever the cost; Falcone devoured biographies of Sicilian heroes as well as adventure books by Alexandre Dumas and Joseph Conrad.

As a child, he 'breathed the air of the Mafia with every breath ... I was horrified by the brutality, the murders, the aggression; Cosa Nostra was like a seven-headed Hydra, or an inexorable lava flow, responsible for all the evils of the world.' But he also breathed in what he called 'an "institutional" culture that denied the very existence of the secret society. To even try to give a name to this Sicilian social disease meant surrendering to the "attacks from the north"!' – as if, in divided Italy, the Mafia was an invention of northerners who used it to denounce the supposedly backward and lawless south.

When the time came for him to choose a career, Falcone decided to study at the Naval Academy. One of his teachers praised his 'remarkable aptitude for leadership' but his father feared his independent character would make life in the Navy impossible for him, and put him down for law studies instead. Falcone became a magistrate in 1964, the same year he married his girlfriend, Rita Bonnici, whom he had met two years earlier. He started his career in Lentini, a small town in south-east Sicily, where he handled both civil and criminal cases. He soon decided to specialise in criminal law, and after two years he moved to the port city of Trapani in western Sicily, where he became a prosecutor.

The Mafia was quick to notice Falcone. It was in Trapani that the twenty-eight-year-old received his first death threats. The local clans sent him postcards with drawings of coffins and crosses; Falcone just ignored them.

More than a decade later when he took on his first big investigation into the Mafia, the threats became harder to ignore. He was focusing on Rosario Spatola, a businessman accused of links to the organisation, and the 'Cherry Hill Gambinos' gangsters in Brooklyn. Falcone led the investigation with such determination that he became the first prosecutor to seize bank records in a Mafia case. He deluged the managers of all the banks in the province of Palermo with demands for full details of recent transactions on suspect accounts, as well as receipts for foreign exchange operations. His office quickly became submerged in rolls of computer printouts, which he spent long hours poring through.

Francesco Lo Voi, a trainee magistrate assigned to Falcone at the time, was stunned to see the prosecutor examine all the cheques that he had seized, one by one. Falcone had no computers at his disposal then; instead he painstakingly listed the names on the cheques in piles of notebooks with alphabetical indexes. Lo Voi was impressed by what he saw as Falcone's enormous sense of duty. Commitment was vital – partly because the Mafia was watching. 'In this job, you can't bluff. If you do, they'll find you out straightaway,' Falcone told Lo Voi. Only hard work would enable the anti-Mafia team to measure itself against Cosa Nostra.

To Lo Voi and other potential recruits to the anti-Mafia team, Falcone stressed that their lives would be full of sacrifices for themselves and for their families. 'It will be difficult, you'll have to make a big commitment and work all hours. If you accept that, that's great. But if you don't, there are plenty of other things you can do as magistrates,' Falcone would tell them. However daunting the task, there was still plenty of room for humour. 'Anyone who doesn't know how to smile isn't doing his job seriously,' Falcone confided.

The Spatola case proved fascinating for Falcone. 'The Mafia, seen through the Spatola trial, appeared to me as a world that was enormous, boundless and unexplored,' Falcone recalled. This time, warnings and threats came from his own colleagues as well as defence lawyers. 'He who strokes a tiger risks losing his arm,' one told him. 'I have boundless admiration for you. But if I were you, I wouldn't leave my bodyguards, not even to go to the toilet,' another told him. Falcone pressed on and obtained an unprecedented, heavy prison sentence for Spatola.

Falcone's first big professional victory coincided with tumult in his private life. His fourteen-year marriage collapsed when his wife left him for a judge who had once been his superior. The break-up was particularly agonising for Falcone, as he now became the butt of gossip in the law courts.

A year after the divorce, Falcone fell in love with Francesca, a beautiful, sweet-natured but reserved prosecutor at the juvenile court. Divorced like him, Francesca was the daughter and sister of a judge. Her father had died shortly after she graduated. A surgeon in a Rome hospital accidentally cut through his iliac vein, and was unable to prevent him bleeding to death. Deeply committed to her job, Francesca said of the children whose cases she covered that she would have preferred never to condemn any of them 'because they've already been condemned by life'.

The pair soon became inseparable, and Falcone's family befriended Francesca. Both were shy of displaying their love in public. Giuseppe Ayala, a close friend and colleague of Falcone's, never saw them embrace in front of other people. Occasionally he'd urge them: 'Come on, give each other a kiss!' – but they were too reserved to do so.

If the two were going to a dinner together, they would make their separate ways to the restaurant, mindful of the threats against Falcone. In a rare comment on their life as a couple, Francesca remarked: 'We live one day at a time . . . I don't ever want to think about what could happen to Giovanni.' She said of his professional commitment: 'I know that this is his life. He wouldn't survive without it.'

Only once did Francesca betray the fear she felt for Falcone's safety – without actually naming him. Moments after learning of the murder of General Carlo Alberto Dalla Chiesa and his wife and driver, when their car was ambushed in Palermo in September 1982, Francesca approached her partner's friend, Ayala. He expected her to be worried about Falcone, but instead she expressed concern for Ayala himself: 'Giuseppe, stop. As long as you're still in time – and you are – stop. You're good, you're brilliant, go and do something else. Forget about this damned Mafia. Think about it, I beg you.'

At the time, Ayala was not considered to be sufficiently at risk to warrant an armed escort. Francesca, he realised, had long understood that it was impossible to expect Falcone to stop fighting the Mafia. Ayala decided he did not want to give up either, and never told Falcone what Francesca had said to him.

Someone put up a poster, in big capital letters, at the spot where Dalla Chiesa was shot: '*HERE DIES THE HOPE OF HONEST PALERMITANS.*'

Falcone and 'The Godfather of Two Worlds'

Falcone did not hesitate when Rocco Chinnici, head of Palermo's investigating magistrates, asked him to join the anti-Mafia team he had created. When she found out about her brother's new job, Falcone's sister Maria allowed him to see her worries for his safety – for the first and last time. She asked him simply: 'Why?'

Without batting an eyelid, Falcone replied: 'Because you only live once.'

Falcone threw himself into his task, regularly working fifteen-hour days. For lunch he'd allow himself a half-hour break for a sandwich at his desk in the cavernous Palace of Justice, built under the dictator Benito Mussolini in the Fascist style in white marble with tall square columns. After long flights abroad on business, he would go straight to his office and get to work, joking: 'To beat the time difference, you have to pretend it doesn't exist.' Much of his desk was covered with stacks of case files, court rulings and volumes of the penal code, but he made space on some bookshelves for a collection of miniature geese made of glass, ceramics, terracotta and wood. Collecting them was one of his few hobbies. On his foreign trips he'd try to look for new pieces to add to his collection; friends and relatives also gave them to him as presents.

Falcone swiftly won respect as an exceptionally gifted and tenacious investigator. Aware that Mafiosi put a premium on facts because truth was what he called 'a law of survival' for them, he never lied to bosses. Each time he began his questioning, he would warn the Mafioso bluntly: 'You can say whatever you like, but remember that this interview will be a Calvary for you because I will try by any means to make you contradict yourself. If you manage to convince me of the truth of what you say, then and only then will I be able to consider the possibility of safeguarding your right to life, and protecting you from both the bureaucracy of the state and from Cosa Nostra.'

Mafiosi quickly found out that Falcone was a redoubtable interrogator. When one witness he was questioning proved particularly cagey, Falcone simply listened to his story. As he listened, the prosecutor kept his eyes down, peering at documents from the case file through a small pair of glasses. At a certain point, Falcone suddenly raised his gaze to stare above the rim of his glasses at the ceiling; then, slowly and ostentatiously, he lowered his gaze to stare straight into the witness's eyes.

After a long, silent stare, Falcone burst out: 'Are you taking me for a fool?'

The shocked witness immediately admitted he had been hiding what he knew.

Falcone made a point of never yielding an inch. It was essential, he believed, that Mafiosi see him as a representative of the state, with all the authority that gave him. 'When I was interrogating Michele Greco, the head of the Palermo Mafia,' Falcone related, 'from time to time we would say to each other, "Look me in the eyes!" because we both understood the importance of backing up what we were saying with our expressions.' Questioning another boss, Falcone saw red when the Mafioso addressed him as 'Mr Falcone . . .' Falcone stood up and retorted: 'No, wait; *you* are Mr So-and-so, *I* am Judge Falcone.' The boss promptly apologised.

With unrivalled determination, Falcone exploited a new law that for the first time defined Mafia association as a crime, and also gave prosecutors sweeping powers to investigate the bank accounts of individuals suspected of laundering funds. Until then, the state had never been able to tackle Cosa Nostra as an organisation. The law was the brainchild of the Communist politician Pio La Torre, a campaigning member of the Rome parliament's anti-Mafia commission. Stalled for two years, the law was only finally approved by parliament – in just ten days – after both La Torre and General Dalla Chiesa had been murdered.

Falcone's growing reputation sparked envy among his colleagues in the Palermo law courts, nicknamed 'the Palace of Poisons' because of the gossip and backbiting which was rife there. Falcone, who was among the most reserved of Palermo magistrates, was mocked as 'the star judge' and 'the sheriff'. Colleagues accused him of wanting to lead every investigation in Italy. A senior magistrate suggested to Falcone's boss, Chinnici: 'Bury him under mountains of minor trials; that way he will leave us in peace.'

According to a close friend, the fact that Falcone never had many influential friends in the law courts was because he was exceptional. He was clearly head and shoulders above the others and that created a lack of understanding, rivalry and petty jealousy.

The constant sniping by colleagues dismayed Falcone. The ashtray on his desk had to be emptied several times a day. He smoked some fifty Dunhill cigarettes a day, a habit which Francesca, and his sisters, tried again and again to make him give up. They all failed. 'He realised it was harmful, but he went on smoking . . . I understood why. He worked off the daily disappointments with his cigarettes. They'd become his inseparable friends,' his sister Anna said. Falcone would also combat stress by going for long swimming sessions at a local pool or in the sea near Palermo; a former rower and gymnast, he could swim for miles.

Falcone's tenacity drove him on. One of his greatest qualities, according to another friend, was 'the capacity to suffer, to bear much more than others, to never give up'. Falcone did not give up when his boss, the chief prosecutor Chinnici, was blown up in front of his home, along with two bodyguards and the porter of the block of flats where he lived, in the summer of 1983. A car bomb exploded as Chinnici walked the few yards from his home to his armour-plated car one morning; a third bodyguard at the wheel of the car survived, shielded from the blast by the car door. Falcone's mother died two months after Chinnici's murder. Her family believed that her death had been hastened by constant worry over her son's safety.

Falcone believed he was simply doing his job as 'a servant of the state'. He had nothing in common with the heroes he'd read about as a boy. 'I'm not Robin Hood,' he liked to joke. 'I'm not a kamikaze pilot; I'm not a Trappist monk. I'm just working for the state in enemy territory.' It was all too easy to be labelled a hero in Sicily, he quipped: 'In this island where everything is extreme, it's normal to become vile or a hero. And anyone who does his duty becomes a hero.'

In fact, Falcone was a shy, serious figure. He and Francesca rarely accepted social invitations – partly because of his job. He knew he could easily fall into a trap. In this he followed in the footsteps of the slain General Dalla Chiesa, who had explained: 'The Mafia is cautious, slow, it takes your measure, it listens, it makes sure about you from a distance . . . For instance, a friend who has done business with you or worked in your office says, as if by chance: "Why don't we go and have a coffee with so-and-so?" The name is illustrious. If I don't know that heroin is flowing in rivers through that house, I'll go, and serve as their cover. If I know it and go, it's a signal that I'm prepared to give my sanction.'

A man of few words, Falcone seemed to want to keep people at a distance. He didn't suffer fools gladly, and could become irascible if the person he was speaking to was vague or ill-informed. But when he felt at ease – with his family, friends, bodyguards or assistants – he could be very affectionate. He was often witty and fun to be with.

Falcone's friend Ayala, who never heard him raise his voice, pulled his leg about how reserved he was. 'Look, we always thought that self-control was typically English. We got it wrong – you invented self-control and the English copied it,' Ayala told him. Falcone laughed.

Falcone treasured the small pleasures in life – a good meal with Francesca, chatting with friends, reading books and listening to music. His friend Giuseppe Ayala often went to see him in the evening at his fourth-floor flat in a modern block on Via Emanuele Notarbartolo, in the heart of Palermo. The street was named after a marquis killed by the Mafia in the late nineteenth century because he fought corruption in the Bank of Sicily, which he had headed; they stabbed him twenty-three times in a train and then threw his body off it. The marquis was the first of the Mafia's 'distinguished cadavers', as leading personalities slain by the secret society are known.

Because of the need for escorts, Falcone and Ayala preferred to have dinner at each other's homes rather than go out to a restaurant. Once, Falcone called Ayala and told him: 'Come over for dinner. I've got sod all but we'll invent a meal.'

'Giovanni, you invite me to dinner and then you tell me you've got nothing to eat?' Ayala asked.

'You bring a piece of bread and one fish and I will multiply them and we'll both have plenty to eat,' Falcone joked.

At Falcone's flat, the coffee table was, like his office desk, covered with case files. The pair would sometimes work together in Falcone's study in the evening, but Ayala soon became exasperated when his friend played his favourite music – Giuseppe Verdi's *Requiem* – again and again.

'I'm going to go and do some reading in the sitting-room; this music is really getting on my nerves. I'm sure it's the most beautiful music in the world but bloody hell, Giovanni, a *requiem*? I'm not asking for pop music but . . .' Ayala protested once.

Falcone smiled and turned the music off.

For the first two decades of his career, Falcone believed that members of Cosa Nostra never betrayed its law of silence: there could never be such a thing as a Mafia collaborator because silence was a golden rule of the secret society. Mafia prisoners did everything except talk, he explained: 'There is the Mafioso who barricades himself in his cell; the one who fakes insanity; the one who is forced by the Mafia to fake insanity; the insolent one who claims he was kidnapped . . . Then there is the genteel Mafioso, obsequious, with a humble glance, until lightning shoots from his eyes as he pretends to be looking away.'

But in 1984, Falcone met the dapper and urbane Tommaso Buscetta, known as 'The Godfather of Two Worlds' because of his criminal dealings on both sides of the Atlantic. His questioning gave investigators a revolutionary insight into the Mafia – starting with the discovery that its members called it 'Cosa Nostra' (Our Affair).

Buscetta, born the last of seventeen children in the Porta di Termini neighbourhood of Palermo, a few hundred yards from where Falcone grew up, was accused of being one of the co-ordinators of Cosa Nostra's drug empire with accomplices in Brazil, Peru, Bolivia, Colombia, the United States and Europe. At the Ucciardone prison in Palermo, Buscetta took good care of himself. A fellow convict explained: 'Buscetta was very meticulous about his person, using only the finest products. He never finished a bottle of toilet water or cake of soap; he gave the rest away as gifts. His casual clothes, his jeans, were always designer made, perfect . . . Only his coffee was prepared in jail; men would take turns to bring it to him piping hot. Otherwise, his breakfast, lunch and dinner came from the best restaurants in Palermo. Buscetta was a boss – in fact, The Boss.'

Despite such home comforts, Buscetta decided to betray the secret society after Riina's Corleonesi clan murdered not only two of his sons, but also a brother, a son-in-law and four nephews.

When Falcone began questioning Buscetta, the supergrass warned him: 'After these interviews with me you will become a celebrity. But they will seek to destroy you, both physically and professionally. And they will do the same to me. Do not forget that an account opened with the Cosa Nostra can never be closed. Do you still wish to interview me?'

Falcone did indeed wish to interview him, and after their first meeting Falcone was so impressed by Buscetta's testimony that he was convinced the end of the Mafia was at last within reach. 'We're just that far away . . .' Falcone told his colleague Lo Voi, gesturing with his thumb and index finger an inch from each other. Buscetta shared that belief, but not for long. 'We deluded ourselves that this time the Mafia would be defeated; that there would never again be the Mafia in our land,' Buscetta recalled.

Over the next three months, Buscetta revealed the Mafia's pyramid-like structure, with a godfather at its summit ruling over the *Cupola* – the commission of bosses from the Palermo province – and its 5,000 members from the rank of soldier upwards. Soldiers were divided into Mafia families, each headed by a *capo-famiglia*, or boss. Three neighbouring families formed a *mandamento*, or district, headed by a *capo-mandamento*, or district boss. Buscetta detailed the initiation

ritual and the distorted 'code of honour' its members paid lip
service to. He defined Cosa Nostra as 'crime plus intelligence
and *omertà*' – the Mafia's law of silence.

For Buscetta, the Mafia had the same values and duties as
the sect of the Beati Paoli, which according to popular legend
dated back to the twelfth century. According to folklore, the
Beati Paoli were like Robin Hood, siding with the poor against
the tyranny of the foreign powers that ruled Sicily from afar
– who over the centuries have included Phoenicians, Greeks,
Ancient Romans, Vandals, Arabs, Normans, Spaniards and
Bourbons. The sect was, in the words of one chronicler, 'an
occult and mysterious force ... Common people, artisans,
sailors, bourgeois, lawyers formed this terrible body, which
took it upon itself to judge the actions of men, to re-exam-
ine judicial sentences and to repair the ills caused by those in
power.'

The truth is that the Mafia has nothing to do with the Beati
Paoli – apart from hostility to foreign rulers. The Mafia has
its roots in the nineteenth century, as a tool of absentee land-
owners eager to defend their Sicilian estates. But that was
too prosaic a reality for Mafiosi, and Buscetta himself never
stopped believing in the Beati Paoli and in Cosa Nostra's
'code of honour'.

Asked long after his betrayal whether he still saw himself
as a Mafioso, he replied: 'If you mean by Mafioso a man who
keeps his word, who has dignity, even being as they say *pentito*
[repentant], but I am not at all *pentito* ... I define myself as
a man disappointed by the Mafia, a man who has contrib-
uted so much to the Mafia and who sees his own children
murdered for no reason, disappear into thin air. I don't think
any father could go on living in such an environment.'

During his meetings with Falcone, Buscetta grew so close
to the prosecutor that he gave him advice on how to avoid
becoming an easy target for the Mafia. Buscetta warned him

against slipping into a daily routine. 'Sir, you mustn't get into habits which the Mafiosi will find out about. You mustn't go for a coffee at 8.05 a.m., and then buy your paper at 8.10 a.m.,' Buscetta told him.

The two men discussed their possible early deaths, and Buscetta was so shocked by Falcone's fatalism that he described it as 'incredible'. Buscetta explained: '[Falcone] said his mind and soul were prepared for death. He was prepared. He believed that escaping the *mafiosa* vendetta was very difficult.'

The prosecutor Ayala was so stunned by Buscetta's testimony that he asked Falcone: 'Are you sure Buscetta isn't talking crap? It's like a novel!'

'What do you mean, a novel? It's all true,' Falcone retorted.

Before Buscetta, as Falcone explained, he and his colleagues had only a superficial knowledge of Cosa Nostra. Buscetta allowed them to begin 'to look inside it . . . He gave us the essential keys to the interpretation of the Mafia, a language, a code. For us he was like a language teacher.' The 'language' which Buscetta taught Falcone enabled the prosecutor to send to trial an unprecedented 475 alleged Mafiosi in the maxi-trial, for which a special bunker courtroom was built by the Ucciardone prison. The prosecution file for the case ran to 400,000 pages; 200 lawyers represented the accused.

In his summing up, the prosecutor Ayala said the evidence demonstrated that Cosa Nostra was 'a state within a state, an anti-state, with its own government, army, territory, rituals, moral code and juridical order' – which meant that the court should convict Mafiosi as collectively responsible for its crimes.

When the court withdrew to consider its verdict, Michele 'The Pope' Greco, who owed his nickname to his faith and dignified bearing (and was accused of seventy-eight murders), called out a thinly veiled threat: 'Let your conscience guide you. I wish you peace, tranquillity of spirit ... I hope that peace may be with you for the rest of your lives.'

The court responded with nineteen life sentences and 2,665 years in prison for over three hundred Mafiosi. Buscetta's testimony also made possible many other cases, among them the Pizza Connection drug-trafficking case in the United States. The supergrass paid a heavy price for his betrayal. Cosa Nostra went on to eliminate even more of his relatives.

Years later in court, Buscetta took to task his chief enemy, the Corleone boss Luciano Leggio. 'I have something more than him,' Buscetta said. 'I know where his son is, but I did not go to kill him because he did nothing to me ... If I had the possibility, I would kill [Leggio], in any circumstance, even in court. If somebody brought me a gun, I would do him in in front of the judge. It's not fury, it's not anger. It's just that I am a father.'

Buscetta could never forgive the men who murdered his sons.

Nor was the Mafia ever to forgive Falcone.

Giovanni Brusca, 'The Executioner'

Every member of the Mafia has to know how to kill, but nobody was as skilled at the task as Giovanni Brusca. He committed so many murders they called him 'The Executioner'. By his own reckoning, Brusca either personally carried out or ordered the murder of 'a lot more than a hundred people, and definitely less than two hundred' people.

For Brusca, who was also known as 'The Pig' because of his fat stomach, murder was nothing to be ashamed of, and simply part of a Mafioso's job. 'In his heart, a Mafioso isn't a bloodthirsty person or a terrorist. The rule is that he kills on behalf of the organisation,' Brusca explained years later. He was a man whose lack of education showed in his speech, which was peppered with Sicilian dialect and sometimes incoherent. 'We "men of honour" made up a state of our own. I was a soldier who served that state. A loyal soldier . . . The only reason I committed crimes was to obey the interests of Cosa Nostra.'

Judge Falcone understood that disobedience was almost never an option within Cosa Nostra: 'In ninety-nine per cent of cases, when a man of honour receives an order to kill, he has no other choice but to obey,' Falcone remarked. 'If he has to kill, he kills. Without questioning himself or anyone else. Without exhibiting compassion. If you hesitate over whether or not to kill, you'll be a dead man too.'

*   *   *

Born in early 1957 at a time when Cosa Nostra was so powerful that many officials denied it even existed, Brusca had
'always' been in the Mafia state, as he said himself. He was
born into it, as his father Bernardo headed the clan in San
Giuseppe Jato, an ancient town set in the hills near Palermo
whose inhabitants scraped a living chiefly from corn, olives
and grapes.

Brusca never breathed a critical word about his father.
Bernardo, he said, was 'a man of honour of the old school'
who believed in friendship, and was neither ambitious nor
greedy for wealth – unlike his son.

Brusca was only five years old when he first set foot in
prison. When his father was in Palermo's Ucciardone jail, the
boy's mother thrust him through a hole in the wall with a
bundle of laundry so that his father could see him.

It was more difficult getting the boy to go to school. He
hated it so much that she resorted to beating him every day
to make him go. His most vivid memory of school was also
of violence: an exasperated teacher once grabbed hold of his
ears and lifted him up in the air then slapped him hard in
the face. His mother would also beat him to make him go to
church, and even briefly managed to make an altar boy of her
wayward son.

Brusca left school altogether at the age of ten. While still
a teenager, he started supplying nuts, almonds and olive oil
from southern Sicily to pastry makers in Palermo. But his
father had less legitimate plans for him, and when Brusca was
twelve, ordered him to bring food, clothes and other supplies
to the fugitive Corleonesi boss Bernardo Provenzano, who
was hiding in a neighbour's home.

He was only fourteen when his father made him an accomplice to murder. One morning after killing two people Brusca's
father went home and ordered: 'If someone comes and asks
you questions, I never moved from here.' From that day on,

Brusca proudly helped his father clean and oil the pistols and rifles that he kept buried in bags near the house.

His first experience of murder, at eighteen, was an unpromising one. He had no idea why the victim had to die, but that didn't bother him. Together with two others he ambushed the designated victim in the street as he drove past them in a van. They fired dozens of bullets but failed to kill the man, who managed to escape even though he was wounded, and died of his injuries months later in hospital.

In his next assignment a year later, Brusca did better. Armed with a double-barrelled gun, he waited with two accomplices for a local thief whom his father's clan had decreed must be eliminated. They squatted behind some bushes outside a cinema. When the film ended, they shot the thief dead in the middle of the crowd, miraculously avoiding injuring anyone else. Brusca raced off through deserted lanes to his home, which was less than a mile away. He then hid his gun, changed his clothes and went back to the cinema to 'enjoy' the sight of the police arriving, as he candidly admitted.

At nineteen, with a solid Mafia pedigree and two murders under his belt, Brusca qualified for membership of the organisation. His father gathered more than a dozen bosses at his home. One was the Corleonesi boss Riina, whom Brusca called 'godfather' as a mark of respect. He thought his father had invited them for a Mafia banquet. In fact this was no meal, but the secret society's ancient ritual of initiation.

With his mother out of the way – women were banned from such ceremonies – the bosses started asking Brusca questions: 'Are you capable of killing a man? Are you capable of committing crimes?' Brusca couldn't understand why they were asking; hadn't he already shown he was capable of murder?

It was only a little later, when he was called before Riina and the bosses who were sitting around a huge round table, that he began to understand it was his initiation into the Mafia. On the table lay a pistol, a dagger and a small image of a saint.

'Do you want to become part of Cosa Nostra?' one of the bosses asked. They told him that he must remain faithful to the organisation if he was ever arrested, and that he must never betray its law of silence.

A boss took hold of one of Brusca's fingers and pricked it with a needle. A few drops of blood were squeezed out, enough to stain the holy image. Riina set fire to the image and then, his hands cupped above Brusca's, made him hold the image while it burnt. The flames began to burn Brusca's hands and he tried to drop the image, but Riina prevented him.

'If you betray Cosa Nostra, your flesh will burn as this image burns,' Riina warned.

Brusca learnt the rules that a 'man of honour' must obey. Never touch the woman of another Mafioso, never do anything without the permission of your clan boss, and always be ready to serve Cosa Nostra. The dagger and the pistol on the table, he realised, were symbols of certain death to anyone who violated those rules. Cosa Nostra also banned stealing and exploiting prostitutes. Finally, Brusca was warned never to talk about the organisation's business in front of strangers.

The initiation ritual over, Riina and each boss in turn solemnly embraced him, kissed him on both cheeks and toasted his entry into the Mafia with champagne.

Brusca joined the Mafia of his own free will, without any pressure from his father. He joined because for him life in the secret society seemed 'the good life' – membership brought money, respect and authority over others. Mafiosi like Brusca genuinely believed they were not committing crimes but rather helping the community at large. As Paolo Campo, a boss from southern Sicily who was in his mid-eighties, once explained in court: 'I was born and will die Mafioso, if by Mafia one means, as I mean, be good to your neighbour, give something to people in need, find jobs for the unemployed and give help to people in difficulty.'

Mafia membership however also meant murder on a grand scale. Brusca killed without hesitation. 'I've always been very cool-headed before, during and after a crime. I might hesitate a bit before becoming "operative". But once I'd made my mind up, all the worries and fears and doubts would disappear,' he explained. On one occasion, a boss asked him to look out for a tractor and kill anyone he saw riding on it. 'I found three and I killed three,' Brusca said starkly.

His priorities could be bizarre. On one occasion, he decided to go ahead with the murder of a young man even though his accomplice had failed to turn up because of a road accident. 'We were in a hurry, [the victim] was getting married a week later . . . We certainly couldn't turn his bride into a widow!' he explained.

But usually all that mattered was to get the job done. Brusca would often begin by torturing victims to 'make them talk'. Not that whether they talked or not made the slightest difference to their fate, as Brusca would kill both those who remained silent and those who confessed to what was often a trumped-up offence.

His interrogations lasted half an hour at most, and victims almost never confessed, even under torture. Brusca described it all in his customary deadpan tone: 'We'd hit the guy on the legs with a hammer, saying to him: "Talk or we'll break them . . ." We might pull his ears with pliers, but only to hurt him and to make him understand that we were serious. It was useless. At that point the guy knew perfectly well that we'd kill him. The condemned showed superhuman strength. We'd realise that and we'd say the fateful word: "*Niscemuninne*"

[Let's be done with it].' The torturers would then strangle the victim.

It took five men to carry out the task. Two would hold his arms, another two would hold his feet, and the fifth would pull a thin cord of nylon around his neck. It took about ten minutes for him to die.

Strangulation was one of Brusca's favourite techniques – it was fast and discreet. Early in his Mafia career, he disposed of bodies by burning them on specially built, giant grills. It was a lengthier business than the act of killing – he'd start in the early morning and wouldn't be finished until sunset. It took lorry-loads of wood to keep the fire going.

But from the early 1980s onwards, Brusca switched to a far quicker method – he began dissolving the bodies in acid, a substance used by jewellers to clean precious metals. It was readily available from building sites, where it was used to wash bricks. Each victim needed eleven gallons.

First he warmed the acid up with a burner to accelerate the process of disintegration. When a body was plunged into the white, milky liquid, the acid would start sizzling like boiling oil. Brusca was always careful to make sure that the victim was indeed dead before he started the process. The acid would cause a live person to go into spasms and the last thing he wanted was to be splashed by acid. It would dissolve a body in three to four hours, or even faster if someone stirred the mixture with a stick.

To Brusca's frustration, the disintegration was never complete. 'The body dissolves slowly; the victim's teeth don't dissolve. The bones of the face get deformed. Part of the pelvis can stay intact ... When it's over there's practically nothing left. At that point we take what's left and we throw it away somewhere,' Brusca explained. Remains such as a wedding ring, or gold teeth, would be swiftly hammered to bits.

When fellow Mafiosi in Palermo mocked Brusca and his friends, calling them 'peasants' and 'louts', or joked about their shoes being caked with mud because they came from a small town in the countryside, he would reply: 'And what about you? What lovely water you drink in Palermo . . .' – the stream that Brusca threw remains into fed one of the main reservoirs supplying the Sicilian capital.

Brusca felt no qualms about the way he treated human life – or death. In his memoirs, he makes a list of some of his worst crimes – torture, strangulation, dissolving corpses in acid, or roasting them on big grills – and remarks clinically: 'Some supergrasses say today they feel disgust for what they did. I can speak for myself: I've never been upset by these things.'

Life in the Mafia was good to Brusca. Mafiosi believe they live life to the full – the more impunity they enjoy, the better – and Brusca was no exception. A judge once questioned a Mafioso about the murder of the boss Salvatore Inzerillo at the age of thirty-seven – he was shot dead with a Kalashnikov in 1981. 'Isn't it a pity to die so young?' the judge asked. The Mafioso replied: 'Inzerillo died at thirty-seven, agreed. But his thirty-seven years were like eighty years for an ordinary person. Inzerillo *lived well*. He had a great many things from life. Others wouldn't have a hundredth of those things. It isn't a pity to die at that age if you've done, had and seen all the things Inzerillo did, saw and had. He didn't die tired or dissatisfied with life. He died sated with life. That's the difference.'

Brusca always had the equivalent of a couple of million pounds on him, carried no weapons, and was always on the move between the many flats he rented in Palermo and the surrounding area. In a sign of the Mafia's power, relatives and friends who otherwise had nothing to do with the secret society gave him hospitality for months at a time.

When Brusca went clothes shopping, he spent lavishly on designer labels such as Lacoste and Missoni, as he did on his collection of Rolex, Cartier and other precious watches. He made a point of avoiding restaurants and shops that were popular with other Mafiosi. 'I've always tried to keep my activity as a "man of honour" separate from my private life,' he explained. And when, in 1991, his girlfriend Rosaria gave birth to their son Davide, he kept the boy's existence secret, even from his own parents. The boss was worried that rival Mafiosi might kidnap or kill him. Brusca insisted that Davide would never join Cosa Nostra.

Despite being on the run, Brusca moved about freely; he travelled hidden in a van escorted by Mafia bodyguards who were armed with AK-47 Kalashnikov rifles. If a police patrol stopped the van and opened the back door for a routine check, the bodyguards had orders to shoot immediately. When he had to visit San Giuseppe Jato, Brusca would hide in the boot of a car while an accomplice drove him there and back. He did this as rarely as possible, complaining it made him feel claustrophobic. Brusca had more than his fair share of luck. He went through dozens of roadblocks but was never stopped. The police did arrest him once, but he spent only three weeks in Palermo's Ucciardone prison, accused of the trivial offence of setting fire to a lorry.

A passionate rally enthusiast, Brusca didn't hesitate to use his Mafia membership in order to give himself an unusual advantage over his opponents. Whenever he needed spare parts for the car he was driving, he would simply steal another and help himself. It was one of the few crimes he admitted to committing for selfish reasons, rather than for the secret society.

Such was Brusca's weight in the organisation that no one ever reproached him for such misdemeanours. Brusca could do no ill. 'This boy's very bright, he'll go far,' the influential boss

Buscetta said of him. Buscetta's sworn enemy, the godfather Riina, agreed and took him under his wing.

Their partnership went back many years. It was Riina who had presided at Brusca's initiation ritual. Soon afterwards, during the so-called 'Mafia war' of the early 1980s which pitted Riina against rival clans, and in which about a thousand Mafiosi died, Brusca helped to save Riina's skin. When Riina's enemy, Stefano 'The Prince' Bontate, discovered where Riina was living with his wife and children in Palermo, Brusca rushed to fetch them and drove them to his own family home, where they stayed for several months.

It was on Brusca, one of the most trusted allies of the Corleonesi clan, that Riina's choice fell when it was time for the godfather to pick an assassin to rid him of Judge Falcone.

For 'The Executioner', it was to be his most challenging assignment ever.

Death as 'second nature'

Falcone had no illusions about the risks he ran. Mindful of the supergrass Buscetta's warning that 'an account opened with the Cosa Nostra can never be closed', Falcone wrote in his memoirs: 'Sure, they haven't killed me yet, but the show's not over yet. My account with Cosa Nostra is still open. And I know that I will only close it with my death, natural or otherwise.'

To journalists who invariably asked him how he coped with the fear that he lived with day after day, Falcone replied candidly: 'Naturally I carry the thought of death with me wherever I go. But, as Montaigne said, it soon becomes second nature. So, of course you stay on your guard, you calculate, you observe, you organise your life, avoid getting into a routine, keep away from crowds and any other sort of situation where you're not in control. But you also acquire a large dose of fatalism, because there are so many ways to die, let's face it: a car crash, your plane might be blown up, an overdose, cancer, or even no reason at all!'

In private, however, Falcone had little doubt as to how he would die, confiding to a colleague in Palermo's law courts: 'I will die at the hands of the Mafia; the Mafia will kill me.' To his colleague Lo Voi, Falcone said: 'Listen, the decision has already been taken, there's a contract out.' According to Lo Voi, Falcone didn't know when or how his murder would be carried out, but he realised that he had come out so strongly against the Mafia that it would inevitably target him.

Falcone had a heavy, and typically Sicilian, dose of fatalism in his character; the whole of Sicily was 'impregnated with the culture of death', he remarked. 'Here the day of the dead is a huge celebration: we offer cakes called "skulls", made of rock-hard sugar. Solitude, pessimism and death are the themes of our literature ... It is almost as though we are a people who have lived too long and suddenly feel tired, weary, emptied, like Tomasi di Lampedusa's Don Fabrizio' in the novel *The Leopard*.

But Falcone was damned if he was going to make it easy for his enemy. For him, managing personal security was the first task for anyone taking on the Mafia; it was a question of professionalism, like knowing the law inside out. 'I know the risks that I run doing the job I do, and I do not believe I should give a gift to the Mafia by offering myself as an easy target,' Falcone explained. 'Those who represent the state in enemy territory are duty-bound to be invulnerable. At least within the limits of what is feasible.'

Falcone looked after his own safety meticulously. Shortly before the murder of his boss Chinnici, the justice ministry in Rome sent him what it described as 'a bullet-proof raincoat'. Falcone was unconvinced. One Sunday afternoon, he took his bodyguards to the countryside near Palermo and asked them to test the raincoat; they effortlessly riddled it with holes.

Falcone was first assigned bodyguards – two of them – in the summer of 1980, on the day after two killers on a motor-cycle shot dead Gaetano Costa, the then chief prosecutor in Palermo, as he browsed at a bookstall near his home. A few years later, Falcone's protection swelled to thirty-six police officers, serving in shifts, each equipped with bullet-proof jackets and machine-guns. They manned four escort cars which rushed him across the Sicilian capital, blue lights flashing and sirens screaming. A police helicopter hovered above his convoy on its way to and from his home and the airport.

When the convoy reached Falcone's block of flats, where an armed officer in a sentry box kept a permanent watch on the entrance, three bodyguards would go up in the lift to his flat on the fourth floor with him, while another two ran up the stairs to precede them. A bodyguard spent the night on the landing outside his front door.

The commotion that Falcone's comings and goings involved exasperated his neighbours, one of whom sent a letter of complaint to a local newspaper. Defining herself 'an honest citizen who pays her taxes', the neighbour suggested that Falcone and his anti-Mafia colleagues should be housed in purpose-built villas on Palermo's outskirts in order to guarantee peace and quiet 'for us citizen-workers' and, above all, stop Palermitans being regularly wounded or killed 'for no reason' in attacks on prosecutors or judges.

Such outbursts dismayed Falcone, who had a visceral love for his home city; he ruefully compared the Palermitans to spectators at a *corrida*, or bullfight, for their failure to take a stand against the Mafia. The revelations he had obtained from the supergrass Buscetta, the convictions handed down in the maxi-trial – none of this had changed the popular consensus on which Cosa Nostra thrived. Just like the murdered General Dalla Chiesa, Falcone was, for many, a troublemaker, a threat to society.

When General Dalla Chiesa was still alive, a prominent Palermo lawyer had protested that the general might be 'a disaster for Sicily'. The lawyer added: 'If he gets to be a super-policeman against the drug traffic, he'll end by ruining this city. Imagine everybody who lives off drugs being thrown out of work. They'd sack our homes. They'd hold us up, break into our stores and offices. Restaurants wouldn't be safe. Our wives couldn't go out in furs. We couldn't go out at night. There'd be no more peace, believe me.'

*   *   *

For Falcone, the escort of bodyguards was 'part of the game, he had to put up with it and put up with it he did,' according to his friend Giuseppe Ayala, a fellow prosecutor. Falcone complained about his escort only once. A keen swimmer, Falcone told Ayala how he had set out for a long swim off a beach near Palermo. Two bodyguards followed him into the sea, but they were unable to keep up with him and he unwittingly gave them the slip. By the time Falcone realised, the officers were back on the beach. He saw they were talking into their radios and swam back as fast as he could. They told him they had called for a patrol boat to come and pick him up; but he was in time to cancel the call-out.

'You realise what this means? I can't even swim anymore!' he told Ayala, before adding with a rueful grin: 'Can you imagine the newspapers? "When he wants a swim, Judge Falcone even bothers a patrol boat." ' From then on, he decided to swim almost exclusively in a covered swimming-pool, going at 7 a.m. to ensure that he and his escort were not a nuisance to anyone.

When he discovered that Ayala had – voluntarily – shaken off his own bodyguards several times, Falcone reprimanded his friend affectionately: 'Listen, you can't allow yourself to make these mistakes. If such a big security cordon has been organised for you, you have to accept it. You can't allow yourself the luxury of avoiding it, not even just a few times.'

Unlike Falcone, Ayala never stopped complaining about his escort. One of the things Ayala hated was that his bodyguards were under orders never to take the same route to a given destination. Ayala felt this was not only an infuriating waste of time, but also senseless.

He vented his frustration with Falcone. 'What's the point of all these sirens, all these alternative routes?' Ayala asked.

'I get all this too,' Falcone shrugged.

'I know, but what's the point of having alternative routes when we always take the same motorway to get to the airport and back?' Ayala insisted.

'Yes, you're right. I'll mention it,' Falcone said. But Ayala never heard anything more about this. He dismissed the idea, something for which he was to bitterly reproach himself.

The constant shadowing by bodyguards didn't dent Falcone's sense of humour. When he called at Ayala's family home, his friend's eight-year-old daughter Vittoria would rush to answer the Entryphone. '*Pronto* [Hello],' she would say.

'And who are you?' Falcone would ask.

'I'm Vittoria.'

Falcone would gently pull her leg. 'And you say "*pronto*" to me? You're a girl; you have to say "*pronta*". "*Pronto*" is masculine. Your brother Paolo can say it, not you.'

And all this while the traffic in the street was held up by half a dozen armed bodyguards waiting for Falcone to enter the block of flats.

A good sense of humour helped Falcone to cope with the risks he ran. 'There's only one thing missing from my personal history: death,' Falcone liked to joke in a deadpan tone. He would often joke that life didn't matter to him. He was convinced a natural death in his bed was not for him. 'But it wasn't an obsession. He'd laugh about it. That prediction made him even more determined to achieve the concrete results which he cared about the most,' his colleague Pietro Grasso explained.

Falcone and Paolo Borsellino, his closest friend and a fellow prosecutor, pulled each other's legs about which of them would be murdered first. Borsellino often told his more famous friend, half seriously: 'Giovanni, as long as you're alive I don't have anything to fear.'

One day, Borsellino entered Falcone's office and told him: 'Giovanni, you've got to give me the keys to your safe.'

'Why?' Falcone asked.

'Because if they bump you off we won't know how to open it,' Borsellino replied.

'I'm not giving you the keys, and if they kill me I don't give a damn how you open the safe,' Falcone shot back.

Falcone and Borsellino even managed to joke about an enforced stay on the Asinara prison island in Sardinia, where they spent several weeks living as convicts with their families after hearing that the Mafia had issued a death sentence on the two prosecutors on the eve of the maxi-trial. The pair and their families were given twenty-four hours notice to set off for the island under heavy armed escort. Falcone and Borsellino quipped that the Italian state had sent them on a wonderful summer holiday. In fact, they were billed for their stay; Borsellino kept the bill as a souvenir.

Borsellino's daughter Lucia, who was fifteen at the time, was so traumatised by the experience that the anorexia she was already suffering from worsened; her condition deteriorated so much she refused food completely, and her weight dropped to thirty-five kilos. She recovered eventually, but it was a harrowing time for her parents.

The new Mafia threat prompted Falcone and Borsellino to carry guns in their briefcases. When they met for dinner in a restaurant the pair, worried a killer might burst in, ate with their guns resting on their laps under their napkins. But Borsellino quickly tired of carrying a gun around with him, and usually left his at home.

Only on one occasion did Falcone venture out without his bodyguards in Palermo – for his marriage to Francesca in May 1986. Without telling his escort, Falcone himself drove Francesca to the city hall where only one guest awaited them: Falcone's mother. The witnesses were Falcone's boss, Antonino Caponnetto – a father figure to both Falcone and

Borsellino – and a friend of Francesca's. Afterwards, the couple joked they had got married 'like thieves'.

The day of the marriage was the only one on which Falcone struck Caponnetto as completely, utterly happy. 'Falcone was never serene. His gaze was never completely limpid, it was as if there was always a shadow across it,' Caponnetto said. During the five years they worked together, it seemed to Caponnetto that Falcone constantly placed an invisible barrier between himself and others. Caponnetto thought it was like a shield, behind which Falcone could hide his shyness. The elderly judge was amazed to see Falcone cry when Caponnetto eventually left Palermo to go into retirement.

Although Francesca wanted to have children, Falcone refused point blank. 'What do you want me to do, bring orphans into the world?' he told a friend who had urged him to have children.

But Falcone and Borsellino believed – or wanted to believe – that the maxi-trial acted as a safeguard against Mafia reprisals. On a work trip to Rio de Janeiro, Falcone, Borsellino and Ayala met for pre-dinner drinks in their hotel near the Copacabana beach.

They never talked seriously about the risks they ran, but Borsellino, unprompted, suddenly remarked: 'I think that as long as the maxi-trial is on, no one will kill us. It's like an insurance policy. They'll try to do everything they can to influence it, but if they kill one of us it's clear the state's reaction will be to inflict life sentences. That's how they'll assess things, so as long as we've got the maxi-trial, we've got an insurance policy.'

Falcone and Ayala looked at each other. 'Yes, that makes sense,' Falcone said. The three prosecutors jokingly called Borsellino's reasoning 'The Copacabana Theory'.

*   *   *

A series of 'distinguished cadavers' – prosecutors, police chiefs or politicians slain by the Mafia in Palermo – did nothing to dissuade Falcone from pursuing the organisation. Among the victims were Falcone's superiors, colleagues and friends at the law courts and in the police. One was Falcone's friend Antonino Cassarà, deputy-chief of the Palermo flying squad. Nine killers armed with Kalashnikov rifles ambushed him in summer 1985 as he walked from his car to the entrance of his block of flats, while his wife and daughter watched from a balcony above. A bodyguard was also killed.

When a shaken Falcone arrived at the scene of the murder, he stepped in his friend's blood by mistake. Falcone and Cassarà had been fond of joking together about what the Mafia might be preparing for them. But in front of the officer's coffin, Falcone only had the strength to whisper: 'This time it isn't a joke. I've lost a friend.'

The way the government in Rome reacted to such killings dismayed Falcone. It would brand the fight against Cosa Nostra an 'emergency' and deploy more police officers on the ground – only for the 'emergency' to be forgotten a few days later. 'It makes me laugh when I hear people talk about "the Mafia emergency". How can people talk about an emergency when the Mafia has existed since before Italy was unified [in the nineteenth century]?' Falcone asked.

Falcone proudly described himself as 'a servant of the state', but the state failed him repeatedly. After one 'distinguished cadaver', a high-ranking anti-Mafia official in Rome called him to ask: 'Now what can we come up with to calm the country down?' Another time, after a series of crimes all in Palermo and all on the same day, the interior minister called and hinted that Falcone himself was to blame for the violence. Falcone gave a damning assessment of the state's commitment to fighting the Mafia: 'Emotive, episodic, inconsistent. Motivated only by the impression created by a given crime or by the effect that a particular initiative on the part of the government will have on public opinion.'

Falcone tried to think dispassionately about such slayings and draw lessons from them. Each of the victims was hit at their most vulnerable moment, he reasoned. The fact that his then boss Chinnici travelled in an armoured car had forced the Mafia to resort to what Falcone called 'more spectacular methods'. He explained: 'They killed him in the only way they could, causing five deaths and destroying ten cars, because Chinnici was very prudent and took care to protect himself.'

What struck Falcone was that many of these victims had been lone fighters against the Mafia. 'One usually dies because one is alone, or because one has got into something over one's head. One often dies because one does not have the right alliances, because one is not given support,' Falcone said. He added starkly: 'In Sicily the Mafia kills the servants of the state that the state has not been able to protect.'

In 1988, Falcone learnt the hard way that he did not have 'the right alliances'. Despite the prestige he enjoyed both nationally and internationally, jealousy and personal attacks robbed him of the job of chief prosecutor in Palermo. The new incumbent, Antonino Meli, dismantled the anti-Mafia team. He argued that Cosa Nostra was not a single, unified structure and assigned cases to prosecutors outside the team, and even to tribunals elsewhere in Sicily. His attempts to force Falcone and the anti-Mafia team to investigate cases from wife-beating to car thefts prompted Falcone and seven other colleagues to threaten to resign.

Falcone's friend Borsellino bravely denounced the destruction of the team of which he himself had been a prominent member, together with the flagging efforts of the judiciary and the police. 'Today, all the trials are dispersed into a thousand little streams. Everybody must look after everything – that's the official explanation. The truth is that Giovanni Falcone is

sadly no longer the point of reference . . . I have the unpleas-
ant feeling that somebody wants to take a step backwards,'
Borsellino complained.

Falcone made no such public protest. He believed that to
survive, he should keep as low a profile as possible. He did
however agree to meet President George H. W. Bush when
the latter invited him to a reception at Villa Taverna, the
American ambassador's residence in Rome, during his visit
to the city in May 1989. Bush and Falcone – the only Italian
magistrate invited to the reception – also met in private. But
Falcone brushed off his friend Ayala's attempts to find out
what happened: 'Bush asked to meet me, and I went,' was all
Falcone would say.

Cosa Nostra tracked Falcone's isolation with keen interest.
In Brooklyn, the FBI recorded a short but telling conversation
between two Sicilian Mafiosi:

'Has Falcone resigned yet?'
'No, he changed his mind.'
'Shit.'

Dynamite and 'a walking corpse'

One hot Monday in June 1989, Falcone invited two Swiss colleagues to join him the next day at a small villa he rented near a rocky stretch of coast at Addaura, north of Palermo. Prosecutors Carla Del Ponte and Claudio Lehman had flown to the Sicilian capital to meet him for an investigation into the laundering of drug money.

'Tomorrow, between 2 and 4 p.m., we'll go to my house by the sea for a snack and a swim,' Falcone told them.

But on the Tuesday, the Swiss prosecutors' work took longer than expected and they declined his invitation. Falcone drove to the villa with his escort as usual, and spent just half an hour lying in the sun on his terrace.

Falcone was still at the villa when one of his bodyguards spotted a diver's bag lying on a rock only a dozen yards away from the villa. Inside the bag were fifty-eight sticks of dynamite. The plan had apparently been to detonate the explosives by remote control the moment Falcone walked past on his way to the sea.

Shortly after the bomb was discovered, Falcone confided to his friend, the prosecutor Ayala: 'They mean business . . . The thing that worries me most is that they've got a mole who told them in advance what I was going to do that day. This is the work of extremely sophisticated minds.'

'It was only chance that prevented a slaughter,' Falcone reflected. 'They gave up because they couldn't be sure of succeeding, because I was some distance away from the "parcel" on the rocks. But if I'd gone down towards the water, even just a few steps . . .'

The assassination attempt prompted Falcone to insist that his wife Francesca spend the night away from the villa. Francesca asked Falcone only once to end his anti-Mafia career – 'Drop it!' she urged him – but he brushed this aside. The couple agreed that Francesca would only stay at the villa during the day, and leave every evening at 9 p.m. to go and spend the night at her mother's flat in the city.

For some time after the discovery of the bomb, Falcone spent his nights on the floor, trying to avoid falling asleep as he feared the Mafia would seek to kill him while he slept. He worried about Francesca and considered staging a fake separation, which he thought might reduce the risk to her.

Francesca struggled to persuade her husband to allow her to stay by his side. But Falcone stood firm, telling a friend after she had tried to remain with him one evening: 'She doesn't want to understand that this time those gentlemen really mean it.'

Francesca refused to give up, and asked Falcone's sister Maria to talk to him. When Maria called on her brother at the villa for dinner, after Francesca had left, she was struck by how extremely worried and tense he was about the threat he faced – it was the first time Maria had seen him like this.

'But Giovanni,' Maria told him over their meal, 'you can't expect Francesca to go home every evening.'

'You don't understand. I must be lucid, I must be always on the alert; I can't be worrying about Francesca's safety. Sometimes I don't sleep at night; I stay in an armchair because they must know that I won't move from here, that I'm not afraid.'

Falcone added: 'You don't understand. From now on I'm a walking corpse.'

The comment made his sister's blood turn cold.

The day after the Addaura bomb was discovered, Falcone was surprised to receive a call from Giulio Andreotti, the prime minister – a bespectacled, stooping figure with hunched shoulders and protruding ears dubbed 'Beelzebub' by his enemies. Andreotti was very affectionate towards Falcone, expressing his delight that the prosecutor had survived the attempt. Falcone thanked him emphatically.

But that evening, when Falcone went to dinner at the home of his friend and colleague Mario Almerighi, Falcone confided: 'I'd never spoken to Andreotti before ... It's definitely a strange phone call, because I've never had personal or direct contact with Andreotti.'

Falcone mentioned what a Mafioso had once told him: 'If you want to find out who ordered a murder, look at the name on the first wreath.' Andreotti was never linked to the assassination attempt. In a 2004 ruling, the Supreme Court found that Andreotti had forged links with the Mafia and was guilty of participation in a criminal association up to the spring of 1980. But the judges acquitted Andreotti on the grounds that the offence had been committed so long ago he was legally no longer answerable for it.

Falcone stressed how isolated he felt, he knew it made him even more likely that he'd join the ranks of the 'distinguished cadavers' he had seen slain by the Mafia over the years.

He explained to his friend Almerighi that the Mafia isolated a target first before killing him. 'Until yesterday I was the state; I was part of the state which fights the Mafia. But [now] I feel more isolated, also within the state,' Falcone said. 'I'm more alone, I'm more exposed; the risks are increasing.'

Falcone was particularly hurt to read in the newspapers that he had himself staged the assassination attempt. He also heard a rumour doing the rounds in the law courts that he'd been given free use of the villa by a Mafioso – in fact, Falcone had rented the villa, which belonged to a magistrate's uncle. For him, these were yet more attacks that highlighted his isolation and his vulnerability. He worried that he was somehow paying the price for having become too notorious and regretted attending the reception hosted by President Bush that spring. 'I made a mistake in accepting Bush's invitation; it was overexposure. I shouldn't have gone,' he told another friend.

Two days after the attempt, Falcone confided to visitors on the terrace of his villa: 'They'll try again, you'll see. They'll try again. The Mafia doesn't forget and it doesn't forgive.'

As always, Falcone tried to think like a Mafioso. He made a prediction, taking into account the heavy security surrounding him: 'They know that to kill me they have to pay an extremely high price. They'll have to carry out a slaughter. And if it becomes necessary, they won't hesitate.'

Falcone was so devastated by the failed attempt on his life that he smoked more than ever and his friends noticed that he put on weight over the next weeks and months. That summer, the personal attacks on Falcone culminated in a flurry of anonymous letters sent to senior state officials. 'The Crow', as the press branded the author, accused Falcone of illicit working methods and negligence in dealing with collaborators. The charges were a fabrication, but they weighed on Falcone's mind.

The godfather Riina made no secret of his disappointment at the failure to kill Falcone. 'It's a pity it didn't work out, because the timing was right,' Riina told Brusca. Many years later, Riina and four of his henchmen were convicted of staging the attempt; investigators concluded that Mafiosi had watched the villa from a rubber dinghy some distance away, waiting to blow up the bomb via remote control. But the question of how they had found out he was at the villa remained a mystery.

This was not the first time that Riina and his loyal servant Brusca discussed killing Falcone. Only two weeks after Brusca had helped the Mafia to blow up the prosecutor's boss Chinnici, Riina had decided Falcone would be the next target.

Ignazio Salvo, a Mafioso who had a monopoly over tax-collection across Sicily, tried to persuade Riina that there was no need for another assassination. The Mafia's political friends in Rome, Salvo argued, would launch a plot against Falcone to discredit him. Besides, Salvo added, if the Mafia killed Falcone, another prosecutor would simply be appointed to replace him.

An exasperated Riina retorted: 'Are they trying to swindle me? I have to kill Falcone, no matter what anyone says. The politicians are looking after their own interests and they're leaving us out in the open. It's chaos – as if we were cannon fodder,' he protested.

'I've got to kill them all. The time has come to kill them,' Riina added. On the list would be not only Falcone, but also the political allies the godfather felt had betrayed him.

As one collaborator explained: 'Riina is as powerful as Jesus Christ because he has supreme power. He holds men's lives in his hands. He can take away or spare anyone's life with just a nod.' But the godfather paid a heavy price for such power. 'At the same time he's reduced to misery because he can't go for a walk, he can't sleep, he can't sit in a garden of orange trees in the evening and enjoy the cool breeze and the smell of orange blossom: he has no peace and quiet . . . He's consumed by the terror of getting killed.'

Riina entrusted to Brusca the task of finding a breach in Falcone's armour. Brusca was honoured to take on the job. For Brusca and his fellow Mafiosi, Falcone was the first prosecutor (after his boss Chinnici) who had managed to seriously hurt the secret society. It was Falcone who had prompted many collaborators to break the Mafia's law of silence, and it was Falcone who had been behind the maxi-trial.

'Falcone had managed to penetrate Cosa Nostra, both because he understood its way of thinking, and because he'd found the right keys to get inside it. We hated him, we'd always hated him,' Brusca said.

A couple of weeks after Chinnici's murder, Brusca had the idea of blowing up the Palermo law courts by using a van identical to the one that delivered coffee and croissants to judges there. But he couldn't think of a way of getting clear of the explosion in time, and the idea was dropped.

He was forced to suspend the mission the godfather had given him when Falcone – who had no idea that Brusca was trying to eliminate him – ordered his arrest. Falcone had acted on the testimony of the supergrass Buscetta, who named Brusca as a Mafioso in 1984. Brusca spent three months in prison but then – despite protests from Falcone who wanted him to stay behind bars – he was sent into internal exile on the island of Linosa, south of Sicily, for ten months.

With or without Brusca's help, Cosa Nostra tried again and again to eliminate Falcone. One summer in the early 1980s, the Mafia considered shooting Falcone at a villa he rented in the countryside near Mondello, a beach resort outside Palermo. The brother-in-law of a Mafia soldier owned a restaurant near the villa, and the organisation discovered that part of the back of the villa could be seen from one of its windows. An assassin, with a precision rifle, stood a good chance of hitting Falcone as he went up and down a staircase where he did fitness exercises. But the plan was abandoned as the police would easily establish where the shot had come from, and trace the link with the brother-in-law.

A couple of years later, the Mafia hatched yet another plot.
This time its killers would ambush Falcone on the tree-lined
road which led to the country villa. The secret society knew
that he travelled in an armoured car, and planned to use two
bazookas. Several Mafia soldiers, who were no experts, experimented with the weapons in the countryside. They fired one
at a mountainside, convinced that the bazooka would blow up
the mountain.

There was an enormous blast, but the mountain didn't
collapse. 'This bazooka couldn't even kill a lizard,' one of the
disappointed soldiers reported back. The project was dropped;
the Mafia concluded the bazookas were not powerful enough,
and feared the attack would inevitably cause a shoot-out with
Falcone's bodyguards.

Undefeated, the Mafia devised still another plot soon afterwards. It would copy the technique it had used with success against
his friend, the police chief Cassarà. A squad with machine-guns
would wait just inside the gates of a small park near the entrance
to Falcone's home in Palermo. This plan was also abandoned
because Falcone, as an extra precaution following Cassarà's
death, had ordered his driver to park the armoured car on the
pavement only a few feet away from the entrance to his home.

After his internal exile ended, Brusca plotted with several
other Mafiosi to kill Falcone in 1987 at the public swimming-
pool a mile from his home where he spent a couple of hours
almost every day. But yet again the Mafia was frustrated; the
idea was soon dropped because it was seen as too difficult to
carry out.

At the end of the 1980s, worried about Falcone's fight against
the Mafia, the Gambino family in New York sent an envoy to
Palermo to find out more about it, and to gather information
about the supergrass Buscetta which they could use to challenge his testimony in American courts.

The envoy met the boss Antonino 'Little Hand' Giuffrè, a former teacher in a technical school who owed his nickname to a deformed right hand caused by a hunting accident. The boss of the Caccamo clan outside Palermo, Giuffrè had risen to become a member of the *Cupola* commission which ruled Cosa Nostra, and met the envoy on behalf of Riina and Provenzano.

The envoy complained about Falcone, who had wreaked great damage on both the American Mafia itself and its white-collar accomplices. The American Mafiosi had suffered from Falcone's work on the 'Pizza Connection' and 'Iron Tower' drug-trafficking rings – the first in which a Sicilian prosecutor had teamed up with his American colleagues, and in particular with the man Giuffrè called 'a historic figure', Rudolph Giuliani.

Riina ordered Giuffrè to reassure their American cousins 'because Uncle Totuccio [Riina] is doing all he can to limit the damage.'

'They kill only in Palermo.'

In February 1991, justice minister Claudio Martelli asked Falcone to move to Rome and offered him a senior post at the ministry – that of director of penal affairs. Falcone hesitated but then accepted. He believed he could do far more against the Mafia from Rome than from Palermo, and saw the new job as an opportunity to declare war, a real nationwide war, on the secret society. He planned to launch the *Direzione Investigativa Antimafia* – the Italian Anti-Mafia Directorate, or DIA – a new agency, similar to America's FBI, which would co-ordinate investigations across Italy.

A couple of days before he was due to leave Sicily and start a new life in Rome, Falcone lunched with his fellow judge Pietro Grasso and three journalists at a restaurant in Catania on the island's east coast, glancing only occasionally at the splendid view over Mount Etna.

Falcone was in an ebullient mood but the journalists kept distracting him with their questions. They wanted to know what he made of critics who, in the latest personal attacks against Falcone, accused him of running off to Rome because he was scared of staying in Sicily.

A visibly upset Falcone burst out: 'What do these people think? They think I'm saving my life? I'm not scared of dying. I'm Sicilian, I am.'

With his thumb and index finger, he pulled a button on his jacket, almost wrenching it off. 'Yes, I'm Sicilian, and for me, life is worth less than this button.'

During the meal, Falcone made just one remark about Riina's clan, the Corleonesi. 'The real strength of the Corleonesi is precisely in their almost total control of the province. They have men everywhere and we don't know them. That allows them to use what really is a ghost army which arrives in the city, shoots and goes away without being bothered by anyone,' Falcone said. His words were to prove not only accurate, but also fateful.

Falcone's wife Francesca, tormented by the fear that he would be killed, had long urged him to leave Sicily. The previous year, she had talked to a friend of the couple about the constant, malicious attacks he endured from his colleagues. Wouldn't it be better for her husband if he got himself a new job in Rome, she asked the friend. 'That way, he'd leave Palermo.'

But when Falcone did take up the Rome job, Francesca stayed behind in Palermo with her widowed mother. 'Without me, my mother will die,' she explained.

The new separation weighed on the couple. Whenever she could, Francesca would go to work in the appeal court from Monday to Wednesday, then fly to Rome for the rest of the week, taking with her thick files from her office. But more often it was Falcone who travelled between the two cities, usually every two weeks.

In Rome as in Palermo, Falcone threw himself into his work. He oversaw the passing of a series of laws – enabling police to restrict the movements of suspected Mafiosi, allowing the government to dissolve town councils infiltrated by the Mafia, and cracking down on extortion rackets.

Falcone lived in the heart of the capital's historic centre near the Pantheon, in a small two-room flat on police premises allocated to him by the interior ministry. He woke up every morning at 5 a.m., and worked at home for a few hours before heading to his office in the justice ministry a short drive away. Visitors had to go through two bullet-proof doors to reach his office and an armed bodyguard was always stationed in the corridor.

Before reaching the office every morning, Falcone would call his secretary Francesca Carraturo and ask her: 'Hello, has Kim Basinger called for me?'

The secretary would reply that the film star hadn't called, to which Falcone would retort: 'Well then, I don't want to know who else has been looking for me' – before listening dutifully to the list of callers.

Falcone's office – its collection of miniature geese contrasting with the coats of arms and insignia given to him by the police forces of five continents – had French windows which gave out onto a terrace, but he kept away from them for his own safety. Rome authorities believed Falcone was less at risk there than in Sicily, and assigned him a smaller escort. Until the previous year, thirty-six bodyguards had watched over him in Palermo. Now, he was protected by twelve bodyguards, who worked in shifts of six men each and carried personal ordnance pistols as well as four M-12 pump-action shotguns. He travelled in a three-car convoy, with two bodyguards in each vehicle – two unmarked cars, and a police car. None of these was armoured. Falcone still carried a gun in his briefcase.

One evening after Falcone had settled in Rome, his friend Francesco La Licata, a journalist, was stunned to see him arrive outside the offices of La Licata's newspaper *La Stampa* in a light blue, battered Fiat 127 car. Falcone was alone. The two had agreed to go out for dinner.

'Who did you steal this old shoe from?' La Licata asked him.

'The ways of the Lord . . .' Falcone replied with a mischievous grin.

'Where's the escort?'

'No escort. I'm a free man this evening.'

'Have you gone mad?'

'No, quite the opposite. I think I'm really safe: nobody knows I'm out in the streets. Everybody thinks I'm locked up at home, and if there's a plot to kill me they will certainly have postponed it at least to tomorrow morning, when I'll leave to go to the office,' Falcone said.

Falcone explained he had dismissed his bodyguards, pretending that he wouldn't be going out that evening. He had left his home without telling anyone.

'Believe me, this is the best defence,' Falcone insisted. 'Who do you think will recognise me inside such a wreck? Everyone expects to see armour-plated cars in front of me and behind me. Naturally, I would never do such a thing in Palermo.'

For the 52-year-old Falcone, the new life he led in Rome was like a rebirth after what he had endured in Palermo. He increasingly went out in the evenings – to the restaurant with friends, and on a couple of occasions to classical music concerts. His sister Maria hadn't seen him so serene for years. The moment when her anguished brother had told her, just two years earlier, 'You don't understand. From now on I'm a walking corpse,' now seemed like a distant memory.

On another evening in late summer, Falcone surprised another of his friends – his former colleague Giuseppe Ayala. Falcone turned up at Ayala's hotel at the wheel of an Alfa Romeo 164, accompanied by his bodyguards. Security rules were clear, and dictated that a bodyguard should always be in the driver's seat. Ayala, who had himself lived under escort for eighteen years, was all the more astonished because he had often driven himself, and Falcone had repeatedly chided him.

Ayala poked fun at his friend. 'So you've realised I was right after all. Maybe you've discovered it's more comfortable to drive it yourself?'

Ayala was even more surprised when Falcone, after looking at his watch, turned to his bodyguards and told them: 'We'll see each other at midnight.'

Falcone looked fairly unconcerned, Ayala thought – it was nothing like the testing times that they had lived through in Sicily.

Ayala suggested to his friend: 'Giovanni, why don't we go for a walk together? I've got the impression we've got away with it!'

'According to your theory – that events of a certain kind happen only in Palermo – we're OK in Rome, but in Palermo ... Well, who knows? Let's hope you're right,' Falcone said.

Falcone and Ayala then left the hotel alone, on foot, and strolled through the historic centre to a restaurant. After the meal, the pair walked back to the hotel, where Falcone's bodyguards awaited him.

A stunned Ayala realised this was the first time that he had ever walked the streets of his home country with Falcone. The sense of freedom was intoxicating – however illusory it might prove to be.

Falcone and Ayala met often in coming months, going out for dinner two or three times a week. Sometimes, when they walked through the heart of Rome, people would recognise them and come up to them to shake hands. '*Bravo*, Falcone,' some said to him. Falcone was pleased: 'They're rooting for us; something's changing,' he said.

One evening, as they left one of their favourite restaurants, a Tuscan establishment called *Nino* near the Spanish Steps, Ayala again told his friend that he believed they were not at risk – in the capital.

'Nothing will happen, because they kill only in Palermo. And what's more, I'm in parliament now' – Ayala had successfully stood for election – 'and OK, you're the director of penal affairs but you don't do investigations any more; you're not breaking people's balls anymore,' Ayala teased his friend.

Ayala continued: 'They've never killed for vendetta. When they kill for vendetta, it's to kill one of theirs. But no servant of the state has been killed for vendetta; when they kill a servant of the state it's to stop them, or to intimidate others.'

Falcone looked at his friend, a half-amused, half-mocking expression in his eyes. 'I really hope you're right. I have to admit that you're often right, but I've never hoped that you're right as much as I'm hoping it now.'

He added: 'Whatever happens, Giuseppe, you've got to bear one thing in mind above all: you mustn't become a victim of "veteran syndrome", because that's crippling. Whoever remains has to keep going.'

In an interview with the author that November, Falcone was keen to stress that he was only doing his job in fighting Cosa Nostra: 'What drives me? Just the knowledge that everyone must do their duty. *Basta* [enough].' He didn't want to talk about himself. 'We'll talk only about the Mafia. Not about me. I don't have anything to do with it ... A phenomenon like the Mafia isn't resolved by heroism – only by hard, tiring, humble day-to-day work,' he said.

Falcone was disarmingly frank about his fate: 'Those who believe they are doing something useful are more exposed than others, for many reasons – because of the inertia, ignorance and cowardice of others. And they are murdered – inexorably. That's all there is to it.'

Unknown to Falcone, the Mafia had in fact granted him a reprieve. As it awaited the verdict of the Supreme Court on the maxi-trial, the organisation ordered its members not to act against him because it feared that an assassination would backfire and lead to heavy sentences against the accused. The godfather Riina himself dreamt that Cosa Nostra would once again triumph in court, and that he could one day return to Corleone a free man, with his wife and four children.

At first, the Mafia had breathed a sigh of relief when Falcone moved to Rome; bosses and soldiers believed he would give them no more trouble. But they soon realised their mistake as he shaped a new national strategy against organised crime and talked to the politicians he met in the capital about the threat posed by the Mafia.

At the very start of 1992, there was what Riina's henchman Giuffrè described as 'a heavy atmosphere, a chill that turned icy' in the ruling *Cupola*, or commission, of Cosa Nostra. 'We were getting close to the day of reckoning,' he explained. 'A lot of people, most of them politicians, had made themselves scarce after the Mafia war [of the 1980s], but when you're dealing with Cosa Nostra, once you've begun something, you can't back out. A number of politicians had eaten from the same plate as Cosa Nostra, and they spat on us. [The ex-mayor] Salvo Lima was one of the ones who had done a runner. But running away didn't help him because his time had come.'

The Supreme Court's verdict of January 1992 was a devastating blow against the Mafia. The ruling definitively confirmed a flurry of life sentences and set in stone the so-called 'Buscetta theorem' – the supergrass's revelation that a single *Cupola*, or governing commission, ruled the Mafia – and pronounced credible the testimony of collaborators.

Until then, many verdicts against the Mafia had been quashed by just one judge, Corrado Carnevale, who was nicknamed 'Sentence Slayer' and who had a near monopoly over such cases. In a bid to prevent more acquittals, Falcone persuaded the justice minister, Martelli, to ensure Mafia appeals were assigned to judges at the Supreme Court in rotation. Under the new system, the maxi-trial was kept away from Judge Carnevale. In 2001, a Palermo court sentenced Carnevale to six years in prison for links to the Mafia, but he was acquitted by the Supreme Court a year later.

For Falcone, one of the main architects of the maxi-trial, the ruling was a long-awaited victory. He bought a bottle of champagne which he shared with ministry colleagues. 'But it wasn't a light-hearted evening,' one of them said. 'We knew something big had happened and that, somehow, we would have to pay.'

For the Mafia, the ruling meant it was high time to lift the stay of execution it had granted Falcone.

'From now on, anything can happen.'

Incensed by the Supreme Court's ruling, the godfather Riina held secret meetings with bosses over the weeks that followed. He called Brusca, who had recently become the head of his Mafia family, to attend one of these gatherings in late February, in a safe house in Palermo. At the meeting Riina, Brusca and three other allies of the godfather's Corleonesi family all agreed that now the Mafia couldn't afford to wait any longer. It must wage war on the Italian state.

Addressing Riina as '*Zu* [Uncle] Totò' – a mark of respect and affection – the boss Raffaele Ganci, a butcher who headed Palermo's powerful Noce family, reminded him of the failed assassination attempts on Falcone's life over the past decade. 'This time we get down to business and we stop only when the job's been done,' Ganci said.

Ganci's words carried particular weight, as he had helped Riina eliminate many enemies both inside and outside Cosa Nostra, including the Palermo boss Stefano 'The Prince' Bontate, and Falcone's boss, Chinnici.

The bosses agreed that both Falcone and the ex-Palermo mayor Salvo Lima must be killed immediately. But the death list they drew up included many others, among them the prosecutor Borsellino, Falcone's close friend, two former government ministers, the head of the Palermo flying squad, and a Rome police chief.

The bosses briefed Brusca on a new plan for Falcone's assassination. They believed they had found his Achilles' heel.

They had discovered that Falcone's love for Francesca and his birthplace had made him a creature of habit since starting the new job in Rome. Virtually every two weeks he flew home to Palermo.

The bosses told Brusca they had picked the coastal motorway leading from the airport to Palermo as the place where Falcone should be assassinated. The four-lane A29 motorway was 'the best spot' to ambush him, they proclaimed.

Finding out precisely when Falcone would be driving down the motorway would be child's play. One of the butcher's shops that the boss Ganci owned was almost opposite the block where Falcone still had his flat. The white armoured Fiat Croma he used when he was in Palermo was still parked there, watched over by armed police. All Ganci and his two sons would have to do would be to wait for the driver to come and fetch it to go and pick Falcone up from the airport.

Brusca learnt that this time the Mafia had decided to blow up Falcone. The bosses discussed several ways of doing so. One idea was to place a bomb in a large rubbish bin on the side of the exit road from the airport. Another was to blow up a bridge over the motorway with more than 2,000 pounds of explosives, just as Falcone passed under it.

Brusca was doubtful that the bridge idea would work. 'Wait. Let's think this over a bit,' he said.

But when Riina turned to Brusca and asked him if he could help him find explosives and a remote control, Brusca replied without hesitation, naming an acquaintance. 'Pietro Rampulla is an expert; let's see if he can give us a hand,' Brusca suggested.

'Fine.' The godfather was satisfied. One Mafioso had suggested that Falcone be killed in Rome, but Riina had dismissed this idea. Earlier that February, Riina had sent several of his soldiers to Rome to work out if it was possible to assassinate Falcone in the capital. But they got the name of one of his favourite restaurants wrong and wasted long hours waiting for him at *Il Matriciano*, a restaurant near the Vatican. Falcone's restaurant was in fact *La Carbonara*, on the picturesque Piazza Campo dei Fiori. Both establishments are named after typical Roman pasta dishes, which may explain the Mafiosi's confusion.

Shortly afterwards, Riina suddenly ordered the squad back to Palermo. He wanted the assassination to be a spectacular, unprecedented show of strength by the secret society, and he wanted it to take place in his stronghold, on Sicilian soil. 'I'm not interested in Rome; I have to kill him in Palermo,' Riina insisted.

Brusca did consider the possibility that trying to assassinate Falcone on the airport motorway might claim the lives of what he called 'civilians' – as if Falcone and his bodyguards were military objectives. 'It was a one-in-a-thousand possibility, and we hoped that no one would get alongside Falcone's car. Usually, the escort cars make sure other cars don't get close. We'd taken this into account too,' Brusca explained later.

But Falcone, his bodyguards and anyone who might be travelling with them, were fair game.

Brusca lost little time in obeying Riina's orders. Two days after the meeting, he drove out of Palermo and down the motorway to see the bridge the bosses had in mind. The more he studied the spot, the less he liked the idea of blowing up an entire bridge. It was too big a target.

He considered placing a bomb in one of the tunnels on the motorway, but decided against this too, because it would be impossible to see when Falcone's car reached the explosives. The butcher Ganci didn't like the idea of blowing up such a large tunnel either. 'Are we crazy? This means we'd bring down the mountains,' he protested.

The conspirators reasoned that the alternative to placing a bomb above the motorway was to place one underneath it, and blow up Falcone from below. Two of the bosses were ordered to scan the motorway.

In the meantime, Brusca worked on finding a supply of explosives. He didn't have to look very far. A cousin of his who worked in a quarry near Corleone was willing to supply a mix of TNT and T4 explosives without asking what Brusca needed it for. Another boss found an additional supply.

Brusca decided to test the explosives he planned to use. He gathered several of the plotters at an isolated cottage near the town of Altofonte, south of Palermo. He picked the small, two-bedroom cottage with a wooden veranda that the local Mafioso Mario Santo 'Half Nose' Di Matteo used as a country home as a base, because it was far from prying eyes. So confident were the bosses that their base would never be discovered that they took no security precautions. Di Matteo, a balding, vivacious soldier with a slightly deformed nose who worked at a nearby slaughterhouse, always left the keys to the front door under a brick on a window ledge.

At the cottage, the conspirators packed twenty-four pounds of explosives into three-feet-long tubes with a diameter of twenty inches. They then made a crude replica of a small stretch of motorway they wanted to blow up, in a field at a safe distance away from the cottage. Using an excavator, they dug a broad ditch, placed the tubes at the bottom of it, and covered them up with 140 cubic feet of concrete.

By the next morning, the cement was completely dry. Brusca blew up the explosives, and he and his accomplices were delighted with the result. The blast had punched a large crater through the cement. Brusca had little fear of being detected. The field was close to a quarry, and anyone hearing the explosion would automatically assume the blast came from there. But to be on the safe side, the team used the excavator to fill in the crater and cover up the rubble.

*   *   *

Needing help with the remote control, Brusca turned to the fellow Mafioso he had mentioned to Riina – Pietro 'The Artificer' Rampulla. The heavily built Rampulla had an unlikely background for an artificer; he bred buffaloes and produced mozzarella cheese. And yet he was widely respected in the Mafia as a kind of boffin who knew all there was to know about explosives and how to detonate them.

Brusca wanted to use the same kind of remote-controlled device with which he'd activated the car bomb that had killed Falcone's boss Chinnici nine years earlier: a type which children used to drive cars from a distance, or to fly model airplanes. He asked Rampulla to find him a couple of such devices.

As Falcone himself put it, Cosa Nostra could count on a host of helping hands – or 'friends of the friends' – like Rampulla: '. . . the Mafia is not a cancer which has spread through healthy tissue. It lives in perfect symbiosis with a myriad of protectors, accomplices, debtors of all kinds, informers and people from all strata of society who have been intimidated or subjected to blackmail.' In total, Brusca was to work alongside seventeen accomplices on the plot to kill Falcone.

The Mafia's death sentence on Salvo Lima – who had served as mayor of Palermo three times and was an ally of the prime minister Andreotti – was speedily executed. On 12 March, two gunmen on a motorbike ambushed his car shortly after he left his home and shot him in the chest. Lima stopped the car and tried to run away. 'They're coming back! *Madonna Santa* [Holy Virgin]! They're coming back! ' he shouted as he fought to free his coat, which had got stuck in the door. He wrenched it off and started to run, but the killers caught up with him and shot him a second and last time, in the back of the head at point-blank range.

The next evening, Falcone invited his friends Borsellino and Ayala to his flat. Ayala, who was himself very worried by the murder, was struck by how strained Falcone and Borsellino looked.

'F—, what's going to happen now? They're going to go crazy,' Ayala said.

'From now on, anything can happen,' Falcone agreed.

Which meant that he and his friends could be killed too, Ayala thought to himself.

For Falcone and Borsellino, the murder looked like the first step in a 'strategy of terror' launched by the Mafia.

On a trip to Catania in eastern Sicily shortly afterwards, the justice minister Martelli was surprised to see Falcone – who had arrived before him – come to pick him up at the airport alone, at the wheel of his white armoured Croma car.

'What's happening? What about the bodyguards?' Martelli asked.

'I feel safer this way. It's easier for me to get around; I'm less visible in a way,' Falcone replied.

In the car, Falcone briefed the minister about the significance of Lima's murder: 'Something enormous has happened . . . This changes everything, it means something deep inside Cosa Nostra has changed . . . We need to find out what's happened inside Cosa Nostra. I've got to talk to [the supergrass] Buscetta again,' Falcone told Martelli.

Back in Rome a few days later, Falcone called at the minister's home to check on his security. After Lima's murder, he told Martelli, no one could feel safe anymore. Falcone was convinced that the Mafia would seek to strike at the highest levels of the state. He told Martelli that the minister was a possible target, but he made no mention of fears for his own life.

To his colleague Grasso, Falcone confided: 'This means everything's going to change now, and to find out more we've got to wait for the result of the next general election . . . You don't kill the hen which lays the golden eggs if you don't have another one ready which lays even more eggs.'

After Lima's murder, a seventh bodyguard was assigned to Falcone's escort in Rome – a police officer who joined two colleagues in the police car, part of his three-car convoy. But Falcone sent the new officer away, as he could see no point in the extra bodyguard.

Soon afterwards, the authorities assigned Falcone an armoured car in Rome as part of his three-car convoy. To avoid being easily spotted, the bodyguards asked their superiors not to always assign them the same cars. But their appeal fell on deaf ears; they couldn't even count on having an armoured car for Falcone every day, because of a shortage of such cars due to inadequate funding.

A few weeks later, around the end of April, Pietro 'The Artificer' Rampulla drove out to meet Brusca at a cottage near the town of Altofonte; the cottage belonged to Baldassare Di Maggio, a soldier in Brusca's clan. Rampulla had bought two remote controls in a toy shop. Apart from the devices, which he hid under bales of straw in case the police stopped him, Rampulla also brought a mare which he gave Brusca as a present.

Rampulla carried two polystyrene boxes into the cottage and placed them on a table. He opened the boxes to show Brusca and several other fellow plotters the remote-control devices inside. Sprayed with dark grey metallic paint, they had two small levers on the top, which moved along grooves in the shape of a cross, and an extractable aerial.

The bosses discovered that one of the two remote controls didn't work properly, so they discarded it. On the other, they removed the lever on the user's left, and used sticky tape to block the lever on the right so that it could move only in one direction, straight ahead. All they needed it for was to send an impulse to the receiver, and the plotters wanted to eliminate the risk of any mistakes when the time came.

The conspirators made themselves a receiver which was even more rudimentary. A small, thin box of plywood contained a small battery-operated motor screwed to a thin, 5cm-long plate of copper taken from a 1.5V battery. When the impulse from the remote control reached the receiver's aerial, the motor made the copper plate turn 180 degrees to strike the head of an iron nail around which a copper wire had been wrapped. Two wires emerged from the box: a black one, which served as an aerial, and a red and white one which was linked to the detonator.

The Mafiosi tested the remote control and the receiver inside the cottage. They connected the receiver to old-fashioned flash-cubes – bought from a photography shop – to simulate explosions. Shifting the lever on the remote control made the flashes burst. The devices worked smoothly.

The plotters moved outside under the veranda. One of them sat in the shade of the veranda with the remote control, while the receiver was placed close to a trough some fifty yards away. Again, the devices worked well.

Brusca was satisfied; now everything was going to plan.

A few days later, Brusca and his accomplices tested the remote control and the receiver on quiet country roads near the cottage. Brusca, who would be operating the remote control on the day selected for the assassination, practised timing the explosion as precisely as possible. This was no easy task, because he had to make sure the bomb exploded at just the right fraction of a second when Falcone's car passed by. According to the butcher Ganci's monitoring, Falcone's convoy travelled down the motorway at an average speed of 80–87 m.p.h.

On 8 May, Brusca spent the whole day working on the timing of the explosion with the help of two accomplices who drove their fast cars – a Lancia and a Mercedes – on a tarmac road, in open countryside, between the towns of Altofonte and Piana degli Albanesi. Again using flashbulbs placed by the side of the road, Brusca struggled for hour after hour to work out how long it took the impulse from the remote control to reach the receiver and shift the thin blade of metal just over an inch to set off the flashbulbs.

After trying again and again, he estimated that a car at a speed of 80–87 m.p.h. covered between 21 and 30 feet in the time it took for him to make a flashbulb burst. But this wasn't good enough for Brusca. He worried that he couldn't be certain of the speed at which Falcone's car would be travelling, so he experimented with the cars going slower and faster than the speeds he'd been given.

The soldier Antonino Gioè – whose previous crimes included drug trafficking, kidnapping and murder – couldn't help chain-smoking during every phase of the preparations, but the team was meticulous in picking up all his cigarette ends afterwards. Gioè had much to recommend him for the job in hand. Until the month of March, he had worked for a company whose task was to clean the subways and drainpipes which passed under the motorway. Few knew the area as well as he did.

Brusca had yet to decide precisely where on the coastal motorway the ambush would take place. He was still experimenting with the remote control when the boss Salvatore Biondino, Riina's driver, and the butcher Ganci told him they'd discovered a pedestrian underpass just over three miles from Palermo. Unlike the godfather, Biondino had a clean record and could move about freely, and he and Ganci were certain this was the ideal spot.

Brusca went back to the cousin who worked in a quarry and asked for some advice, again keeping his mission secret. The tighter the space in which the explosives are placed, and the deeper underground, the more powerful the blast, the cousin told him.

From what his cousin and 'The Artificer' Rampulla told him, Brusca realised that the pedestrian passage, which had a diameter of almost five feet, was no good. The conspirators estimated they would need more than two thousand pounds of explosives. Besides, they would also have to close off the passage with the risk that someone might realise what they were up to.

'This will be a fiasco,' Brusca told Biondino, 'because when we blow up the explosives, too much of the blast will go out through the two exits, and we won't get what we're looking for. We need a smaller place, something more closed and deeper underground.'

'I'll look for it,' Biondino replied.

Brusca also rejected three other tunnels under the motorway which were suggested to him: two were too big, as they were wide enough for a car to get through, and a river flowed through the third.

But less than two weeks later Biondino reported back that this time he had found a great spot. Biondino drove Brusca out of Palermo, stopping just over two and a half miles from the city, by a stretch of the airport motorway that was flanked by olive and prickly pear trees, and cane thickets. Some two hundred yards further on was the exit for the small medieval town of Capaci. A short distance away, a road ran along the coast past a virtual wall of small, mostly ugly villas which had been built without planning permission.

Biondino led Brusca to a spot at the bottom of the motorway's 13ft-high escarpment; visible among the undergrowth was the mouth of a small drainpipe which ran under and across the motorway. It was small and tight, just as his cousin had recommended. Brusca saw instantly that the pipe, only 20 inches wide and made of reinforced concrete, would act as a pressure chamber and make the blast even greater. In his mind's eye, he could already picture how effective explosives placed there would be.

Brusca was exultant. 'Perfect. Too good to be true.'

Brusca asked Biondino if there was a spot he could use as a vantage point from which to operate the remote control.

Biondino pointed up the hillside to a clump of trees. 'What do you think about that spot up there?'

The two walked 400 yards up the hill to the spot. From there, as one of the Mafiosi said, 'we had a perfect view, the motorway pointed straight towards us.' The lookout commanded a clear view of just under a mile-long stretch of the motorway. Beyond it, the Tyrrhenian Sea stretched out beyond Women's Island, a low, dark mass which owed its name to a sixteenth-century prison for women convicts.

The Mafia's latest plot to assassinate Falcone was foolproof – provided the explosives could be detonated at precisely the right time. The plotters would run no risks, as they would be 400 yards away when the bomb blew up.

It was a scenario that Falcone himself had foreseen, albeit in general terms. 'It is commonly believed that the Mafia prefer certain techniques of assassination to others,' he writes in his memoirs. 'That is not true. The Mafia always choose the shortest and least dangerous path. That is its only principle.'

A drainpipe, explosives and a skateboard

One afternoon in early 1992, Liliana Ferraro, the head of Falcone's private office, was stunned to find him in tears when she walked into his office at the justice ministry. A few days earlier, Falcone had announced his candidacy for the office of 'super-prosecutor', a Rome-based group of investigating magistrates which would co-ordinate anti-Mafia investigations nationwide.

Falcone's announcement prompted yet another wave of personal attacks. Critics wrote lengthy articles in the newspapers admitting that yes, he was indeed Italy's best anti-Mafia investigator, but he shouldn't get the job because he was too ambitious, too close to the justice minister Martelli, and too close to the political establishment in general.

Ferraro tried to comfort her boss: 'Ignore it all, it's nothing surprising. After all, it isn't the first time they attack you,' she told him.

'You have to understand, I have nothing ... All I have is my honour and my life; these people want to take my honour away.' Falcone added: 'One day, Cosa Nostra will take my life away.'

His wife Francesca bluntly questioned Falcone's determination to continue fighting the Mafia. 'How can you do everything you do when you don't even have a consensus behind you? You want to save a country that doesn't love you,' she challenged him in front of friends of the couple.

'Some people don't love me, and these people aren't my country,' Falcone replied.

Francesca urged her husband to defend himself publicly, but he replied: 'If you defend yourself, you only make it worse. It gives the impression that you've done something wrong.'

Behind Falcone's apparent coldness and lucidity were strong feelings he was careful to hide. 'Falcone suffered a great deal. He wasn't a cold fish; not at all,' his close friend Ayala said. And Falcone suffered most when his professionalism, and the high standards he set himself, weren't understood.

The personal attacks also heightened Falcone's sense of isolation – which he firmly believed left him yet more vulnerable to the Mafia. But to all appearances, Falcone felt much safer in Rome than in Palermo. When Francesca and her brother Alfredo came to stay with him for a few days in late April, Falcone dismissed his bodyguards every time they went out to a restaurant or cinema – something he never did in Palermo.

From Rome, Francesca told her friend Laura Cassarà, the widow of the slain police chief: 'We went to the supermarket and Giovanni did the shopping with me.' For the couple, it was a taste of normality which was still inconceivable in Palermo.

One day in late April, Brusca told his accomplice Di Maggio that the boss Giuseppe Agrigento would be bringing 'some things' to his cottage the following day. Brusca did not explain what these were. The next morning, Agrigento arrived with four bags in his car weighing 50kg each. Di Maggio helped to pour the contents into two big white plastic drums.

Inside the bags were small granules of a dirty white colour. Di Maggio thought it was fertiliser. But as the two men poured the granules into the drums, Di Maggio breathed in a small cloud of dust thrown up by the granules. He felt a burning sensation in his nose. It was only then that Agrigento told him it was not fertiliser, but explosives.

Late one afternoon in early May, Brusca, Di Matteo and four other plotters loaded the explosives, the remote control, the receiver and several detonators into two cars. Brusca and 'The Artificer' Rampulla set off first, ahead of the rest, to check if police had set up any roadblocks on their route. Five minutes later, the rest followed in the two cars with the explosives – Brusca carrying a Kalashnikov for the trip.

After a forty-five-minute drive, the conspirators reached an old shack just outside the town of Capaci, which belonged to the tall, dark-skinned Antonino Troia, deputy boss of the local Mafia family. The shack lay off the main road, up a path too narrow for cars to pass along. To ensure they would not be seen from the road, the plotters put up a big green canvas screen. The new base was cramped and noisy as it only had two rooms and was flanked by a poultry pen and a stable housing a mare and two calves. But as far as the bosses were concerned, it was perfectly situated. The hillside vantage point over the motorway was only 200 yards away. Brusca called the shack his 'logistics base'.

Brusca and the soldier Gioè gingerly carried in the detonators, carefully wrapped in newspaper. Gioè put the packages down on a table and unwrapped them; to Di Matteo, the silver detonators looked like cartridge cases for a Kalashnikov rifle.

'Be careful with these. If someone drops them, the whole place will blow up,' Gioè warned.

The butcher confided to one accomplice who saw the explosives in their drums lined up outside against a wall: 'That's the powder to blow up Falcone.'

Back at the shack one evening soon afterwards, Brusca, Gioè, Di Matteo and three other Mafiosi slipped on white surgical gloves before spreading a canvas sheet out on the tiled floor under the veranda. They poured explosives onto the sheet and then, scooping up and cupping them in their hands, transferred them into one 77lb drum, and twelve 55lb metal drums.

The explosives they were working with were TNT and ammonium nitrate, and weighed some 500 kilos. Half was of a granular substance, while the rest was darker, more powdery. When the Mafiosi pressed it down into the drums as they packed it inside, the imprints of their hands were visible on the surface. At first they thought they would have to mix the two kinds of explosives inside each drum, but 'The Artificer' Rampulla told them that alternating drums with different explosives inside the drainpipe would be enough.

It took them more than two hours to fill the drums. When they had finished, Rampulla inserted two detonators in the biggest of the drums – he pushed one down into the middle of the drum, and placed the other near it. He made a small hole in the drum for the wires that would link the detonator in the middle of the drum to the receiver, and then covered the hole with sticky tape to make sure the wires would not come loose.

The job done, the plotters hid the drums in a hole near the gate and covered them with manure. They burnt the canvas sheet, the bags which had contained the explosives and the surgical gloves, meticulously covering their tracks.

On the evening of 8 May, Brusca, 'The Artificer' Rampulla and four other conspirators dressed in workers' dark blue overalls, and met by the drainpipe under the motorway at sunset.

As three accomplices stood guard – one of them carrying a Kalashnikov rifle, and two others .357 Magnum revolvers – the plotters, working by torchlight, measured the width of the motorway and then worked out how much of the pipe corresponded to half that width. All they had to do was count the tubes that made up the pipe, each of which was a yard long. The bosses knew from their previous monitoring of Falcone that his car always travelled in the fast lane, but they decided to place the explosives under both Palermo-bound lanes to make certain.

Although exhausted after the last few days of preparations, Brusca tried to crawl into the drainpipe. However, it was so narrow – only 20 inches wide – and the air inside so oppressively warm that he immediately began to find it difficult to breathe. 'If I go inside this, I'll die,' he thought to himself.

He extricated himself quickly saying he wasn't up to it. Gioacchino La Barbera, a boss nicknamed 'The Industrialist' because he ran a small earthmoving business, tried next. La Barbera was picked because he was short and thin, but he too gave up after crawling only a couple of yards into the pipe, complaining that the air inside was suffocating.

'I want to try,' the soldier Gioè announced. He slipped inside and shouted: 'I could go for a *passeggiata* [walk] with my girlfriend in here; there's no problem!' A ladies' man who always dressed smartly, Gioè liked to boast about his female conquests, which included – simultaneously – a main partner in his home town of Altofonte and several other women in Palermo. Gioè managed to crawl down the pipe, reaching the spot that corresponded to the middle of the motorway.

Using his mobile phone, Brusca summoned two accomplices who had been waiting to drive over with the thirteen drums full of explosives, hidden in black bin-liners. Once they had arrived the plotters, wearing thick builders' gloves made of leather to avoid leaving fingerprints, lifted the heavy metal drums out of the car and placed them under an olive tree near the drainpipe. The Mafiosi hoped that any passer-by seeing the bin-liners would think it was just more rubbish dumped by the side of the motorway.

The bosses had brought a skateboard with them and took turns using it to place the drums inside the pipe. Each Mafioso inched forward bit by bit, his face scraping against the dirt as he pushed the skateboard forward, a drum resting across it. When Brusca took his turn he felt 'like a dog with my hands stretched out ahead and my face touching the earth'. One of the accomplices crouched by the mouth of the pipe, lighting it with a torch. It was slow and exhausting work, and it took a couple of hours to place only three of the drums.

The sudden arrival of a *carabinieri* police patrol van, which stopped by the side of a road 200 yards away, made the Mafiosi panic. They rushed to hide behind the trees and bushes that grew by the motorway. The moustachioed Corleonesi boss Leoluca Bagarella, his Kalashnikov at the ready, ordered the two other armed plotters to open fire if the officers came any closer.

If the officers were shot dead, Brusca reflected with regret, the attempt on Falcone would have to be cancelled. But it was a false alarm. A couple of officers got out of the van, relieved themselves, and then drove off again.

The bosses got on with their task, but after a couple of hours Brusca had a brainwave. 'Why don't we lie down on the skateboard on our stomachs?' he asked Gioè. 'Let's go inside feet first; we can push the drums with our feet. We'll tie a rope to our chest; when I yank it that will mean it's time for you to pull me out.'

The work went much more smoothly from then on and the team finished in an hour and a half. They placed the biggest drum in the middle of the row and, using sticky tape, ran the wire from the detonator inside it along a tube that ran along one side of the drainpipe, to avoid it being damaged. When they had finished, they then threw some rubbish and weeds over the mouth of the pipe to hide it from view.

'The Artificer' Rampulla warned his accomplices that other signals near the motorway, such as the opening or closing of an electronic gate, could interfere with the receiver, so they decided to activate it at the last possible moment. It would take only a few seconds to connect the receiver with a couple of plugs. From then on, a boss checked on the explosives daily; he had no difficulty finding the spot as some old mattresses had been thrown away nearby.

At 4 a.m., the tired Mafiosi got into their cars. 'We didn't chat or make any wisecracks on the drive,' Brusca related. 'We talked little; we were too tense, concentrating on the job, careful not to get anything wrong. Like military types. I was calm, couldn't have been calmer.'

In another car, Gioè told La Barbera who the explosives were destined for. 'We have to kill Falcone,' Gioè told him bluntly – until then, La Barbera had known only that the victim would be 'an important person'.

Gioè confessed to La Barbera that he feared the worst. He couldn't understand why Riina was making them risk their lives by working for so many hours with a detonator in the middle of so many explosives.

Besides, they were bound to make a bad end, he predicted. 'What can we do?' Gioè asked. 'We can only end up with a life sentence, or be shot dead by the Corleonesi. Or we put a rope around our necks and we hang ourselves.' The remark was to prove eerily premonitory for Gioè himself.

A Mafia vigil

Soon after they had placed the bomb, the plotters began their vigil, waiting for Falcone's arrival. After they saw neighbours staring at them as they came and went from the shack near the vantage point, they decided to switch to a new base only a hundred yards away – a small villa that a friend of the Capaci deputy boss Troia had lent him the keys to. They began a three-day vigil on a Thursday; they had easily established that Falcone flew to Palermo on a Thursday, Friday or Saturday because his convoy, when it arrived at his block of flats in the city, did so with sirens blaring.

Near Ganci's shop in Palermo, the butcher and his sons Calogero and Domenico would set the whole assassination plan in motion as soon as they spotted Falcone's driver set off for the airport. The butcher's shop was just fifty yards away from the corner of Via Gioacchino di Marzo where Falcone's armoured car was parked, guarded by police in a van, behind his Palermo home.

From 8 a.m., Calogero watched over Falcone's car from the nearby bar Ciro's. The plan called for Ganci's sons to follow the car to the motorway to make sure it was on its way to the airport. They had learnt to recognise Falcone's driver, and had memorised the car's registration number.

For Calogero, born into a Mafia family and initiated into the secret society at the age of twenty, murder was a necessity and didn't contradict what he saw as the Mafia's 'moral values'. He later explained: 'Cosa Nostra was a criminal organisation, so that meant murders had to be committed. But that was a necessity for Cosa Nostra, to fight the enemy . . . When they ordered me to go and fight, to commit a murder, I saw that victim as an enemy of mine, an enemy of my family or of Cosa Nostra.'

While the Gancis watched over Falcone's car, ordering a series of coffees to make the wait more bearable, Giovan Battista Ferrante, a soldier from Palermo's San Lorenzo family, was waiting twenty miles away, close to the airport.

The son, grandson and great-grandson of Mafiosi, Ferrante had joined the Mafia when he was twenty and had proved himself a trusted killer, carrying out dozens of murders. His 'distinguished cadavers' had included Falcone's boss Chinnici, Falcone's friend the police chief Cassarà, and the ex-Palermo mayor Lima. He ran a road haulage company and had helped to obtain the explosives for the failed attempt on Falcone's life at his seaside villa.

He knew the Capaci area well, as he had worked as a lorry-driver there after dropping out of school, and this, together with his murderous past, had made him a natural choice to work on the latest Falcone assassination plot.

And yet, unknown to his fellow Mafiosi, Ferrante was constantly wracked by doubts about his life in the organisation. He saw his youth – before he discovered the Mafia at the age of eighteen – as the happiest period of his life. He said of his long years in the organisation: 'I couldn't work out who I was; I'd look at myself and I couldn't see which was the good part of me and which the bad part. On one hand I refused to do what had to be done – at least, a part of me refused to do it – but on the other hand I felt obliged to do it because I couldn't see any alternative.'

He had once tried to give vent to his misgivings when a boss ordered him to murder a childhood friend. Ferrante dared to ask if the murder could be avoided, if there was any particular reason for killing his friend. 'It has to be done because it has to be done. Otherwise, you go and speak to [Riina],' the boss retorted – something which, Ferrante knew, was out of the question.

Again and again since joining Cosa Nostra, Ferrante had been told that soldiers simply didn't ask questions, or express any doubts. 'What is done is done, and has to be forgotten. *Basta* [enough], you don't ask why,' he was told.

When Brusca gave him his orders for the vigil, Ferrante kept his mouth shut. Brusca told Ferrante and the latter's cousin, the Mafioso Salvatore Biondo, that once the pair were alerted that Falcone's armoured car had left Palermo they must follow it to the airport. When it left for Palermo, it would be Ferrante's job to stand by the airport entrance reserved for the police, and make sure that Falcone was inside. Ferrante had been chosen for the job because there was no warrant out for his arrest.

Brusca had drummed home to Ferrante the importance of recognising Falcone. 'When you get to the airport, you have to get out of your car,' Brusca stressed. 'You must look inside Falcone's car. We have to be sure it isn't someone else inside. We can't screw things up. You must see him. Understood?'

When Ferrante spotted Falcone leaving the airport, he would call another plotter, La Barbera, who would be waiting in his car on a road that ran alongside the motorway further inland for more than three miles. La Barbera, a keen rally driver like Brusca, would be driving his Lancia Delta, which was powerful enough to keep up with the convoy.

Brusca told La Barbera: 'As soon as you see Falcone's car you stick to it. See what speed it's going at and tell us on the mobile phone.'

Ferrante was unhappy with the plan. He didn't want to have to use his mobile phone at the airport and the CCTV cameras there would catch him on film. But he said nothing.

Together with Biondo, Ferrante spent part of the first morning, a Friday, waiting in their car near a hotel five minutes from the airport. The cousins then moved from place to place as the day wore on. There was little risk that anyone would notice them, as the nearby beaches were deserted at that time of year.

The pair watched the cars leaving the airport after the arrival of scheduled Alitalia flights from Rome – they'd been told that Falcone would be on one of them and they looked in the day's local newspaper to find out the flight times. A previous attempt by a Mafioso who had settled in Rome to monitor Falcone's departures from the capital had failed because there were police officers at the spot he had chosen as a vantage point.

Ferrante and Biondo's part in the vigil was far from rigorous. They were so certain that Falcone would be on an Alitalia flight that whenever there was a gap of an hour or more between the airline's flights, they would take a break. Ferrante would drive to his road haulage company, or go to the bank or the post office. The pair would also stop for lunch, buying sandwiches to take to their accomplices waiting at the villa.

The whole day passed without any sign of Falcone. They gave up in the early evening, but resumed the vigil on Saturday morning and on until late in the afternoon – but again, there was no sign of Falcone. The conspirators were to resume their vigil towards the end of the following week.

Throughout all their preparations, no one ever bothered them. Only once did a local man chance on two of the Mafiosi by the motorway; but they were dressed in workers' blue overalls, and he didn't think there was anything suspicious about them.

*   *   *

On the morning of 15 May, Brusca met seven of the plotters at the shack and they set out to test the remote control at the vantage point for the first time. Brusca and Gioè brought the remote control and a pair of binoculars. They saw that several branches of a tree were blocking their view of the motorway. One of the Mafiosi fetched a carpenter's saw and cut them down, as well as the branches of another tree close to the mouth of the drainpipe.

In the meantime, Di Matteo drove off in his white Lancia to wait near a motorway entrance while Rampulla and La Barbera made their way to the drainpipe. They placed the receiver inside, with the aerial pointing out of the pipe, and connected it to an old-fashioned flash-cube placed on the escarpment by the guardrail of the motorway. They stayed nearby, only a few yards from the motorway, so they could see both the flash-cube and Di Matteo's car when it passed by. So that Brusca could see the spot where the pipe lay, the plotters sprayed some white paint on the side of the guard-rail facing the hillside. From the vantage point, Gioè called Di Matteo on a mobile phone he had given him and told him to set off. Once on the motorway, Di Matteo drove towards Capaci at high speed. For reasons that remain unexplained, Brusca now estimated that the convoy would be travelling at 100-105 m.p.h. Di Matteo made a couple of trial runs; La Barbera called Brusca on his mobile to report back on the timing of the flash-cube's explosion, and adjusted it for the next test.

Brusca had planned to use Di Matteo for more trial runs, but he came to suspect that Di Matteo had talked about the planned assassination to his wife, and swiftly dropped him. For the next day's tests, Brusca switched to the apparently loyal Ferrante. When Brusca asked him to drive his Mercedes repeatedly down the motorway – and over the explosives – Ferrante asked no questions and did as he was told. But he had his heart in his mouth every time he did so. 'We were very afraid, also because it was a stretch of road on which anyone could travel, even my family could pass by at any time,' Ferrante said.

According to Ferrante, several of the conspirators – he didn't name them – had even deeper misgivings about the assassination attempt. 'We all knew that this thing would be a complete disaster for us,' Ferrante said. 'We knew we were doing something which was irreparable and destructive for Cosa Nostra, but no one had the power to prevent it or to do anything else.'

The godfather Riina had no such fears. At a meeting in a Palermo villa with three of the plotters, Riina exuded optimism about his strategy of terror.

Important people, Riina said, would ensure that Falcone's assassination didn't backfire on Cosa Nostra. These 'important people' would also pass laws in the organisation's favour.

'I'm putting everything on the line; we can sleep easy. I've got Dell'Utri and Berlusconi in hand' – the future senator Marcello Dell'Utri, and the future premier Silvio Berlusconi – 'and that's a good thing for all of Cosa Nostra,' Riina said. 'Because these people are the ones who will do good for us. We have to cultivate them; we have to assist them today and even more tomorrow.' In 2010, a Palermo appeal court sentenced Dell'Utri to seven years in prison for collusion with the Mafia. Two years later, the Supreme Court ordered a retrial. Both Dell'Utri and Berlusconi have denied any links with Cosa Nostra.

From the hillside, Brusca could see the cars on the motorway perfectly well with his naked eye, but he asked an accomplice to get him an L-shaped periscope – 'an excess of zeal', as Brusca called the request.

As he experimented again and again, Brusca spotted a large white fridge which lay among other rubbish near the motorway. He ordered his accomplices to place it on the escarpment some 65 feet ahead of the drainpipe as a marker which was clearly visible from the vantage point. Brusca estimated that he had to shift the lever on the remote control at the precise moment that Falcone's car would race past it; it would take the car less than 0.9 seconds to reach the bomb.

Brusca knew his measurements were in part guesswork, but he felt confident enough he would succeed. As he put it, Brusca was now 'fully operational'.

'This is the happiest period of my life.'

In early May, Tommaso Staffoli, one of Falcone's body-guards in Rome, discovered that the judge had never seen the *mattanza* (massacre) of tuna fish at the island of Favignana, west of Sicily, where Staffoli was born and had grown up. During the *mattanza*, an ancient ritual which is popular with tourists, fishermen use giant nets to trap the tuna fish in a so-called 'death-chamber' where they are slaughtered with harpoons, the sea turning into a churning mass of red.

'We could go and see the *mattanza* together. That's where I come from. Let's organise it,' Staffoli said.

Falcone agreed immediately. 'Yes, let's go on a Friday or a Saturday. Let's go and watch it.'

They decided to go on Friday, 22 May.

Staffoli and Falcone's other Rome bodyguards sometimes talked among themselves about how Cosa Nostra might attack 'us'. Almost all of them agreed that the most likely assassin was a lone sniper, using a rifle with a telescopic lens, who would shoot Falcone outside his home. Most of the bodyguards thought that was the only place the Mafia could strike, because no one ever knew in advance where Falcone was going. Even they usually found out only at the last minute. Or perhaps, they guessed, the Mafia would block the road and suddenly attack the convoy from the sides; but the bodyguards were confident such an attack would fail as they would be inside the armour-plated cars and would have time to react.

Falcone repeatedly told his Rome bodyguards not to be afraid in the city, because nothing would ever happen to him there. But in Sicily it would, he added.

Ahead of his planned trip to watch the *mattanza*, Falcone flew to Palermo on 18 May, a Monday, for a day-long work trip with several colleagues from the justice ministry. Falcone usually flew to Palermo on state-operated flights reserved for officials which he or his secretary booked through the Security Division of the SISDE secret service.

But as Falcone was flying with several colleagues, for the sake of convenience they flew together that Monday morning on a scheduled Alitalia flight. As a precaution, his secretary didn't give his name when she booked scheduled flights; instead she gave her own maiden or married name.

From Palermo airport, Falcone was escorted to the law courts where he greeted several of his former colleagues. Later, over lunch at the Charleston restaurant, they celebrated Falcone's fifty-third birthday, which was two days away.

The prosecutor Paolo Borsellino, Falcone's closest friend, quipped with typically morbid humour: 'My dear Giovanni, you've diddled me. You've managed to live beyond the age of fifty-two. Well done. I envy you a lot. I don't know if I'll manage it . . .'

In a blend of fatalism and superstition, Borsellino was convinced that he would die at the age of fifty-two – both his father and his grandfather had died at that age.

It was only when it was too late to strike that Brusca found out not only that Falcone had come and gone, but also that during the trip he had given Borsellino a lift in his armoured car on the coastal motorway.

'If we'd known, we'd have killed two birds with one stone. *Pazienza* [patience],' Brusca said.

The plotters resumed their vigil.

Back in Rome, Falcone and his wife Francesca had more than his birthday to celebrate. With Falcone's help, Francesca had managed to get a new job as a member of the commission overseeing examinations for would-be magistrates in Rome. The new job would last about a year, so Francesca decided to move to the capital. She would be based at the justice ministry and could at last live with her husband, returning to Palermo at weekends to see her mother.

The couple was jubilant. 'This is the happiest period of my life,' the forty-seven-year-old Francesca told a friend. Falcone confided to another friend: 'As Francesca is coming here now, we'll practically be living here.'

Falcone started thinking about looking for a bigger flat. He had made up his mind. He would settle in Rome for good.

On 19 May, Falcone's secretary Francesca Carraturo called the SISDE secret service to book an official flight to Palermo for him, leaving on the evening of 22 May. She also booked a return flight for the morning of 25 May. Later, Carraturo said her boss was as calm as ever that week. All that struck her as unusual was that she saw him walking up and down the terrace outside his office for some time. In his fourteen months in Rome, he had only ventured out onto the terrace twice, to show it to visitors.

Falcone invited his friend and ex-Palermo colleague Ayala to travel with him. Ayala often flew with Falcone on his official flights to and from Palermo. Ayala didn't save any money – as an MP he was entitled to free flights – but he liked being able to fix the time of the flight, and enjoyed talking freely with Falcone during the trip. But on the morning of 22 May, a

Friday, Falcone called Ayala to tell him that he had decided to postpone his departure to the following afternoon because Francesca was busy with her new job and would not be free until then.

'There's no point in me going first and then Francesca flies the next day, I might as well wait for her and we travel together . . . Why don't you come too?' Falcone said.

'Giovanni, the idea of getting to Palermo on a Saturday evening only to leave again on Monday morning makes me think it's best if I stay in Rome. Thanks, we'll see each other next week,' Ayala told him.

'OK, I'll call you when I get back,' Falcone said.

Falcone regretfully told his bodyguard Staffoli that he couldn't go to see the *mattanza* after all because of Francesca's work commitments. The couple would go only to Palermo this time; they would have lunch with Francesca's mother on the Sunday, and would return to Sicily to see the *mattanza* the following weekend.

Falcone spent much of the Friday evening tidying up his office. He used the irritatingly loud shredder so much that Ferraro, the head of his private office, went up to him and protested: 'But don't you realise you're deafening everybody?'

Falcone was always tidy but Ferraro was shocked at how thorough he was in putting everything in order. Later, she said it struck her as 'unreal'.

It was as if, Falcone's former boss Caponnetto said, Falcone 'was about to clean things out, to get rid of all that was superfluous . . . As if he wanted to leave scorched earth behind him, the most absolute void.' Caponnetto added: 'For some time now, Giovanni was awaiting the day of his execution. Let's be clear about this. His more and more frequent comments – "They'll hit me in Palermo and not in Rome," – demonstrate that he was aware his destiny was sealed.'

*   *   *

Giannicola Sinisi, a young magistrate at the justice ministry working for Falcone, also noticed that he had become increasingly obsessive about keeping his desk tidy. Over recent days, Falcone had vented his frustration at being the constant target of personal attacks in the newspapers for putting himself forward for the job of 'super-prosecutor'.

Falcone told Sinisi: 'After all, for someone like me who knows he's going to be killed, what do you think I care about being a super-prosecutor?'

One evening, after reading yet another newspaper article attacking him, Falcone burst out: 'I have nothing. I don't even own a flat; I've only got my work and my dignity. And they can't take my dignity away from me.'

Ferrante kept up his vigil for Falcone, but it apparently took second place to the First Communion of his son which was due that Sunday. Ferrante was anxious not to miss it, and asked Riina's driver Biondino if he could go to it. Biondino consulted Brusca, and was told nothing would be attempted that Sunday because the receiver wasn't trustworthy, and also because there was always more traffic on the motorway on a Sunday. Blowing it up then would be too dangerous.

If Falcone didn't fly to Sicily soon, Biondino added, they would have to remove the explosives from the drainpipe. It was too risky and dangerous to keep them there for too long; they couldn't just go on like this without being certain when Falcone would come.

Part 2

Ambush:

23 May 1992 – 26 July 1992

'The meat's arrived.'

On the morning of Saturday 23 May – a morning of limpid blue skies in Palermo, so warm it felt more like summer than spring – the butcher Ganci, his sons and the other plotters resumed their vigil, waiting to see if Falcone's driver would turn up to fetch the armoured car he used in the city. Ganci went to the bar Ciro's near his shop and ordered the first of his several coffees of the day.

That morning Francesca's mother Lina, who lived downstairs from the flat which Falcone and her daughter had kept on, went upstairs to water the plants. She saw that Francesca had covered the sofas with white sheets to keep the dust off; for a moment the sight unsettled her and she felt a heart murmur.

In Rome 265 miles away, Falcone spent the morning at the justice ministry. He stayed until shortly before 2 p.m., taking his leave of his secretary. 'See you on Monday morning at the usual time.'

'Have a good trip,' she replied.

While Falcone had a late, lone lunch at his flat, cooking himself some spaghetti – his wife was busy at the exams commission – a couple of Falcone's bodyguards set off in an escort car to check the road which he would be taking soon to Ciampino airport, south of Rome. They noticed nothing unusual and headed back to his flat.

At about 4 p.m., Falcone and his police escort car went to fetch Francesca at the justice ministry. As Falcone waited for her to join him, he started looking for a book he wanted to take with him to Palermo. His bodyguards helped him search in the car but they couldn't find it; Falcone went up to his office and found it there.

He announced that he would drive his armoured car, with Francesca as the only passenger, and told the two bodyguards who normally accompanied him to ride in the escort car instead.

The convoy sped through Rome. Down the Via dei Fori Imperiali, which the dictator Benito Mussolini had built as a symbolic link between his offices and the Colosseum after destroying an entire neighbourhood; past the Colosseum, where tens of thousands of gladiators were put to death; out through the ancient walls of the Eternal City; and on to Ciampino airport, which it reached shortly after 4.30 p.m.

Falcone and Francesca boarded a small Falcon 200 jet, which took off at 5.02 p.m. They had no idea that Cosa Nostra was waiting for them.

From Ciro's in Palermo shortly after 4 p.m., the butcher Ganci suddenly caught sight of Falcone's driver setting off down the street in the judge's white armoured Fiat Croma.

Almost breaking into a run, Ganci strode fast back to his shop and ordered his two sons Domenico and Calogero: 'Now, move. Follow him, the car's gone.'

Riding his Peugeot scooter, Domenico managed to follow only for a short time before he lost track of the car. His brother Calogero, driving his Alfa Romeo, also failed to keep up with Falcone's car and rushed on to the airport in the hope of catching sight of it there.

Giuseppe Costanza, Falcone's Sicilian driver, headed down the coastal motorway along with six bodyguards in two more Fiat Cromas. A former hairdresser, the forty-five-year-old

Costanza was married with two children; he had served as Falcone's driver since 1986, but after the judge's move to Rome he only worked for him on his trips back to Sicily.

At Falcone's request, Costanza had got rid of the flashing blue light he'd been given along with the white Croma; Falcone had explained it was too obvious a marker for the Mafia. Also at Falcone's request, before he took the car Costanza always inserted into the exhaust pipe a long baton the judge had given him to check for any explosives which the engine heat would blow up. As ever, he found nothing.

Brusca and five of the conspirators were waiting at their base near the town of Capaci when they received a call from Domenico Ganci.

'The lorry is on its way,' Domenico told La Barbera.

'I'm sorry, you've got the wrong number,' La Barbera replied before hanging up.

La Barbera drove to a spot by the road that ran parallel to the motorway and waited, his engine running.

Brusca and Biondino, carrying the remote control, made their way to the vantage point on the hillside.

Gioè and two other plotters went to the drainpipe to place the receiver inside, connect it to the detonator and extract the aerial. The task completed, Gioè joined Brusca at the vantage point.

They watched the motorway. Gioè stared through the periscope Brusca had requested. It rested on a specially made pedestal he had brought with him. He kept it pointed at the stretch of motorway which ran past the fridge; it was his job to tell Brusca when Falcone's car passed the fridge. Gioè started chain-smoking Merit cigarettes, chewing heavily on the cigarette ends before spitting them on the ground.

Brusca kept his hands on the remote control – close to the switch, but not too close.

*　　*　　*

Over the last few days, Ferrante and Biondo had regularly slipped away from their assigned position near the airport in the afternoons, returning only when they knew an Alitalia flight from Rome was due. But this afternoon, after bringing sandwiches to their accomplices waiting at the villa, they were waiting dutifully in their car – Ferrante's business was closed on Saturdays and he apparently had nothing better to do – when Ganci's son Domenico called them at 5.01 p.m.

Domenico told them that Falcone's car was on its way to the airport and the pair set off towards it; Ferrante called La Barbera at 5.05 p.m. to pass on the news.

Calogero Ganci reached the airport at about 5 p.m. He had just got out of the car when he saw the convoy arrive; it went through a police barrier and sped on towards the airport's apron area.

Calogero called his father's butcher's shop at 5.15 p.m. His brother Domenico answered the phone.

'Listen, the meat's arrived,' Calogero said.

'Everything's OK, everything's OK,' Domenico replied. He had already warned the plotters.

After his jet had taxied up to the waiting convoy, Falcone walked briskly down the steps and greeted his driver, Costanza, and the six bodyguards. His smile was tight but cordial as ever.

'Let's stop off at home first; we'll drop my wife off there.' Falcone said he would then go on to a clothes shop in the centre of Palermo to buy some shirts.

Falcone got into the driver's seat of the white Croma, and Francesca sat in the front passenger seat; she suffered from car-sickness and preferred to sit in front. Falcone always drove when they were together, and for her sake he drove slower than his drivers. Costanza got into the back; no body-guard joined them.

The tall, athletic thirty-year-old Vito Schifani got behind the wheel of the lead car, a brown Croma. That morning, his wife Rosaria had accompanied him with Emanuele, their four-month-old baby, to the police barracks where he was based. Rosaria had a vague sense of foreboding, and had asked her husband if she could stay at the barracks and wait for him until his return. But he had just kissed her goodbye outside the barracks as usual, and gone off to start his shift.

One bodyguard sat himself next to Schifani in the lead car but Antonio Montinaro, the chief bodyguard, told him to go and sit in the last of the three cars. 'This seat's mine,' Montinaro, a lanky fishmonger's son with long curly hair, announced. Montinaro was so dedicated to Falcone that he'd named the second of his two sons Giovanni, as a tribute to the judge. He had celebrated his wife's birthday the previous evening, and they'd talked about Falcone; he told her that he was ready 'to die with Falcone'. This was no surprise to her; for Montinaro, Falcone was a God-like figure, a rare honest man, and he often told her: 'If I have to die, I want to die with him.'

For three of the six bodyguards on duty that day, it was their first assignment with Falcone. Montinaro told one of the 'new boys', Rocco Dicillo, to join him in the lead car. Dicillo complied; he secretly hoped that Falcone would stay at home that evening, so that he could spend a Saturday night with his girlfriend, a shopgirl who worked all week.

The other three bodyguards got into the last blue Croma driven by Gaspare Cervello – his surname meant 'brain' in Italian, and he'd long got used to the jokes people cracked about that. He was joined by the two other 'new boys', Paolo Capuzza and Angelo Corbo.

A blue light flashing on the last car, the convoy – with Falcone's car in the middle – set off out of the airport shortly before 6 p.m., and then down the motorway towards Palermo.

Several of the bodyguards held their machine-guns at the ready.

No police helicopter shadowed the convoy. The helicopter which had tailed Falcone for most of his years in Palermo had been axed five months earlier – to save money.

Hiding between parked cars so as not to be filmed by the airport's CCTV cameras, Ferrante recognised Falcone at the wheel of the white Croma as he passed through the police barrier.

Ferrante called La Barbera at 5.48 p.m. 'The car's there and it's gone,' Ferrante said, then hung up.

On the motorway, Schifani, the driver in the lead car, flashed his headlights at a Lancia Thema driven by Vincenzo Ferro, an employee of the regional health authority. Ferro saw the three Cromas overtake him in turn and guessed it was the convoy of a judge or a politician.

Later, the sight of the three cars overtaking him was the last thing he could remember.

From his spot on the road parallel to the motorway, five miles from the airport, La Barbera spotted Falcone's convoy. La Barbera not only recognised Falcone's car, he saw the body-guards inside the other cars and could even make out their machine-guns.

La Barbera called Gioè at 5.49 p.m. and the two men kept talking as La Barbera drove down the road, shadowing the convoy as it travelled down the motorway on his left. The two men chatted on and on, without ever hinting at what they were up to in case their phones were being tapped by the police.

'What are you up to this evening?'

'Nothing. If you're free we could go and have a pizza.'

'OK.'

La Barbera realised the convoy was travelling not at the 100–105 m.p.h. the conspirators had expected, but at about 80 m.p.h. As he chatted, he indicated that he was driving relatively slowly; he stayed on the phone for five minutes, until the road no longer flanked the motorway. It was 5.54 p.m.

In the last car, the 'new boy' Corbo sat with his back to the driver Cervello, his eyes fixed on the motorway behind the convoy. A Lancia Thema came up too close for his liking, so Corbo told Cervello to slow down to keep it at a safe distance from Falcone's car.

Cervello had noticed there were several cars behind the convoy; that made him slightly nervous until he saw that they didn't try to overtake, but rather kept away. Nothing to worry about, he decided.

In the middle car of the convoy, Falcone chatted with his driver Costanza. Falcone told him that he would be dropping off Francesca at their block of flats and asked him to get out of the car with her. 'I'll drive on,' Falcone said.

Costanza asked whether Falcone needed him on Sunday and Monday. Falcone told him he could take Sunday off but that he would need him to go back to the airport for his return to Rome.

Costanza asked Falcone when he should come and fetch him.

'Monday morning,' Falcone replied.

'So, when we get to your flat, could you please give me my car keys so that on Monday morning I can get the car?' Costanza asked.

To Costanza's astonishment, Falcone took his own set of car keys out of his pocket and pulled Costanza's set out of the ignition with the car still in fourth gear; in Costanza's bunch, along with the key to the ignition, were those to Costanza's flat. Falcone reached behind to hand Costanza's set back to him.

'What are you doing? We're going to get killed!' Costanza cried out.

The car slowed to 50–55 m.p.h. Falcone inserted his own bunch of keys into the ignition. Falcone turned, caught Francesca's eye and then turned again towards Costanza. 'I'm sorry,' Falcone said. 'I'm sorry.'

Later, Costanza thought that the reason for Falcone's action must have been that the judge, whom he had never seen do anything reckless, was worrying about something.

Brusca and Gioè had been waiting less than ten minutes when Gioè suddenly burst out: '*Vai* [Go]!'

But with his naked eye, Brusca couldn't see Falcone's car. So he didn't move.

'*Vai*!' Gioè urged a second time.

Brusca still didn't move.

Then he saw the white Croma, and as he stared at it he real-ised it was slowing down. He estimated it was travelling much slower than he'd expected, at about 50–55 m.p.h.

Brusca had planned to flick the lever when the car passed by the fridge, but because it was going slower than expected he stayed immobile a little longer. He felt 'mummified', momen-tarily thrown by the slower speed.

'*Vai*!' Gioè urged him a third time.

This time, The Executioner flicked the lever.

'The end of the world.'

From his vantage point, Brusca saw tall flames leap up into the air in fits and starts, as each barrel blew up one after the other in quick succession. He distinctly heard the explosions, which sounded to him like 'ba-ba-bang, ba-ba-bang', over and over again; the sounds reached him with a delay of just over a second. A huge, mushroom-shaped cloud of dust and black smoke rose over the motorway. Brusca felt he was seeing 'the end of the world ... something very, very awful.'

'What's happening? What the hell have I done?' Brusca cried out.

He heard rubble falling back down to earth; it sounded like rain to him. He heard the burglar alarms of nearby villas screeching out all together, set off by the shock waves from the explosion. He saw that behind Falcone's car, the flashing blue light of the last escort car kept turning.

More than 50 miles away in Agrigento on Sicily's southern coast, the explosion was registered by the Geophysical Observatory, timed at 5.56 p.m. and 48 seconds.

Cervello, the driver of the last car in the convoy, was just behind Falcone's in the fast lane. He instinctively swerved to the right when he saw the motorway explode in front of him. He lost consciousness immediately afterwards but came to very soon, blood trickling from a broken nose.

He managed to open his door by shoving it hard, and got out of the car. The car and the ground as far as 200 yards away were strewn with everything that the explosion had punched into the air – asphalt, blackened fragments of concrete, stones, lumps of clay, earth, parts ripped from cars and from the lights above the motorway – and, unknown to Cervello, pieces of the mattress that the plotters had used to hide the explosives. The tarmac of the motorway had cracked into slabs with jagged edges; the surface looked like a patch of African soil parched and broken up by drought. The air stank of petrol and cordite.

Dazed by the blast, Cervello roamed aimlessly around for a few moments, his gun drawn. He saw a man approach and shouted at him: 'Stop or I'll shoot!'

'I'm a colleague,' the man replied – Cervello hadn't recognised his fellow bodyguard.

'Stop or I'll shoot,' Cervello insisted.

The shock wore off and Cervello saw that his car, its front mangled, had halted just a couple of feet from the back of Falcone's. A mass of rubble almost surrounded Falcone's car, holding it in a tight grip. Rocks rested on the roof, and more rubble had penetrated inside; the bullet-proof front and rear windscreens had both shattered. What remained of the devastated front of the car rested on the edge of an oval-shaped crater, fourteen yards long, a dozen yards wide, and a dozen feet deep.

Cervello rushed up to Falcone's car. He saw that Falcone was trapped – the car's engine unit was crushing him, the back of his seat was twisted and leaning forward, and he could move only his head. Blood trickled in rivulets from a single stain on the driving wheel, the bottom of which was also twisted.

In the seat beside him, Francesca sat with her body slumped forwards; Costanza lay on his side on the back seat. Both had lost consciousness.

Cervello walked up close to Falcone and, for the first time in the many years they had known each other, used the judge's first name. 'Giovanni, Giovanni . . .' Cervello murmured.

Falcone turned to stare back at him, but his gaze seemed somehow impenetrable, and lifeless.

'They've all had it,' Cervello thought to himself. For years afterwards, Falcone's eyes tormented Cervello day and night. 'They follow me, they accompany me, they're part of me,' he said much later.

There was no hushed silence. Apart from the burglar alarms triggered by the blast, the radio station which the health worker Ferro, whom the convoy had overtaken shortly before, had been listening to played on and on for the next hour – a mix of music, jingles and advertisements. Ferro himself suffered only a fracture to one arm in the explosion.

There was no sign of the lead car. Cervello presumed it had escaped unscathed, and had raced on ahead to get help.

Capuzza, who had been sitting in the passenger seat next to Cervello, was looking out through the right-hand window when he heard the explosion and felt a blast of warm air engulf him. He turned instantly to look ahead and saw the tarmac rising up into the sky.

As the car came to an abrupt halt, Capuzza was thrown onto the dashboard, injuring his left arm and body. He felt no immediate pain but heard rubble raining down onto the car. There was so much black smoke he couldn't see anything. He tried to grab his Beretta M-12 sub-machine-gun but found that for some reason he couldn't hold it properly. So he jumped out of the car clutching his ordnance pistol instead and stared around wildly, expecting gunmen to come up and shoot them all dead.

But no shots came, and Capuzza saw flames just in front of Falcone's car.

His superior Cervello called out to him: 'Angelo, Angelo, go get the fire extinguisher and let's put this fire out before it gets out of control and we cop it too.'

Capuzzza went back to his car to get the fire extinguisher and managed to put the fire out quickly. He then tried to call for help on his car radio, but the blast had destroyed it.

But soon, Capuzza saw two cars had stopped nearby and told their drivers: 'Call for help, tell them there's been a bomb attack and Judge Falcone is a victim.'

With his back still turned as he stared out of the rear window, Corbo, the third man in the last car, saw nothing of the explosion. He heard the blast, and felt a pressure wave as he was catapulted towards the front of the car. Despite hitting his head so violently that his nose was badly broken, Corbo managed to get out, after struggling to open his door, and he too rushed up to Falcone's car with his gun drawn, worried that a killer would come up to the judge to give him the *coup de grâce*.

Corbo couldn't make out whether Falcone was making any noise. The bodyguards tried to help him but his door wouldn't open. Corbo saw the judge turn to look at him, apparently realising that the bodyguards could do nothing for him now. The bodyguards thought that Falcone was urging them to look to his right, as if he wanted them to help Francesca.

The bodyguards managed to pull out the window on Francesca's side and gingerly lift her out of the car. They also managed to get Costanza out. Both Francesca and Costanza were unconscious but still breathing as they were raced to hospital.

It was only when firemen arrived that Falcone was freed from the wreckage and lifted out.

He was still alive, still conscious and aware of the explosion. 'If I survive, this time I'll make them pay . . .' a young fireman heard Falcone say before an ambulance took him away.

Usually The Executioner liked to stay behind to watch the pandemonium that followed his hits. But this time, Brusca didn't wait around. He and Gioè left the remote control, the telescope and the pedestal to the soldier Battaglia, rushed to a car they had parked nearby and drove off to Palermo.

'We were satisfied with the result we'd obtained, even though we still didn't know what had happened exactly. We drove calmly, but at the time we were stunned, because we'd raised Hell,' Brusca related.

Battaglia destroyed the remote control, burning all the remaining pieces. But none of the plotters realised then that they'd left behind on the hillside the dozens of cigarette ends Gioè had dropped on the grass – the only time during the long weeks of preparation that they had forgotten to pick them up and take them away.

Judge Borsellino loses his 'shield'

Falcone's close friend and colleague, Paolo Borsellino, sat with his head back, a white towel around his neck and a lit Dunhill Light cigarette in his hand as the barber Paolo Biondo shaved around his black, silver-lined moustache. Borsellino closed his green-brown eyes and relaxed.

This was a ritual Borsellino had refused to give up despite security worries. For the past fifteen years he had been going to Biondo's shop near his home. Today his youngest daughter Fiammetta, a nineteen-year-old law student, had driven him there, and as ever he would walk home alone afterwards.

The prosecutor relished any small taste of normal life – beyond the barrier his bodyguards represented. He hugely enjoyed going out, accompanied only by one of his children, to buy a packet of cigarettes or something – a lotion to stop his hair falling out, shaving cream or razors – at a department store. He would simply roam the shelves, then stand in line and wait for his turn at the cash till, refusing politely when other shoppers recognised him and invited him to pass in front of them.

The senior prosecutor Caponnetto, who had had both Falcone and Borsellino under him, was fond of saying that they lived 'parallel lives'. Only six months younger than Falcone, Borsellino had grown up like him in the Kalsa neighbourhood in the heart of Palermo and the two had played football together in the streets, often with a ball made of rags.

The son and grandson of pharmacists, Borsellino was raised like Falcone with strong patriotic values; two of Borsellino's uncles had fought in Africa in the Second World War, and were taken prisoner there. Borsellino admitted many years later that despite his upbringing, when he was fifteen he had envied a schoolmate who boasted he was the son of a Mafia boss.

His father died when Borsellino was twenty-two years old, and he became 'the head of the family, with a mother, two sisters and a brother to worry about.' He studied law, and learnt the job of magistrate working for the father of Francesca, Falcone's future wife. As anti-Mafia prosecutors in Palermo, Falcone and Borsellino became the chief architects of the maxi-trial of hundreds of bosses. Like Falcone, Borsellino had huge respect for the state and its representatives. When he was told that a *carabiniere* general was a member of Cosa Nostra, he retched in shock.

Caponnetto, their boss at the time of the maxi-trial, was struck by the differences in their characters. Falcone was an introvert, while Borsellino was outgoing. Falcone allowed himself few pleasures in life, while Borsellino enjoyed riding a motorcycle, sailing and other pastimes. Falcone appeared troubled, Borsellino much more serene; Caponnetto attributed this to Borsellino's strong Catholic faith. He often told his children: 'In love, you must always give and not take.' The two also had contrasting political views. Borsellino was right-wing, and had been a member of a neo-Fascist group as a young man; Falcone was left-wing.

But despite such differences, their friendship endured. When Borsellino was transferred to Marsala on the western tip of Sicily, he and Falcone called each other almost every day. Borsellino was less rigorous than his friend about his personal security. A fatherly figure to his younger colleagues, he showed far more concern for their safety than his own. In the evenings, his bodyguards would accompany him home to his flat in the police station but he would then dismiss them, knock on the door of a neighbour who was a colleague, and the two would go out to dinner with no escort whatsoever.

Borsellino moved back to Palermo in late 1991 and became deputy-chief prosecutor – a job which had once been Falcone's. When asked whether fighting the Mafia made him afraid, Borsellino would reply: 'Fear is a human feeling. So it's normal to have fear. The important thing is to have even more courage.'

Borsellino was convinced that his friend protected him. 'Falcone is my shield; he's my shield against the vendetta of Cosa Nostra. As long as Falcone's alive, I'll always be number two on the list,' he confided. Borsellino often said that Falcone was three months ahead of him in everything they did – Falcone had graduated three months before him, and started his judicial career three months before him too.

But, a fatalist like Falcone, he also told his friends that he wouldn't live beyond the age of fifty-two – his father and his grandfather had died at that age, and he believed that he would too.

Borsellino had turned fifty-two in January.

At about 6.30 p.m., as the barber spread aftershave lotion over Borsellino's cheeks, the prosecutor's mobile phone rang. It was his younger colleague Francesco Lo Voi, another friend of both Falcone and Francesca.

The news Lo Voi gave him made Borsellino turn pale; he suddenly straightened up in his chair and gestured for the barber to stop.

'What are you saying?' Borsellino asked in a strained, pleading tone.

'Yes, it's Giovanni. All we know is that he's wounded,' Lo Voi replied; he didn't know about any other victims.

Borsellino got out of his chair, snatched the towel from around his neck and, his phone still clamped to his ear, extracted two banknotes from his wallet and almost threw them at the barber before racing outside.

'OK, I'm going home, come and pick me up there,' Borsellino told Lo Voi.

He ran home, rushing past the porter without greeting him. When his son Manfredi, a law student like his younger sister, opened the door to their flat, Borsellino did not stop to greet him either and rushed to the telephone in his study.

Manfredi, together with his sisters Fiammetta and Lucia, a pharmacy student, who had been studying in the sitting-room, rushed to their father – their mother Agnese was out.

'What's happened?' they asked.

Their father said nothing. His mouth was clamped shut. He kept punching out a number on the phone on his desk.

'Daddy, tell me what's the matter. Tell me,' Lucia insisted.

Again their father said nothing. Then, with mad eyes, Borsellino suddenly slipped off his belt and started beating it against the wall – one lash, two lashes, ten lashes. He screamed in anger: 'A bomb attack . . . Giovanni, Giovanni . . . he's wounded, he's at the Civic Hospital!'

His three children were too stunned to say anything for a moment. Then Lucia took hold of her father's arm and managed, after a short struggle, to stop him whipping the wall.

'Let's go, Daddy; that's enough now. Let's go to him,' Lucia told him.

Borsellino shook himself and put his belt back on. 'Yes, let's go,' he said.

Falcone arrived at Palermo's Civic Hospital in a state of cardiac-respiratory arrest. Doctors fought to save him as police helicopters clattered noisily, and uselessly, above the hospital. The doctors found Falcone had suffered several haemorrhages due to internal injuries, a sizeable trauma to the skull, a wound to the face and a trauma to the chest as well as multiple bone fractures in his legs.

At first, Francesca had been rushed by mistake to the Cervello hospital in Palermo, which was not adequately equipped to treat her. The first doctor to see her was Andrea Vassallo – an orthopaedist who had been investigated for suspected Mafia offences by none other than Falcone himself. Francesca, suffering like her husband from internal haemorrhages – the blast had also broken both her legs, and her left arm – was then swiftly taken to the Civic Hospital where a new team fought to save her.

After driving into Palermo, The Executioner and several of his accomplices – among them Ganci and Salvatore Cancemi, both of them butchers – met at the same villa where the godfather Riina had briefed Brusca about the assassination plot four months earlier. On the way there, Brusca passed a couple of police roadblocks but no one challenged him.

The bosses switched on the TV set and learnt that Falcone was in hospital but still alive – as was his wife Francesca. Cancemi sprung up from his chair and started venting his frustration. 'That f—er, if he survives, he'll break our balls, he'll destroy us!' Cancemi ranted.

Brusca and Ganci looked at each other in amazement at his behaviour. Ganci couldn't understand Cancemi – the two were close friends, and often went together to markets and slaughterhouses to buy and sell their livestock. Brusca thought Cancemi had gone mad.

Borsellino was among the first to arrive at the Civic Hospital's casualty department. Lo Voi drove him there in his armoured car so fast that Borsellino exclaimed at one point: 'Go slower or we'll get killed!'

At the hospital, Borsellino asked for Falcone. Two doctors recognised him and, taking him by the arm, led him through a glass door, with Lo Voi following. Borsellino's daughter Lucia waited on a bench.

After half an hour, the doctors struggling to reanimate Falcone abandoned their efforts. Falcone was pronounced dead at 7.05 p.m. The cause of death was registered as a haemorrhagic shock from injuries to internal organs, especially in the abdomen. Later, an autopsy found Falcone had eight broken ribs and his lungs had been crushed by his ribcage. His abdomen was full of blood, and he had a fractured lumbar vertebra.

Lo Voi realised Falcone was dead only when he saw Borsellino huddle up in a corner, holding his head in his hands. The pair then went to see Francesca; doctors were fighting to save her, and the pair began to hope she would survive.

Shortly after Falcone was pronounced dead, Borsellino's mobile phone rang. It was his ex-boss Caponnetto, who had been trying to get in touch with him ever since he'd seen the first report of the explosion on TV.

Borsellino greeted Caponnetto; he had hardly any voice left.

'Paolo, how is Giovanni?' Caponnetto asked.

All Caponnetto could hear was the sound of Borsellino crying.

'Paolo, can you tell me? How is Giovanni?' Caponnetto insisted.

'He died a minute ago in my arms,' Borsellino replied.

Nearby, Francesca found the strength to ask: 'Where's Giovanni?'

The person she asked had just seen her husband die but did not tell her the truth.

*   *   *

As she waited, Borsellino's daughter Lucia saw him emerge from behind the glass door. He stooped as he walked; he looked pale and lost.

Borsellino hugged his daughter, telling her only: 'He died like this, in my arms.'

Lucia burst out crying. She wept not only for Falcone. She felt that death was now closer for her father; he had accompanied Falcone down that stretch of motorway so often. And Borsellino had told her a thousand times that Falcone was his shield: 'They'll kill him first, then they'll kill me,' he'd said.

Now her father whispered to her: 'Don't cry, we mustn't make people stare.' But he too suddenly started crying, without restraint, in his daughter's arms. Lucia felt his tears on her neck.

'Daddy, how are you going to keep going now?' Lucia asked.

'I don't know, I don't know,' he replied.

Francesca's brother Alfredo emerged through the glass door. Borsellino realised from one glance at him – white as a sheet, mute, stunned – that there was little hope for her.

Sobs jerked Borsellino's stooped body. Clasping Lucia tightly, he murmured: 'No, not Francesca as well, no . . .'

Antonio Ingroia, a junior colleague of Borsellino's, saw him shortly afterwards. 'He was shattered, leaning with his shoulders against a wall; his eyes stared into the void, his expression was dark, immobile, stunned. I didn't have the strength to say anything to him,' Ingroia related.

Borsellino's sadness quickly turned to anger. Smoking continuously, he became 'like a beast in a cage', according to the lawyer Francesco Crescimanno, another friend of Falcone's.

That afternoon Falcone's sister, Maria, was waiting for him at her flat. He had said he would come to see her.

The phone rang. A friend she was due to see that evening asked her some odd questions, checking if they were still going to meet up that evening. A few minutes later, the phone rang again. Maria's husband answered. She looked at his face, caught a few words of the conversation, and suddenly realised that her brother was late.

She thought it must be her friend calling again. 'Something's happened, hasn't it? Is it Giovanni?' Maria asked her husband.

'A bomb attack, but it's not serious. Maybe he's wounded . . . slightly. Francesca too,' her husband told her.

For a moment, Maria saw in her mind's eye what seemed like a film of her brother's life, and of their life together. What a torment it must have been, she thought, his fight for principles which should be universal rules. He had been always alone, always hindered by others, and rewarded with nothing – and yet he had given the utmost he could give.

She began to hope there was a mistake, that it wasn't true there had been an attack. She called the police, told them she was Falcone's sister, and asked if they could send someone to take her to her brother and Francesca.

'How do we know for sure that you really are Judge Falcone's sister?' an officer asked.

'Alright, then tell me at least where he is,' Maria said.

At the Civic Hospital, she saw a group of people who looked like investigators. They would know whether her brother and Francesca were still alive, she thought. Before she could ask them, Francesca's brother Alfredo ran up to her, bewilderment stamped on his face. There was no need for him to speak; Maria understood.

Francesca's mother learnt about her daughter's death watching the TV news, which reported it before Alfredo called her. He had delayed calling her to tell her about the blast, hoping that his sister would survive.

A champagne toast

When the news of Falcone's death flashed onto the screen at the villa where the plotters waited, Cancemi exclaimed, 'That bastard wanted to ruin everyone!' He jumped up from his chair again, rushed up to the TV and started spitting at it, and insulting it as if Falcone himself were in front of him.

He thrust a hand into his pocket and gave some banknotes to a young Mafioso, asking him to go and buy a bottle of champagne. He spat at the TV again and again, repeating: 'That f—er, that f—er! At last!'

Brusca stared at him, stunned by his reaction; he felt Falcone's death shouldn't be treated so crudely. But when the bottle of champagne arrived, Brusca had no qualms about toasting Falcone's death with his accomplices.

Later that evening, Brusca had dinner at Gioè's home in Altofonte. As they ate, Brusca told him he hadn't believed the initial report that Falcone had survived the blast. The explosion had gone perfectly, and it was physically impossible for anyone to survive it, he insisted.

When the news of the assassination spread through Palermo's Ucciardone prison, hundreds of euphoric Mafia convicts applauded and cheered. They too toasted his death. Prisoners at the Caltanissetta jail in central Sicily also rejoiced: 'When the news bulletin came ... in the cells, we toasted each other and drank,' one collaborator remembered.

But for Ferrante, who had spotted Falcone at the airport, and his accomplice Biondo, there was no reason to exult at the judge's death. When they heard the news on the car radio, they both agreed that killing Falcone had been a mistake because the state would surely react now. Falcone would harm the Mafia much more now that he was dead than when he was alive, Ferrante said.

For now, Ferrante had another celebration in mind – his son Giuseppe's First Communion the next day, Sunday. Back in Palermo, he went to fetch his wife and the couple drove to the restaurant where they would be having a party for Giuseppe. Ferrante had brought several bottles of champagne with him for the reception, and talked to the staff about arrangements for the banquet – to all accounts an apparently ordinary father, anxious only that everyone should have fun.

That evening La Barbera, who had shadowed the convoy from the road parallel to the motorway, was stuck in a traffic jam on his way back to Palermo. Through his open window, he heard people talking about the assassination. 'Those bastards, they're a disgrace, they've killed that fine man Falcone and his wife,' one man said.

La Barbera saw several people in tears. He felt very uncomfortable. When people asked him if he'd heard about the assassination, he pretended that he hadn't. He too had misgivings, but he confided them only to Gioè. They both wondered what the godfather Riina's objective was – what was the point of such killings? But they were resigned to obeying orders.

At about 8 p.m., the lawyer Crescimanno drove to Falcone's flat with a few colleagues of Falcone's and a couple of police officers to fetch some clothes to dress the body in before it was placed in a coffin.

Once at the flat, they started opening cupboards and drawers looking for suitable clothes. They were still looking when they received a phone call telling them that Francesca had also died; they should find some clothes for her too.

When Falcone's driver Costanza regained consciousness at the hospital and asked where the judge, Francesca and his colleagues were, he was told only that they were all being taken care of like him. He could remember nothing after Falcone handed the keys to him, until he found himself in hospital.

Of the three people in Falcone's car, Costanza – who had been sitting in the back – was the only one to survive the explosion, although he suffered injuries to the skull, stomach and spinal cord. Later, he estimated that Falcone pulling the keys out of the ignition had meant that their car was at least an extra yard away from the centre of the explosion – enough to save it from a frontal impact with the blast. Just that one yard, together with the fact that he was sitting in the back of Falcone's car, had saved Costanza's life.

It wasn't until a few hours after the explosion that the first car in Falcone's convoy was discovered. The only car in the convoy hit by the full force of the blast, it had been catapulted a distance of sixty-two yards across the motorway, over prickly pear trees and cane thickets and into an olive grove where it shattered on impact. The three bodyguards – Montinaro, Schifani and Dicillo – died instantly, their bodies torn to pieces, their faces unrecognisable. It took firemen an hour to cut through the wreckage with big shears and extract the bodies.

That evening, two *carabinieri* stopped Rosaria Schifani, now a widow, from going down the flight of steps which led to the morgue in the basement of the forensic medicine institute. She was told to wait. At 9.30 p.m., Rosaria recognised Borsellino as he arrived at the morgue with his escort and approached her. Rosaria begged him to show her Vito's body.

'No, Rosaria, it's better if you don't go down there. Not yet,' Borsellino told her.

It was another two hours before Rosaria was finally allowed into the morgue; all she was shown of her dead husband were his hands. They were intact.

Falcone's friend and colleague Ayala flew from Rome to see him one last time. Ayala was left alone with the body, stretched out on a slab of marble in the morgue.

Ayala was struck to see how unblemished Falcone looked. All there was was a small scratch above his right eyebrow less than an inch long. Otherwise he was perfect, Ayala thought. Falcone's face was relaxed, he was smiling, his eyes closed. Ayala was reminded of the times he'd seen Falcone sleeping during their travels.

In tears, the tall Ayala bent down to kiss Falcone on the forehead. He stroked Falcone's hair and rearranged a wisp of it above his temple. He then took Falcone's hand in his. Ayala had often teased Falcone about his hands, which were much smaller than his – 'women's hands', Ayala used to call them. Ayala was struck by the beauty of Falcone's hand and had the impression that it disappeared within his own.

Ayala felt a huge wave of fondness for Falcone. He had put his life at stake, Ayala thought. 'What's my life going to be like without him now? What the f— am I going to do now?' Ayala asked himself. He felt as if he'd had a limb amputated. Falcone had changed his life, ever since they had met when Ayala was thirty-six years old, just over a decade ago.

Ayala felt 'infinite rage' at those who had killed his friend. 'If I'd had the killer in front of me at that moment, I would have killed him,' Ayala explained. For years he had braced himself for Falcone's death, but in the past months he had started to believe that 'they' wouldn't kill him after all.

In the days and weeks that followed, Ayala found the strength to cope with the murder in the words that Falcone had said to him a few months earlier: 'Whatever happens Giuseppe, you've got to bear one thing in mind above all . . . Whoever remains has to keep going.'

Another former member of the Palermo prosecutors' anti-Mafia team, Leonardo Guarnotta, who had known Falcone for the past thirteen years, was also surprised to see that Falcone looked unhurt, as if he were simply asleep. Guarnotta thought of all the work they had done together, of the lives they had shared.

Questions assailed Guarnotta as he stared at the body: 'Why? Why do these things happen? Why can't we just work in peace in Sicily to seek a better future for our society, for our young people?'

That evening, Borsellino told his escort to drive him to the scene of the explosion. There, the stench of petrol and cordite still hung heavy in the air and Borsellino's eyes stung; he rubbed his eyes before covering his mouth and nose with a handkerchief.

A police officer guiding Borsellino pointed to where the lead car had been catapulted. Borsellino turned sharply, took a few steps through the rubble on the tarmac, and saw the fate which his friend had met. Falcone's car was still on the edge of the crater: Francesca's shoes lay on the floor mat in front of her seat.

Nearby lay the wrecks of several cars that had not been part of the convoy; another seven people who had been driving down the motorway had been injured in the explosion. Borsellino bent down and picked up a stone from the rubble, which he took away with him.

'This is just the beginning,' Borsellino thought to himself as he was driven back to Palermo.

In his office at the law courts that night, Borsellino summoned three young prosecutors, stared silently at them for a time, then spoke. 'We have to ask ourselves three questions: Why did they kill Giovanni? Why did they kill him now? And why did they kill him in Palermo?' he said.

Borsellino hid his face in his hands for a moment, then, smoking one Dunhill Light after another, tried to answer his own questions. He told his young colleagues, whose eyes were wet with tears, that he had found out Falcone had been about to be appointed 'super-prosecutor'. But he had no idea whether the news had spread outside the law courts.

'But that's only the first question . . . Giovanni died today because today was the last time he would have come back to Palermo with any regularity. And they knew it, someone had warned them . . . His habit of coming down to Sicily almost every week, and always at weekends, would have ended because Francesca had finally found a way of staying in Rome for a long period . . . I don't think that this was ever public knowledge, or that it ever appeared in an newspaper, but in here everyone knew it,' he said.

In a low voice, barely above a whisper, Borsellino told his colleagues: 'There was a report going around that Giovanni could become the new interior minister . . . do you understand what that would have meant for them, the Mafiosi?'

At 3 a.m., Borsellino left the law courts and returned to the hospital where Falcone's body still lay.

Later, he placed the stone he had taken from the scene of the explosion on a bookshelf at home, a constant reminder of the loss of his friend – and perhaps, for Borsellino, of his own vulnerability.

Rosaria Schifani's plea for justice

On 24 May, the day after Falcone's assassination, Borsellino was back in his office in the law courts at dawn. Later that morning, he went downstairs to the cavernous entrance hall, where the mahogany coffins of Falcone and Francesca had been placed for the people of Palermo to pay tribute to them.

For hours on end, thousands of Palermitans of all ages filed past the coffins, many of them in tears. Borsellino, who was crying too, stood a short distance away and talked to several young anti-Mafia colleagues. Some of them were so discouraged by the assassination that they talked about leaving Palermo for good.

Borsellino shook his head: 'Boys, I'm talking to you as if I was your father, or your older brother. I have a duty to tell you that we can't have any illusions. If we stay, the future for some of us will be that one!' – he pointed to the two coffins.

He then gestured towards the people filing past the coffins. 'I'm staying and I'm staying only for them. I can't leave them on their own!' he said.

When the politicians arrived from Rome – among them the speaker of the Senate (the upper house of parliament) as well as several government ministers – to pay their respects to the victims, thousands of Palermitans crowded outside voiced their anger at decades of collusion between politicians and the Mafia, and the state's failure to beat organised crime.

'Assassins!' the crowd shouted. 'Jackals, go away! You're the Mafia; go back to Rome!'

Across Palermo, people hung white bed sheets from their windows. Scrawled on them was: '*Palermo demands Justice*'; '*Basta* [enough]*!*'; '*Get the Mafiosi out of government!*'; '*Falcone, you remain in our hearts*'; and '*Falcone lives!*' For Falcone's friend, the journalist La Licata, this act of defiance showed that the popular consensus Cosa Nostra had by and large benefited from until then had been shattered – at least for the time being. 'The sheets told it: "We're not with you." Imagine, it's as if you lived in the jungle and there were lions and tigers outside your home. And you decided to hang a chunk of fresh meat outside your home even though you knew it would attract the beasts,' La Licata commented.

Many Palermitans paid a pilgrimage to Falcone's home and stuck tributes and messages on a magnolia tree in the street outside. 'There are a million things to say to you, but the first we can think of is: "Thank you",' read one note left by schoolchildren.

That morning on the hillside above the motorway, officers from the Palermo forensic police spotted fifty-three cigarette ends lying on the ground; investigators suspected this was the spot where the plotters had lain in wait.

Gioè was watching the TV news with his niece when a journalist reported that one of the assassins had left behind dozens of cigarette ends which had been 'heavily chewed'. Investigators hoped the cigarette ends would allow them to establish the DNA of at least one of the killers.

'Uncle, the man who killed Falcone has the same nasty habit you've got,' Gioè's niece quipped. She knew nothing about his involvement.

Gioè felt as if he'd been slapped in the face.

It rained on the day of the funeral for the five victims of the Capaci bomb. Police chiefs deployed hundreds of officers near the seventeenth-century Church of San Domenico to prevent a repeat of the protests that had marked the arrival of government leaders at the law courts.

Despite the rain, thousands of mourners thronged the square outside the church and streets up to a mile away. With the square packed, Giovanni Spadolini, the acting head of state, the interior minister Vincenzo Scotti, the justice minister Claudio Martelli and other politicians had to make a detour down side streets and enter the church through the sacristy instead of the main doors. Giulio Andreotti, the prime minister, stayed in Rome.

In front of the altar, an Italian tricolour was draped over each of the five coffins. The black robes Falcone and Francesca had worn in court were displayed on their coffins; police caps had been placed on the bodyguards' coffins.

From the pulpit, Rosaria, Vito Schifani's young widow, struggled to read in halting, tearful tones a text she had written with her cousin, the priest Father Cesare Rattoballi. She stumbled over the words, repeating herself and often departing from the prepared text.

'In the name of all those who have given their life for the state – the state . . . – I ask first of all for justice. Now, speaking to the men of the Mafia – because even inside here there are Mafiosi . . . : know that there is the possibility of forgiveness for you too.

I forgive you but you must go down on your knees. If you have the courage to change . . . but they don't want to change, they, they don't change, they don't change. If you have the courage to radically change your designs of death, be Christians once again.

For this we pray in the name of the Lord who said on the Cross: 'Father, forgive them, for they know not what they do.'

We ask you this for our city of Palermo, which you have turned into a city of blood, to ask you to strive for peace, justice and hope. Too much blood, there is no love here, there is no love here, there is no love at all . . . '

Broadcast live on Italian TV, Rosaria's words touched one of Falcone's assassins. When he heard her, Ferrante felt like a worm. 'Her words weighed on me more than anything else,' he said.

As Rosaria's voice tailed off, many off-duty police body-guards wearing civilian clothes surged forward to get close to the politicians, angrily shouting 'Justice!' over and over again. A few of them, who wore black armbands in a sign of mourn-ing, threw coins at the politicians in a traditional gesture of disdain and spat at them. 'We're the walking dead!' one of them exclaimed.

Their uniformed colleagues managed to push them back and allow the politicians to flee the church unharmed, but there were more shouts, jeers and whistles from the crowd outside: 'Incompetent!', 'Accomplices!', 'Assassins!'

Standing beside Falcone's coffin, a pale, mute Borsellino stared aghast at the tumult in the church. He had such a high esteem of the state and its institutions that the police body-guards' protest shocked him deeply. Borsellino had spent most of the night keeping vigil over Falcone's coffin and had insisted on driving Francesca's mother to the church that morning – it was his way of 'continuing to feel that Giovanni and Francesca were alive,' his daughter Fiammetta explained.

After the funeral service, Borsellino went up to the still-distraught Rosaria and whispered to her: 'The Lord will see to vendetta; we'll see to justice.' The prosecutor repeated his promise: 'Rosaria, you'll see that I'll make sure justice is done for the death of your husband.' Moments later Borsellino, wet through as he rushed about in the rain, searched for a car to take Francesca's mother home.

That afternoon, the prosecutor accompanied his ex-boss Caponnetto to the airport where he was catching a flight home to Florence. Caponnetto was certain that Borsellino was the

next target on the Mafia's death-list, just as he was certain that
Borsellino knew this too, even if the latter joked about it.

As they said goodbye to each other, Borsellino asked: 'Nino,
are you sure we'll see each other again?' He was smiling as he
said this.

'Either in Florence or here, of course we'll see each other
again,' Caponnetto replied.

But Caponnetto's sense of foreboding was so strong that
the two men embraced more warmly than they had ever done
before.

Gianni De Gennaro, Italy's 'Supercop' as the newspapers
called him, chose to stay away from Palermo. The forty-four-
year-old De Gennaro had become friends with Falcone over
a decade of working together, and rather than attend the
funeral, he preferred to start work immediately on the hunt
for the assassins at his base in Rome. 'There are some things
you can do only in the first hours, which there and then look
meaningless but then they bear some fruit, if luck is with you,'
he confided in a voice made husky by sixty cigarettes a day.

Self-effacing but headstrong, De Gennaro had left his native
Calabria in the toe of Italy's boot to study for a law degree in
Rome, before joining the flying squad at a busy police station
on the capital's outskirts. Promoted after taking part in a
shoot-out following a kidnapping at the Belgian embassy, he
had crossed paths with Falcone when he escorted Tommaso
Buscetta, 'The Godfather of Two Worlds', from Brazil to Italy
in 1984. When Buscetta decided to turn his back on the Mafia
and break its law of secrecy, it was De Gennaro whom Falcone
asked to verify his lengthy testimony.

With De Gennaro's help, Falcone ensured that Buscetta
was held not in an Italian prison as the law demanded but
instead in a comfortable cell hastily set up inside the Rome
police headquarters – a home which guaranteed his survival,

as in jail fellow inmates would have swiftly tried to murder him for his betrayal. Working on the subsequent maxi-trial with both Falcone and Borsellino, and on the testimony of other Mafiosi who followed Buscetta's lead, De Gennaro had become, like the two prosecutors, a sworn enemy of the Mafia.

A few months before Falcone's assassination, De Gennaro had been named deputy-head of the new DIA agency, an Italian FBI which Falcone had helped create and whose investigators included hand-picked officers from both the police and their long-time rivals, the *carabinieri*.

His agency was housed in the fifteenth-century convent of Santa Priscilla in northern Rome, a haven of elegant cloisters and gardens built above ancient catacombs. From his top-floor office, after Falcone's murder, De Gennaro started to make dozens of phone calls and order up case files.

'If it's the last thing I do in my life, I'll get them. I owe it to Giovanni, I owe it to myself, I owe it to those bastards who killed him. Giovanni taught me to understand what Cosa Nostra is and how it can be defeated; now we'll see what I learnt, and they'll find out too,' he pledged.

The godfather Riina was so overjoyed with Falcone's murder – a crime nine years in the making – that he summoned the assassins to celebrate with champagne one afternoon, a week or so later. As Riina walked up the stairs leading to a Palermo safe house, his driver Biondino started complaining to him about the failure of the 1989 attempt to blow up Falcone at his seaside villa. The boss who'd overseen the attempt should have asked for his help, Biondino said, instead of relying on 'good-for-nothings'.

'If only he'd asked for a hand, if he'd asked for some help, I mean, we wouldn't have had to wait until now,' Biondino said. He moaned about the failed attempt for so long that Riina shut him up, telling him it was irrelevant as Falcone was dead now.

The godfather didn't let the exchange sour his celebration. The champagne cork popped, and Riina drank to the assassination with Brusca, his brother-in-law Bagarella and the two butchers Ganci and Cancemi, among others. Riina congratulated them all.

'At last, we've put our minds at rest,' one of the killers declared.

Riina kept talking delightedly about the plot he'd devised. He said of the state authorities: 'They're going crazy. They didn't expect it. They've been forced to ask for help from the American secret services' – a reference to the FBI, which along with Britain's Defence Research Agency had been asked to help identify the explosives used.

The godfather had little doubt the assassination, apart from ridding him of Falcone, would also wreck the prime minister Andreotti's hopes of becoming president. 'I'll make sure he becomes president,' Riina said ironically.

After the toast, Riina and Ganci talked quietly together, sitting on a leather sofa. Cancemi heard an agitated Riina tell Ganci: 'Stop. I'm taking responsibility for this; it has to be done as quickly as possible.'

As close friends Cancemi and Ganci drove home after the celebration, Ganci voiced the worries of many bosses about Riina's determination to continue his war against the state: 'He wants to burn us all up.'

But for the supergrass Buscetta, who was lying low in his secret American refuge, Riina's plot had been far from ideal because it had nearly failed. Despite the huge amount of explosives, no one in Falcone's car had died immediately. 'The driver of the armoured car survived, Falcone and his wife died in hospital. The assassination wasn't that perfect,' he reflected.

Buscetta paid tribute to his former enemy: 'Judge Falcone was my beacon. We understood each other without speaking. He was full of intuition and intelligence; he was honest and determined to work hard.'

Falcone's sister Anna was asked how she preferred to remember her brother. She pictured him as she had often seen him: serene and relaxed, and staring out from the balcony of her flat at the sea which had always fascinated him. If he were still alive, Anna said, she would say to him: 'Giovanni, you see how you died? Was it worth it?'

Judge Borsellino's race against time

With Falcone dead, Borsellino suddenly found himself thrust in unwelcome limelight as the new hero of Italy's fight against the Mafia – newspapers, magazines, TV programmes all portrayed him as his friend's heir, and politicians followed suit. One party, the neo-fascist Italian Social Movement, went so far as to call for Borsellino to become president of the republic – a move which infuriated him, as he had no desire to enter politics.

Vincenzo Visco, the interior minister, publicly backed Borsellino for the job of 'super-prosecutor' – despite the fact that Borsellino didn't want the post. Borsellino sent the minister a personal letter of refusal, saying he did not want to benefit in any way from Falcone's death.

The abrupt, massive public exposure he was now subjected to worried Borsellino. 'Giovanni Falcone was my shield, behind which I could protect myself. Without Falcone I'm the one who feels exposed and I'm the one who has to act as the shield for you people,' Borsellino told a young colleague, concerned as ever about the security of his juniors.

In the days that followed Falcone's death, he did his utmost to try and join the investigation into the assassination. As the crime involved a magistrate, the judicial investigation was led by prosecutors not in Palermo, but in Caltanissetta in central Sicily which handled such cases. In a confidential request, Borsellino asked to leave his job as Palermo's deputy-chief prosecutor and be transferred to Caltanissetta. But his demand was rejected on the grounds that he was 'emotionally involved' in the case. Borsellino accepted the decision without protest.

But he refused to do nothing. He spoke again and again to the 'Supercop' De Gennaro, and planned to go to Caltanissetta to testify before the prosecutor Salvatore Celesti, who was in charge of the investigation.

'I'll tell Celesti facts, episodes, events. I'll tell him about my last talks with Giovanni . . .' Borsellino confided to a friend two days after Falcone's death.

Just six days before the assassination, Borsellino said, he had learnt that Falcone had obtained the majority of votes he needed in the CSM, the self-governing body for Italy's judges, to be made national anti-Mafia prosecutor.

'I'd told Giovanni that now the conditions had been met . . . I don't know whether the news that Falcone would be the new anti-Mafia prosecutor was known to everyone,' Borsellino said. Perhaps, he added, the Mafia was afraid of the new powers Falcone was about to wield.

As he waited to be summoned to testify, Borsellino called every day on Pietro Vaccara, a prosecutor from Caltanissetta who had got himself an office in the Palermo law courts to work on the investigation. Vaccara knew little about the Palermo Mafia, and Borsellino briefed him at length, often inviting him to dinner. Through Vaccara, and his many contacts in the police, Borsellino followed the investigation as closely as he could.

Searching for clues, he read and re-read the case file on the murder of the ex-mayor Lima in March – a killing which he and Falcone had seen immediately as a possible first step in a 'strategy of terror' by the Mafia. Borsellino also scrutinised a report by the *carabinieri* on the Mafia's infiltration of public works contracts, which Falcone himself had commissioned.

To his friends, Borsellino mentioned repeatedly that he
intended to testify formally before the Caltanissetta prosecutors. 'I'll make a formal statement to the prosecutors on what
may be the right line of investigation when I've got a clearer
idea of the context of the bomb attack,' Borsellino told his
junior colleague Ingroia.

Gradually he came to believe that he had a great deal to
tell his colleagues, confiding to his wife Agnese: 'I'm racing
against time. I feel I can see clearly what the Mafia is up to.
I've got so much work to do, I've got so much work to do ...
I've understood everything about Giovanni's death.'

Borsellino didn't specify what 'everything' meant, but he
believed the priority had to be the capture of the godfather
Riina, whom he suspected – rightly – had ordered Falcone's
death. According to the *carabiniere* officer Carmelo Canale,
his right-hand man, this was the reason why Borsellino felt
he was 'racing against time'. For him, capturing Riina had
become 'a cause to live for'. Borsellino suggested to officials
at the interior ministry in Rome that the state should offer a
reward of several billion lire for Riina's capture. But the idea
was rejected.

And as the weeks passed, the summons from Caltanissetta
failed to materialise and Borsellino complained repeatedly to
his wife about the delay.

On the morning of 2 June 1992 – ten days after Falcone's
death – Borsellino's elderly mother Maria looked out from her
fourth-floor balcony in Via Mariano D'Amelio, a quiet dead-
end street in central Palermo, and noticed what she thought
were 'strange people' in a garden next to her block of flats, on
the other side of a perimeter wall.

Nervous about her son's safety in the wake of the assassination, she called the police. It was almost a full day later, at dawn
the next morning, before the head of the flying squad and

Giovanni Falcone and Paolo Borsellino, heroes in Italy's long fight against the Mafia. 'Falcone is my shield – he's my shield against the vendetta of Cosa Nostra,' Borsellino said of his friend. 'As long as Falcone's alive, I'll always be number two on the list.'

Set among the olive groves and rolling hills of central Sicily, a farmhouse used for secret meetings by the godfather Bernardo Provenzano near Mezzojuso, east of his hometown of Corleone.

The cathedral in Palermo, the teeming Sicilian capital where both Falcone and Borsellino were born and grew up among the children of Mafiosi.

A typical scene on the main square of Corleone, home to the clan which bludgeoned its way to the top of the Mafia and then turned its sights on the Italian state.

General Carlo Alberto Dalla Chiesa, of the paramilitary Carabinieri police, one of the Mafia's many 'distinguished cadavers', as leading officials slain by the society are known.

Falcone and Giuseppe Ayala, a friend and colleague, relaxing by the sea. Falcone was followed by his bodyguards even when he set out for a swim.

Falcone, his wife Francesca and Ayala on holiday in Egypt. After the death of General Dalla Chiesa, Francesca urged Ayala to 'forget about this damned Mafia'.

Falcone, Ayala and Borsellino in Brazil. It was in Brazil that the three agreed the Mafia would spare them while it awaited verdicts in the so-called 'maxi-trial' of hundreds of Mafiosi.

Giovanni 'The Executioner' Brusca, who described himself as 'a loyal soldier' at the service of the Mafia. He said he killed 'definitely less than two hundred people'.

Bernardo 'The Tractor' Provenzano, Riina's closest lieutenant and then successor. He earned his nickname 'because of his homicidal capability and of what happened to a problem or a person when he dealt with it,' an informer explained.

The godfather Salvatore 'The Beast' Riina from Corleone. 'His philosophy was that if someone's finger hurt, it was best to cut his arm off – it's safer that way,' a supergrass said of him.

23 May 1992 – The Mafia blows up a stretch of motorway near the town of Capaci to ambush Giovanni Falcone, his wife Francesca and his bodyguards.

Flowers left by mourners at the crater caused by the explosion which struck Falcone's three-car convoy.

Rosaria Schifani, the widow of Falcone's bodyguard Vito Schifani. In an appeal to Mafiosi at the funeral of the Capaci victims, she said: 'I forgive you but you must go down on your knees.'

19 July 1992 – A car-bomb wrecks Via D'Amelio as Borsellino, escorted by his bodyguards, arrived to see his mother.

Gianni De Gennaro, Italy's 'Supercop'. He promised after the Capaci explosion: 'If it's the last thing I do in my life, I'll get them. I owe it to Giovanni.'

Gaspare 'Baldy' Spatuzza, who carried out dozens of murders for the Mafia before embarking on what he called 'a beautiful spiritual journey' which led him to break its law of silence.

several officers arrived. All the officers found was evidence that someone had been at the spot recently. The report was filed away and forgotten.

Fear for Borsellino's life took its toll on all his family. In the nights after Falcone's death, all three of Borsellino's children – Manfredi, Lucia and Fiammetta – suffered nightmares about death, bombings and massacres. Lucia told herself again and again that another assassination was impossible. 'After assassinating Falcone, they'll calm down, they won't dare to carry out another massacre,' she reassured herself.

Borsellino, a devout Catholic, had never concealed his fear of death from his family. 'I'm scared of the end because I see it as a mysterious thing; I don't know what will happen in the hereafter. But the important thing is to be courageous,' he told them. The worst thing about death, he added, was the idea of seeing them no longer: 'If it wasn't for the pain of leaving my family, I could die serene.'

The early death of his own father still weighed on him, and Borsellino wanted to make sure that his children should know what to do if he was killed by the Mafia – an event he saw as normal, and predictable. Before a trip, he would tell them: 'If the plane crashes open my drawers, there are signed cheques there. This is what you have to do to obtain grants as orphans of a magistrate . . .'

In the weeks after Falcone's death, when his children told him how they had solved a problem, he would smile and whisper: 'Now I can die in peace.' According to his daughter Lucia, Borsellino felt very guilty that he had sacrificed too much of the time he should have spent with his children for the sake of his work.

Borsellino's children found it impossible to understand how he could go on living from day to day, knowing that his life could end at any time. His every return home was a source of huge joy. 'Daddy, it seems a miracle that you've managed to come back today as well,' his children would tell him. 'It's true, it seems a miracle to me too,' he'd reply.

But Borsellino bluntly brushed off his family's objections when, after Falcone's death, they criticised his security arrangements. When they pointed out that there should be a no-parking area outside his mother's flat in Via d'Amelio, as he visited her often, he gave them his stock answer whenever they raised such concerns: 'There are organs of the state whose job it is to ensure the protection of magistrates. Everyone has to do their job: the judge, the police chief . . . I'm a magistrate and I have to stay a magistrate.'

And yet Borsellino did worry about security – his family's security. He decided to stay in Palermo and sacrifice his summer holiday, because he feared his family could be hurt in a dynamite attack on the family's seaside villa in the town of Villagrazia di Carini, west of Palermo.

On one occasion at the law courts, Borsellino's colleagues criticised their own security arrangements – their armoured cars often broke down, there was often a lack of patrol cars to check on places they had to go to – and then they began to criticise Borsellino's.

They asked him for his opinion. Borsellino replied with a dismissive smile: 'The boys who escort me are all extremely generous. But I have to leave a chink in the system of protection. Because if they have to kill me, I want them to have the possibility of striking only me. I can't run the risk of some members of my family becoming involved as well.'

His answer chilled his listeners.

Lo Voi and several other colleagues also tried to persuade him to be more careful. 'I *am* careful, and anyway they've doubled the size of my escort,' he told them.

'But Paolo, who gives a damn whether they've doubled your escort? Didn't you see what happened to Giovanni? We don't know how Giovanni was killed, so you've got to be much more careful. You mustn't tell anyone about your movements, you mustn't call anyone, you mustn't go to see anyone,' his colleagues insisted.

Borsellino brushed them off with a smile.

Overcoming Borsellino's reluctance, Palermo authorities reinforced his security in the wake of Falcone's death. Police chiefs who studied his habits found that every week he went not only to the law courts but also to church and to his mother's home in Via d'Amelio. Security was reinforced outside Borsellino's home and at the church; parking in front of both of them was banned. *Carabinieri* officers were stationed outside Borsellino's home, and he was assigned an armoured car with four bodyguards.

Borsellino's daughter Fiammetta saw that he now waited a few seconds in the lobby of their block of flats for a nod from the chief bodyguard before walking out to the armoured car. Fiammetta would then have to wait some ten seconds before joining him in the car – she found the experience 'an incredible agony'.

Borsellino didn't believe in such measures. 'When they decide to kill me, these men [the bodyguards] will be the first to die,' he often told his family. Whenever he could, he would give his bodyguards the slip and go out alone.

Requests by his bodyguards for a no-parking zone outside his mother's block of flats in Via d'Amelio fell on deaf ears; locals kept on parking on both sides of the road, as well as down the middle of it.

Borsellino's family and friends worried not only about his security, but also about his wellbeing. Many of his colleagues in the law courts were struck by how dramatically Borsellino had changed after Falcone's death. 'There was an air of terrifying sadness about him. Many of us noted that he seemed to have death in his eyes,' one of them said.

Several of Borsellino's friends urged him to flee Palermo, to give up the fight against the Mafia and leave the task to others, but he rebuffed all such appeals. 'Those who give me this advice aren't friends,' he said. 'The real friends are those who understand the choices I make, who share the same ideals I have, the values I believe in. How could I flee, betraying the hopes of honest citizens?' he asked.

His words echoed those which someone had written on a poster put up at the spot where the *carabiniere* General Dalla Chiesa, his wife and driver had been shot dead in 1982: '*HERE DIES THE HOPE OF HONEST PALERMITANS.*'

Borsellino's former superior Caponnetto, now a close friend, called him often and was struck by how much darker the prosecutor's tone was becoming. Borsellino sounded more and more exhausted, and he would often fall silent during their talks. He also seemed to be more and more frustrated at the way his superiors in the law courts treated him.

'What's wrong?' Caponnetto asked him at one point.

'I find myself more or less in the same situation as Giovanni was,' Borsellino replied; he complained about his superiors, saying he had very few allies he could count on. His mandate covered Mafia families only in the areas of Trapani to the west and Agrigento to the south. He had asked for it to be extended to the Palermo area so that he could contribute to the investigation into Falcone's murder. But the request had been refused.

Borsellino doggedly kept repeating his request; he clearly felt isolated in his work – a plight which Falcone had long suffered, and which had made him feel increasingly vulnerable to Mafia revenge.

In another conversation, Caponnetto talked to Borsellino about his personal security. Caponnetto recalled his anger at seeing Borsellino arrive at the law courts alone, driving his private car.

'You're not going to make me get mad again the way you used to . . .' Caponnetto said.

'No, I've become more cautious, I've grown up. But don't you know that in the end precautions are useless?' Borsellino asked.

Negotiating with the Mafia

About a week after Falcone's assassination, Massimo Ciancimino – the youngest son of a former mayor of Palermo known to all as 'Don Vito' – boarded a scheduled Alitalia flight at Palermo airport, bound for Rome.

Captain Giuseppe De Donno of the *carabinieri* police walked up the aisle and, after asking a hostess's permission, sat himself down next to the twenty-nine-year-old Massimo, who was also unkindly nicknamed 'The Dwarf' by several of his acquaintances because of his short stature. The two passengers already knew each other, and were on first-name terms. They had first met eight years earlier, when Massimo's father was being investigated by Falcone. The task of searching the Ciancimino home had fallen to De Donno and he had treated the family courteously, which they appreciated.

De Donno chatted with Massimo for a while, then asked: 'Would your dad agree to receive me, and perhaps someone else, for a chat?' He did not say what he wanted to talk about.

For Massimo, the request was sudden and completely unexpected. 'Look Giuseppe, I can't promise you anything,' Massimo replied. 'I'll try to convince my father.'

Before they parted, De Donno gave Massimo his mobile phone number.

The request for 'a chat' with the former Christian Democrat mayor Vito Ciancimino had been planned long in advance

– part of a new strategy launched by an elite section of the *carabinieri*, the Special Operations Group (ROS), which was dedicated to fighting organised crime and terrorism.

Colonel Mario Mori, one of the section's heads, had at first greeted De Donno's idea of contacting the ex-mayor with scepticism. But he soon decided to give the idea a try; Mori believed there was a chance, albeit a slim one, that Don Vito might be persuaded to turn his back on his Mafioso friends and become an informer. He might help put a stop to the 'distinguished cadavers'. He might even lead the *carabinieri* to the biggest quarry of all – the godfather Riina. For De Donno there was a chance he would collaborate, if only to demonstrate that – as he had always publicly claimed – he had nothing to do with the Mafia.

If Mori gave the plan the green light, it was also because he was dismayed at what he saw as the failure of the various police forces to step up the fight against the Mafia after Falcone's murder. After the Red Brigades had kidnapped and killed the former prime minister Aldo Moro in 1978, abandoning his body in a car boot parked in the heart of Rome, Mori had decimated the ranks of the terrorists with a long series of arrests, which had included Moro's kidnappers. Mori had then spent four years in Palermo, focusing on the Mafia's links to politicians and businesses, and reporting his findings and those of De Donno to both Falcone and Borsellino.

In the wake of Falcone's murder, Mori felt more keenly than ever that he was on his own in trying to combat the Mafia. There was no strong guiding hand from prosecutors, whose role it is under Italian law to direct the work of the police. He decided to do what he could, in secrecy. 'Instead of shirking and waiting for the storm to blow over, as many did in that period, I decided I had a precise moral and professional obligation to honour the memory of Falcone,' he explained.

⋆   ⋆   ⋆

Few Sicilian leaders embodied the close ties between the
worlds of politics, business and the Mafia as much as Don
Vito. Sour, arrogant, disdainful, with a Hitler-style moustache, he was very rich indeed. Don Vito had, as councillor for
public works, presided over the so-called 'Sack of Palermo' – a
building boom which saw the city hall grant 4,205 construction permits in just the four years between 1959 and 1963.
Tonnes of cement were poured over a lush valley of palm,
lemon, orange and olive groves known as the Golden Shell,
and its beautiful Liberty-style villas were razed to the ground
to make way for tall, ugly blocks of flats.

Many of the property developers whose paths were
smoothed by Don Vito were tied to the Mafia. In the words
of one prosecutor, Don Vito behaved 'like a vampire who had
become the custodian of a blood bank, bleeding dry and sack-
ing a city' with the support of the construction Mafia. Don
Vito is said to have amassed a fortune worth some 250 million
dollars.

Cosa Nostra was a power base for politicians like Don Vito.
'The politicians have always come to look for us because we
have a lot, a huge amount of votes at our disposal,' one collaborator explained. 'To get an idea of how much weight the
Mafia has in elections, just think of the family of Santa Maria
del Gesù [in Palermo], a family of 200 members. It's a terrifying strike force, especially if you consider that each man of
honour can dispose of another forty to fifty friends and relatives. There are between 1,500 and 2,000 men of honour in
the province of Palermo. Multiply that by fifty and you get a
fat bundle of 75,000–100,000 votes to steer towards friendly
parties and candidates.'

Don Vito's ties to the Mafia stretched back many years,
right back to his youth. In what he would no doubt have
called a stroke of luck, he was born in the town whose clan
came to dominate the Mafia – Corleone, a warren of steep

and tortuous narrow streets overshadowed by two crags. Nicknamed 'The Barber of Corleone' because one of the properties he owned was rented out to a barber, Don Vito – who was studying accounting – had taught maths to a schoolboy, Bernardo Provenzano. The boy was in need of coaching as he had spent little time at school; he was only eight years old when his parents first sent him to work in the fields.

In time, Provenzano had risen to become second-in-command to the godfather Riina, earning the nickname 'The Tractor' – 'because of his homicidal capability and of what happened to a problem or a person when he dealt with it,' as one supergrass explained. Don Vito was one of the few Sicilians who called Provenzano by his first name, and fondly remembered the times he had reprimanded the youngster over his maths exercises and boxed him on the ear: 'I'm one of the few who called him a *cornuto* [cuckold] and is still alive.'

Don Vito was one of the few who could mock Provenzano, and get away with it. Once, when Provenzano's car radio was stolen in the street outside Don Vito's home, the ex-mayor gave the boss a mocking smile and joked about 'the overwhelming power of the Mafia'. Provenzano looked crestfallen.

On his next visit, Provenzano brandished a car radio which he said had been 'returned with many apologies'. Don Vito couldn't resist another quip, asking in a sarcastic tone: 'Now tell the truth; how much did you pay for it?'

From childhood, Don Vito's son Massimo had seen Provenzano as his father's friend. The boss was the only visitor who could call unannounced. Sometimes he came for lunch; sometimes Don Vito would receive him in his pyjamas, in his bedroom. They would talk for hours on end. To Massimo, the boss was a gentle, slightly hunched figure who would pat him on the cheek and tell him to always obey his father.

But there was far more to the relationship than he could imagine. For 'The Executioner' Brusca, Don Vito was 'the puppeteer' of the Corleonesi family. Brusca explained: 'They carried out murders for him, to make him stronger.'

It cannot have been easy for Massimo, whom his father had made his right-hand man and driver when he turned eighteen, to find the courage to pass on the news that an officer of the *carabinieri* wanted to meet him. Don Vito was a bad-tempered, domineering, violent father who on one occasion, when a thirteen-year-old Massimo was sent home from school for bad behaviour, first slapped his son repeatedly then chained him up – with a chain long enough only to allow him to reach the bathroom. And Don Vito hated the police.

But Massimo, as jovial as his father was unsmiling, did his duty. Unsurprisingly, Don Vito resisted the idea at first. But he told Massimo to find out the purpose of the meeting. Massimo met De Donno again, and reported back: the officer wanted to discuss the capture and surrender of the Mafia's top bosses.

Unknown to the *carabinieri*, Don Vito promptly consulted his former maths pupil, the boss Provenzano. In the first half of June, the boss sent Don Vito his reply, in the form of a *pizzino* – a message typed on a sheet of paper, half A4-size, which was placed inside an envelope, sealed with sticky tape. In the message, Provenzano addressed Don Vito as '*Carissimo* [very dear] Engineer' – a term of respect for the ex-mayor who was in fact a qualified surveyor – and gave his blessing: '*If you think that speaking with these people will do us good ...*'

As his father's personal assistant, it was Massimo's job to act as postman between Don Vito and the boss. Massimo would deliver his father's messages to another intermediary, or directly to Provenzano himself. Provenzano always followed the same ritual: he first checked that the seal on the envelope was intact, and then opened it in Massimo's presence. Provenzano read the message to himself, then tore the sheet in half and handed the pieces back to Massimo, who would bring them back to his father. Don Vito burnt his returned message in the kitchen, or flushed it down the toilet.

Don Vito treated messages from Provenzano more clinically. Terrified of fingerprints being found on them, he would slip on latex gloves, read the contents, and make a copy of the message immediately. He then burnt the original.

Having obtained the boss's seal of approval, Don Vito agreed to meet De Donno. The ex-mayor hoped to get something for himself out of the meeting – chiefly some help with his judicial woes. Arrested by Falcone in 1984 on the basis of testimony from the supergrass Buscetta, he had been sentenced to eight years in prison as a white-collar ally of the Corleonesi family. Six years later, he had been arrested again, over his handling of public works contracts for roads and schools; his total jail sentence increased to thirteen years.

But he was still a free man because neither sentence had so far been confirmed by the Supreme Court. Under Italian law, a conviction becomes definitive only after all appeals have been exhausted. Don Vito hoped that he might obtain a pledge from the authorities to forget about him if he went into exile.

According to Massimo's account, Don Vito met De Donno at the ex-mayor's apartment in Rome – which commanded a stunning view over the Piazza di Spagna – on a hot afternoon in the first week of June 1992.

De Donno, dressed in plain clothes for the sake of discretion, greeted Don Vito courteously: 'How are you? I hope you're well.'

True to type, Don Vito retorted acidly: 'I would be, but for you' – a reference to the fact that the last time they had met two years ago had been when De Donno served him with a judicial warrant.

But after the meeting, which lasted a couple of hours – with Massimo waiting out of earshot – De Donno confided that the talk had gone better than he'd expected. Don Vito had made an offer: he could perhaps act as De Donno's mole among Sicilian entrepreneurs to feed him information about public works contracts.

'[Don Vito] is taking a couple of days to think about it. He thinks the same as we do: we have to come up with a solution to avoid more bloodshed,' De Donno told Massimo. According to Massimo, his father thought he might be able to draw some benefit from acting as a mediator. Perhaps he could avoid having his wealth seized by the courts – for Don Vito, this prospect was 'an obsession'.

'The TNT has come for me.'

Borsellino had failed to get himself appointed as one of the prosecutors in charge of Falcone's assassination, but this didn't stop him trying to investigate. He was determined to bring the killers to justice. 'Don't worry, we'll find out who did it; don't worry, trust me,' he promised Liliana Ferraro, the former chief of Falcone's private office.

A month after the murder, on the afternoon of 25 June, Borsellino arranged a meeting with Colonel Mori and Captain De Donno of the *carabinieri*. For the sake of secrecy, Borsellino met the two officers not in his office at the law courts, but at the police force's barracks. Borsellino first asked the officers if they had any new leads on Falcone's assassins; they had none. He then asked them to restart their earlier investigation into the Mafia's infiltration of Sicilian public works contracts, which they had carried out at Falcone's request.

Borsellino asked the two officers to work in secret and to report back only to him. Formally, the prosecutor had no right to lead such an investigation. To his increasing frustration, his mandate still covered Mafia families only in Trapani and Agrigento.

Mori and De Donno made no mention of the contact with the ex-mayor Don Vito earlier that month.

That evening, during a crowded debate on the struggle against the Mafia held in Palermo's municipal library, a former Jesuit convent, Borsellino described himself as 'a witness'. He was a witness, he explained, because he had worked alongside Falcone for many years and because, as they were friends, Falcone had confided in him many times.

Borsellino announced that he was going to tell the prosecutors in charge of the investigation into the assassination what Falcone had told him. They could then assess whether what he said could help explain why Falcone was killed. Borsellino stopped short of revealing what it was Falcone had told him. But never before in his career had he given such an explicit, and public, warning.

At home, watching the speech which was broadcast live on a local TV channel, Borsellino's wife Agnese blanched as she heard his words. 'What's Paolo saying?' she whispered. 'If he says these things, they'll kill him . . .'

Four days later on 29 June, Borsellino's colleague Lo Voi called him to mark his saint's day.

Borsellino didn't even say hello, blurting out in a tense tone of voice: 'What's happened? Has something else happened?'

Lo Voi said no, nothing had happened; he just wanted to wish his friend well on his name day.

Borsellino relaxed and the two chatted for a while. Lo Voi understood: because he had called Borsellino to tell him about Falcone's murder, Borsellino often became anxious when he phoned him.

On 1 July, Borsellino flew to Rome to question a new Mafia collaborator, Gaspare Mutolo. A Palermo car mechanic and Mafia soldier, Mutolo had earned so much from trafficking in heroin that he became notorious within the secret society for his reckless spending. He wore Giorgio Armani suits, drove a Ferrari, and ate at the best restaurants. His fellow Mafiosi gave him two nicknames – 'Mister Champagne' and 'The Baron'. More interestingly for investigators, Mutolo had worked as a driver to the godfather Riina.

For the jailed Mutolo, Cosa Nostra had turned its back on its 'code of honour'. He had been shocked by the way Cosa Nostra tried to discourage Mafiosi from collaborating with the state: in 1989, the secret society shot dead three women in central Palermo – the mother, sister and aunt of the collaborator Francesco Marino Mannoia. Never before had Cosa Nostra targeted women. 'The most terrible thing for me was when they started killing women and also a few children,' Mutolo explained. 'I remember that in years past, if, for example, there was the order to kill someone, if he happened to be in the company of his wife or daughter, they watched them, then went away and postponed the execution. But this rule no longer holds.'

Mutolo had first announced in early 1992 that he wanted to collaborate with investigators, on one condition: that he would betray the Mafia's secrets only to Falcone. But Falcone's new job in Rome meant he had no authority to do this, and so Mutolo refused to talk to anyone else. It was only after Falcone's assassination that Mutolo changed his mind. Like many both inside and outside the Mafia, he considered Borsellino the natural heir to Falcone, and announced: 'I want Paolo Borsellino. He's the only one I trust.'

Borsellino had high expectations about what Mutolo might be ready to tell him. 'Here we're on a level with Tommaso Buscetta, maybe above him,' the prosecutor told a colleague.

When Borsellino met Mutolo in Rome, the collaborator quickly revealed that the Mafia had infiltrated both the police and the law courts. He named two alleged stooges: Bruno Contrada, a former head of the Palermo flying squad who now worked for the SISDE secret service in Rome, and the anti-Mafia prosecutor Domenico Signorino – a friend and colleague of Borsellino's.

An unexpected phone call for Borsellino interrupted his questioning. After taking the call, Borsellino told Mutolo he had been summoned by the newly appointed interior minister Nicola Mancino, who was taking office that day; he would be back in a half hour. Borsellino was away for an hour; when he came back, he looked angry and worried.

'What's the matter, sir?' Mutolo asked.

Borsellino told him that instead of meeting the minister, he had met Vincenzo Parisi, the national chief of police, and Contrada – the very officer the collaborator had only just identified as a Mafia stooge. Borsellino was incensed that both Parisi and Contrada had known about his meeting with Mutolo.

'The interrogation is secret, how the hell did Contrada find out about it?' Borsellino shouted, ignoring Mutolo.

The prosecutor was so agitated that he lit two cigarettes at the same time, and held them both in his hand.

'Sir, you've got two cigarettes!' Mutolo told him.

Borsellino laughed, but he was still nervous. He kept insisting that Mutolo allow him to take a written statement from him, but Mutolo refused.

'Listen, we mustn't put anything down on paper because I . . . I mean, they'll kill me and so what I want to get down on paper first is everything that concerns who's who in the Mafia,' Mutolo said.

Mutolo was worried that a written document of his testimony would leak out. He insisted that he wanted to talk about Cosa Nostra first, and refused to be questioned about its allies within the state as he feared this was too dangerous.

Borsellino insisted, but to no avail. Mutolo agreed only to outline the biggest revelations he planned to make, but refused to agree to an official, written record.

It is not known whether Mutolo told Borsellino that he had heard as early as a dozen years earlier, in 1980, that the Mafia wanted to kill the prosecutor, because he had signed an arrest warrant for the boss Francesco Madonia, who was accused of the murder that year of the *carabiniere* Captain Emanuele Basile. Killers shot Basile as, carrying his young daughter in his arms, he walked towards his barracks with his wife. Both his daughter and his wife were unharmed.

In 2007, the Supreme Court sentenced Contrada to ten years in prison for ties to the Mafia; the following year, he was granted house arrest on health grounds. Signorino, the other 'stooge' that Mutolo named, committed suicide in December 1992.

A couple of days later, Borsellino and his family received Rosaria, the widow of Falcone's bodyguard Vito Schifani, at their Palermo home. Borsellino had been deeply moved by her words at the funeral, which she had addressed to the assassins – 'I forgive you, but you have to get down on your knees.' Borsellino told her cousin Father Cesare: 'Rosaria's strength is devastating.' Her words had helped persuade many Mafiosi to collaborate with the state.

At his home, Borsellino took Rosaria to his study and the two talked at length, the prosecutor smoking his Dunhills. Speaking for himself and his family, he repeated the promise he had made to her after the funeral: 'We'll be close to you, dear Rosaria. You will have our affection and we will get justice for your Vito.'

The prosecutor and the widow talked on, about their hopes for the future, about forgiveness and the collaborators. Borsellino spoke to her of Vincenzo Sinagra, a killer known as 'Tempest' because of his volcanic temper and his strength: 'He's changed. He used to be a beast and he's become a human being,' Borsellino said.

At one point, she asked the prosecutor point-blank: 'Are you scared?'

Pulling nervously on his cigarette, Borsellino replied: 'I am not afraid.'

He paused, and then added this time in an uncertain tone: 'But I am afraid for my wife, for my children.'

Borsellino always asked his children to leave the phone numbers of the friends' houses they were going to, adding with an affectionate smile: 'Otherwise, when they kill me, I won't be able to find you.'

Shortly afterwards in a newspaper interview, Borsellino spoke about the two most sought-after Cosa Nostra bosses – the godfather Riina and his lieutenant Provenzano. Borsellino had no doubt they were both hiding in Palermo, the city where he lived. 'For Mafiosi of their calibre, control of the territory is important, even fundamental. You can't "govern" soldiers and look after business if you're far away from Sicily,' Borsellino said.

He confided for the first time that he believed Cosa Nostra might be suffering from friction at its very summit. 'I've got the impression that the Corleonesi bosses don't get on anymore. I repeat, it's only an impression,' he said. Riina and Provenzano, he said, 'are like two boxers who are showing off their muscles to each other . . . as if each of them wanted to show the other how strong he was, and how capable he was of doing harm.' Borsellino speculated that one of the bosses – he didn't specify which – might be behind the murder of the ex-mayor Lima, while the other might be responsible for Falcone's killing.

Asked whether he believed the long chain of 'distin-guished cadavers' would ever come to a stop, Borsellino replied: 'I don't know, but nothing indicates it's all over. To the contrary.'

Soon afterwards, Borsellino received news that he believed meant his fate would soon be sealed. He told Father Cesare, Rosaria's cousin, that a consignment of TNT explosive had arrived with a load of contraband cigarettes.

'The finance police found out and it's arrived for me, [Leoluca] Orlando and an officer of the *carabinieri*' – Orlando was a former mayor of Palermo. He gave no other details.

Borsellino's friend Giuseppe Ayala flew from Rome to see him because their former boss Antonino Caponnetto had been struck by how depressed he sounded on the phone. During a long conversation at Borsellino's office in the law courts, Ayala told him how worried Caponnetto was.

'We're in the shit, but Nino told me you're obsessive about work, you're always here from morning to night,' Ayala said. 'Let's calm down a bit, life goes on for us – unfortunately. I don't dare ask you how many cigarettes you're smoking. You don't even count them.'

Borsellino, cigarette in hand, looked at his friend. 'Giuseppe, I can't work less. I've got only a little time left,' Borsellino said.

Ayala was so shocked he pretended not to understand, and changed the subject. For years afterwards, Ayala kicked himself for what he saw as his own cowardice. He should have said something like: 'What the f— are you saying?' Surely that would have prompted Borsellino to say something more.

Borsellino granted himself no respite. On 7 July, he flew to Germany, to question a jailed informer about the Mafia of Palma di Montechiaro, a town near the southern coast of Sicily. It was founded by an ancestor of Giuseppe Tomasi di Lampedusa, author of the classic novel *The Leopard*. In the novel, Lampedusa vividly brings to life the extremes of the Sicilian countryside: '. . . Sicily, the atmosphere, the climate, the landscape of Sicily. Those are the forces which have formed our minds together with and perhaps more than alien pressure and varied invasions: this landscape which knows no mean between sensuous sag and hellish drought; which is never petty, never ordinary, never relaxed, as should be a country made for rational beings to live in.'

As usual, Borsellino crossed himself before the plane took off – he was always scared of flying. The prosecutor also had the habit of crossing himself before diving into the sea or setting off on a long car journey. His family always pulled his leg about it.

At his arrival in Mannheim, Borsellino was struck by the security that his German hosts had prepared for him. As he was rushed away from the airport in an armour-plated Mercedes, he saw that elite commando units were stationed at street corners along his route. At his hotel, the security forces had installed CCTV cameras to ensure live monitoring of the corridor outside his room, and taped all phone calls to and from the hotel. On several occasions during his stay, he flew in a police helicopter.

When Borsellino told the elite officers guarding him that he'd like to go to a shop and buy a gold chain as a present for the baptism of a friend's son, they insisted on checking the entire shop before he walked in.

Borsellino smiled and joked with heavy irony: 'Just like at home!'

When Borsellino flew back to Rome, the contrast could not have been greater. There was no protection whatsoever waiting for him at the capital's Leonardo da Vinci airport. The prosecutor and his right-hand man Canale drove down south of Naples to Salerno where Borsellino was meeting some relatives. They had no bodyguards, let alone an escort car. The pair were defenceless. Canale had left his gun at home as he had to travel unarmed on international missions.

The next day, they flew from Naples to Palermo. Again, no bodyguards or escort cars met them at Palermo airport. They got stuck in a huge traffic jam, and Canale forced his way through, hooting furiously and rowing with dozens of drivers.

But soon afterwards, at Borsellino's office at the law courts, double bullet-proof glass was installed in the window behind his desk.

'It's so thick I can barely see the light of day,' he joked to a friend.

Borsellino told his junior colleague Ingroia that he wouldn't be taking a holiday that summer. Instead, he planned to spend the whole month of August questioning two collaborators – 'Mister Champagne' Mutolo, and Leonardo Messina, a thief turned Mafioso.

'Everyone goes on holiday in August; that way I can work more calmly and more intensely,' Borsellino said.

On the afternoon of 13 July, one of Borsellino's bodyguards noticed that he looked particularly worried and tense. The bodyguard couldn't help asking him: 'Sir, what is it? Has something happened?'

Borsellino replied: 'I'm worried. I'm worried for you boys because I know that the TNT has come for me and I don't want to drag you in.'

The bodyguard blanched, but said nothing.

Later the priest Father Cesare called on Borsellino in his office. The two men chatted. Borsellino appeared to be calm, although he was worried about his children's future.

As the priest was about to leave, Borsellino stopped him and said: 'Wait, before you go I'd like you to take my confession.'

There in his office, the priest heard Borsellino's confession.

'The Executioner' had been keeping a low profile after Falcone's assassination. Brusca moved from one safe house to another, first near Palermo, then in western Sicily where he stayed in a seaside villa near Castellammare del Golfo, on a beautiful stretch of coast with remote bays and crystal-clear waters.

In these idyllic surroundings, as he put it, 'I worked for Cosa Nostra' – meaning he shot dead a rebel boss, on the orders of the godfather Riina and with the help of several of Falcone's fellow assassins. Several other killers then strangled the boss's pregnant girlfriend because she was related to an officer working for the secret service, and it was feared she might betray the Mafia's secrets to him as an act of revenge. Boss and girlfriend were buried alongside each other in a field.

On the evening of the girlfriend's death, Brusca met Riina's driver, Biondino, and asked him for help in destroying the girlfriend's BMW, which her killers had seized.

Biondino said he couldn't help his friend, and added: 'You know, we've got a job on.'

Brusca guessed immediately that the Mafia was preparing another murder. 'Do you need me?' Brusca asked.

'No. Everything's fine,' Biondino replied.

Brusca knew better than to ask any more questions.

In the first half of June, Brusca was summoned by Riina. 'How are you? What's happening? What news have we got? Reactions?' – the godfather wanted to know what Brusca had found out about the state's reaction to Falcone's assassination.

A euphoric Riina boasted to Brusca about the impact of the murder on Italian leaders: 'At last, they've shat themselves.' The godfather said the interior minister, Nicola Mancino, had sent him a message asking: 'What do you want in exchange for stopping the massacres?' In reply, the godfather said, 'I gave them a huge list with all our demands.'

Riina didn't show Brusca the list, neither did he tell him what the demands were. Nor did the godfather tell Brusca who was acting as his intermediaries in the talks, but Brusca guessed they included the ex-mayor of Palermo, Don Vito Ciancimino. The minister Mancino has denied Brusca's account as 'absolutely laughable'; he said he had never known anything about any negotiation between the Mafia and the state.

★   ★   ★

An intermediary pressed the list, sealed in an envelope, into the hands of Don Vito's son Massimo in the last week of June, outside the Caflish bar at the seaside resort of Mondello near Palermo. Massimo, according to his account, dutifully handed it to his father the next day. Don Vito read through it with a mounting sense of disapproval.

Riina had set a high price for halting his strategy of terror. His twelve demands, written in block capitals, included a review of the maxi-trial to cancel its life sentences, which would have wrecked the work of Falcone and Borsellino; the abolition of life sentences in general for Mafia crimes; and an end to the harsh prison regimes which had helped persuade many convicts to become collaborators.

Prison sentences, Riina also demanded, should as often as possible be commuted into house arrest, or stays in hospitals (many Mafiosi routinely feigned illness to avoid jail); collaborators should enjoy fewer benefits; and parliament should revise the law which made Mafia membership a crime and allowed the seizure by judicial authorities of Mafia assets. Riina added a very personal request to the list: he demanded a new trial for Giuseppe Marchese, a relative convicted of murdering a boss in prison.

When he'd finished reading, Don Vito commented bitterly: 'They're crazy. You'll see, they'll tell us all to go f— ourselves because these demands are unacceptable.' He then folded up the piece of paper and put it in his pocket.

Soon afterwards, Don Vito met Riina's second-in-command, 'The Tractor' Provenzano, in a bank's offices off a square in the centre of Palermo. The two were both shocked at the godfather's demands. 'It's mad to make these suggestions!' Provenzano decreed, shaking his head.

Don Vito made no secret of his revulsion at Riina's strategy of terror. 'The moment's come to take some responsibility,' he told Provenzano. 'The technique of burying your head in the sand's no longer an option. Binnu, you helped create this monster and now have a duty to come up with a solution.'

The boss believed the talks might help, and told Don Vito: 'You go ahead, and we'll try to reason with the crazy one' – by whom he meant the godfather himself.

Sea air and a sleepless siesta

On the afternoon of 17 July, a Friday, Borsellino made a point of walking into the offices of several of his colleagues, one after the other, to say goodbye before the weekend break. He embraced each of them in turn – something he had never done before.

The gesture was so unexpected that one of his fellow prosecutors exclaimed: 'Paolo, what are you doing?'

'What's so surprising? Aren't I allowed to say goodbye to you?' Borsellino replied in a jokey tone.

'I'm off, see you on Monday,' Borsellino told the prosecutor Vittorio Teresi. Borsellino was smiling, but only slightly; he looked worried, unlike the cheerful figure his colleagues were used to.

Another colleague, Teresa Principato, was greatly moved by his unprecedented embrace; she could not help feeling that Borsellino was destined to meet the same fate as Falcone – and that he knew it.

When Borsellino arrived home late that afternoon, his son Manfredi found him tense and extremely nervous; word that Mutolo had become a collaborator had leaked out and this exasperated him.

But Borsellino sounded optimistic about the chances of capturing the godfather Riina. 'My hunch is that the noose around Riina is tightening; this time we'll get him,' Borsellino told his son.

Borsellino confided that he was talking to a new collaborator, but didn't name him. 'I'll tell you only that he's a man of honour who was extremely close to Riina for years, he was even his driver,' he said.

Later, after sunset, Borsellino turned to his wife. 'Let's go to Villagrazia,' he said – the family's villa by the coast outside Palermo. 'I need a bit of sea air. But without an escort; on our own,' he added.

A worried Agnese asked: 'Paolo, what is it? Has something happened?'

Borsellino said nothing.

Agnese insisted: 'Paolo, why without an escort? It's not prudent right now; it's dangerous, you know it is . . .'

Borsellino wouldn't be swayed. 'Let's go, Agnese, you and me on our own.'

The couple left soon afterwards, Borsellino driving the armour-plated Croma he'd been issued with down the motorway which also led to the airport. Borsellino said nothing, but his wife kept asking him what the matter was until he told her that Mutolo was accusing the prosecutor Signorino of Mafia collusion.

Agnese understood her husband's silence. She knew he simply couldn't accept that a fellow magistrate could be corrupt, and that Mutolo's revelation was a source of huge suffering for him.

'For him it meant the collapse of a faith, a faith which had forced him to watch powerless as so many of his friends died,' she explained later.

After a few hours at the seaside villa, set among pine trees, the couple drove back to Palermo in silence.

The next afternoon, Borsellino went to see his mother in Via d'Amelio. He had come to help her as a cardiologist was due to come and examine her at home. His sister Rita, a pharmacist who lived next door, was out. But the cardiologist called to apologise. His car had broken down and he was unable to come. He agreed to see Borsellino's mother at his home the next day, in the afternoon.

Borsellino's sister Rita called to ask about the cardiologist. The prosecutor told her about the postponed appointment. Rita said she wouldn't be free to take their mother the following day.

'No problem, Rita, I'll come and fetch Mother. I'll take her with me,' Borsellino said.

Ever since his father had died when Borsellino was twenty-two, he had felt as the eldest son a special responsibility towards his mother and his family. Over the past six months, Borsellino had been to see his mother practically every Sunday.

That evening, Borsellino greeted the porter of his block of flats, known as Don Ciccio, hugging him and kissing him on the cheeks – again, something he had never done before.

On the Sunday, 19 July, Borsellino took a 5 a.m. phone call from his youngest daughter Fiammetta, who was on holiday in Indonesia. She had begun the trip only a few days earlier, but had felt so homesick that she had slept badly the previous night at her hotel in the capital Jakarta.

Borsellino asked the nineteen-year-old Fiammetta how she was, and reminded her to buy a radio for her brother Manfredi in Hong Kong. Fiammetta got the impression he wanted to cut short the conversation, and they said goodbye.

Fiammetta wasn't surprised by her father's curtness; he was never comfortable on the phone. And in recent weeks he had become colder towards his children. Fiammetta guessed later that he was trying to hide how much he loved them. Perhaps he was preparing them for a death he believed would come soon. But she found out he had confided to his priest that he felt guilty about the way he was treating them.

When Fiammetta had told him a month earlier that she wanted to go on holiday that summer – initially to Africa with a group of friends – Borsellino's first reaction was to tell her with a smile: 'If I die, if they kill me, how will I manage to tell you, to find you in a village where there surely won't even be telephones?'

Father and daughter had argued until Fiammetta yielded, and agreed to go to Indonesia instead with a friend of his, Alfio Lo Presti and his wife Donatella, and friends of theirs. Borsellino felt reassured at the fact that his daughter would be with his friend, but he still appeared dissatisfied; she guessed he worried they might never see each other again.

The phone call to her father, albeit brief, made her feel less homesick and she set off soon afterwards for the airport to catch a flight to the island of Bali.

A couple of hours later, Borsellino received another phone call, this time from his superior, the chief prosecutor Piero Giammanco. He had finally decided to grant Borsellino's request that his mandate be extended to allow him to investigate the Mafia in Palermo. The decision effectively gave Borsellino a chance to help find Falcone's assassins.

Early that morning, Borsellino asked his other daughter Lucia to go with him to the villa by the sea.

'Let's hope I'll see you get a bit of a tan; the exam you've got tomorrow has stopped you from having even one swim,' he said. He suggested they go to the villa now, and come back in the afternoon to take his mother to the cardiologist's; they would come back home and she would go back to her studies while he did some work.

Lucia said no, she had to go study at a friend's house; it was the friend's birthday and she had invited her to stay for lunch.

'But when are you going to close them, these books?' Borsellino protested.

Lucia shook her head. 'Dad, I can't come with you.'

Borsellino had only slightly better luck with his son Manfredi. Manfredi agreed to go to the villa, but later; he had gone to bed late the previous night and was in no hurry to leave now.

'You come when you want, I'm off,' he announced with a hint of disappointment. As often happened when one of his children made him wait too long, he set off just with his wife; he hated leaving after 9 a.m. because the traffic always built up at the motorway exit near the villa.

Manfredi reached the villa at about 11 a.m. His father's police bodyguards told him he had just missed him; the prosecutor had already been out for a quick bicycle ride and a swim, and now he had set off on a boating trip with a neighbour. True to type, Borsellino had told his six bodyguards to stay behind and two of them were standing around on the beach, staring out to sea and hoping to see the boat reappear.

Manfredi learnt later that on the rocks near the villa were two men who were apparently also watching the boat's movements. He never did find out whether or not the two were just holidaymakers.

Borsellino returned in time for lunch with his wife and son at the home of two neighbours who were old friends, Pippo and Mirella Tricoli. As ever, he crossed himself before the meal of Sicilian fritters made from chickpea flour, potato and egg croquettes, followed by fish and then cake. During the meal, and making sure no one else would overhear him, Borsellino told his friend Pippo, a history professor: 'The TNT has arrived for me.'

The lunch over, Borsellino thanked his friends, watched the Tour de France on TV for a short while, then went back to his villa for a siesta. 'I'm going to sleep a bit,' he said.

But Borsellino did not sleep. He lay in bed, smoking five cigarettes in just over an hour. His family later found the cigarette ends in the ashtray.

As Borsellino tried to rest, the six bodyguards waited and watched outside in the garden and close to the villa.

The six had been given a day off. But that morning, the team which had been assigned to protect Borsellino had asked to be replaced – because one of its officers had rowed with his girlfriend. He had asked his colleagues a favour: 'Boys, give me a hand. I've quarrelled with my girlfriend and I want to get back home, I want to get the row over. Let's ask headquarters if we can be replaced.' The others agreed, and the new team was dispatched instead.

As they waited, some of the six chatted with Manfredi. Some children playing with a water gun came up and sprayed the only woman in the team, Emanuela Loi, twenty-four. Cheerful, attractive with curly blond hair, she had just got back from a holiday in her native Sardinia and was about to get married. She pretended that they had wounded her.

For the Australian-born Walter Cosina, it was the last day on duty before he began his summer holiday; he had first worked as a bodyguard in the northern Veneto region before being transferred to Palermo, ten days after Falcone's murder. Two other bodyguards – Claudio Traina, from Palermo, and Vincenzo Li Muli, the youngest in the team at twenty-two – walked around the villa, worried about the motorway which passed only twenty yards from it. The chief bodyguard Agostino Catalano, a widower with two children, and his junior colleague Antonio Vullo, who was married with one son, stayed in the parking lot close to the three cars which made up Borsellino's convoy.

*   *   *

At about 4.30 p.m., Borsellino emerged from the villa. Dressed in jeans, a light blue Lacoste polo shirt and a pair of smart Tod's shoes – a gift from his daughter Lucia – he said a quick goodbye to his wife and son.

As ever, it was only now – at the last possible minute – that Borsellino told his bodyguards that they were leaving. 'I'm going to pick up my mother. I've got to take her to the doctor's,' he said.

Manfredi accompanied him to the parking lot. 'I'll go alone in the blue Croma; you go in the other two,' Borsellino told his bodyguards.

He opened the back door of his car and placed his briefcase on the seat, before getting into the driving seat and leaving with a '*Ciao* Manfredi.'

Borsellino was 'devastatingly serene', Manfredi related.

Via d'Amelio

Two miles from Borsellino's villa, Borsellino's convoy sped onto the motorway near the town of Capaci and, a short distance further on, the tyres of the three cars passed over the new tarmac surface which had been laid after Falcone's murder. A streak of red paint along the guardrail bore witness to the blast fifty-seven days earlier.

After leaving the motorway on Palermo's outskirts, the convoy passed the Favorita stadium and soon turned into Via d'Amelio where the prosecutor's mother lived; the street was sealed off at one end by a wall which bordered a construction site.

Vullo, the driver of the lead car, had never been to Via d'Amelio before and he was surprised to see so many cars parked outside the block of flats where Borsellino's mother lived. He found it odd that there was no parking ban outside it.

Borsellino, who was following Vullo, overtook him. The prosecutor slowed, turned the car around so that it faced back down the street, and stopped in front of the gate leading to the block of flats at Number 19.

Vullo stopped next to Borsellino's car to let his colleagues Traina and Li Muli get out. He then drove on a little more than a dozen yards and stopped, placing his car in such a way that it blocked any other cars from entering the street. He was relieved to see that as the street was a dead end, he was blocking the only access to it. Vullo stayed in the car and waited.

The last car in the convoy stopped next to Borsellino's. The prosecutor opened the door of his car and, a lit Dunhill cigarette in his right hand, started to walk the short distance to the gate. The blonde Loi and her four male colleagues, carrying pistols and machine-guns, escorted him. Borsellino pressed the buzzer on the Entryphone to his mother's flat with his left hand.

Two yards from where Borsellino waited for his mother to buzz the gate open, a remote-controlled car bomb made of 90 kilos of explosives, and hidden in the boot of a small, purplish red Fiat 126 which had been parked there for the past two days, exploded at 4.58 p.m.

From inside his armoured car further down the street, the bodyguard Vullo felt a blast of heat and saw flames engulf his car as it was thrown into the air and turned upside down. Terrified the car might explode before he got out, Vullo managed to open his door and scramble outside.

As car alarms sounded in the street, triggered by the blast, he saw burning cars and clouds of thick black smoke and drew his gun. He started heading towards the spot where Borsellino and his bodyguards had stood and walked on something soft; he looked down and realised it was part of the foot of a colleague. He looked around him and saw bodies, bits of human flesh and pools of blood.

Soon afterwards, emerging from the clouds of smoke, he saw a police officer approaching – the first patrolman on the scene. Vullo fainted.

Borsellino's friend and ex-colleague Giuseppe Ayala had been resting in his nearby flat after spending part of the day at the seaside when the sound of an explosion made him jump out of bed. He rushed to the window but saw nothing out of the ordinary – at first. Then he saw an enormous black cloud billow up into the sky, above a ten-storey block of flats.

Ayala went out into the street and started walking fast towards Via d'Amelio, 200 yards away, his bodyguards following. When he got there, Ayala at first thought there'd been a gas explosion. But then he caught sight of a Fiat Croma to his right which had an aerial on the boot – a couple of years earlier, three such cars had been assigned to Ayala, Falcone and Borsellino, all three of them with aerials on the boot and not on the roof as was usually the case with armoured cars. 'Why the f— is that car here?' Ayala asked himself.

Then he tripped over something and as he bent down for a look, as he put it, '[my] eyes were forced to see something which every human being should be spared.' He had tripped over the burnt trunk of a man. Ayala didn't immediately recognise whose body it was. The blast had severed the arms and legs from the body. The face was blackened, and there was black dust on the man's moustache; his eyes were open, and his parted lips appeared to hint at a smile. The mouth was half open, the teeth slightly crooked towards the inside – like Borsellino's. The nose was aquiline – like Borsellino's.

Ayala looked around him, and caught sight of Guido Lo Forte, a Palermo colleague. 'Guido! Guido!' Ayala shouted. Lo Forte rushed up to him and Ayala asked: 'Who is this? Do you think it's Paolo?'

Lo Forte bent down. 'It's Paolo,' he said.

One of Borsellino's arms was found later on the second floor of his mother's block of flats.

Vullo was the only one of the six bodyguards to survive the explosion – simply because he had stayed in his armoured car. The hand of one bodyguard was catapulted upwards to land on a fifth-floor balcony. Next to Borsellino's remains lay the body of the female bodyguard Loi. Less than two months earlier, an examination Agostino Catalano, the chief bodyguard, had taken to be promoted to superintendent had prevented him from being on duty with Falcone on the day of his murder; today, there had been no such quirk of fate.

The blast wounded dozens of people as it devastated 113 flats in four apartment blocks; thirty cars were ravaged by fire. Wreckage from the Fiat 126 in which the bomb had been placed was hurled up to 160 yards away; one half of the car was found with the wheels clinging to the wall of a garden of lemon trees. A fireman began picking up human remains and placing them in three brightly coloured plastic containers, which he had obtained from a nearby nursery school.

When she heard the explosion, Borsellino's mother Maria knew in her heart that this was the bomb destined for her son. But her brain persuaded her it was a gas leak, and she rushed down four flights of stairs to get outside. She went straight past the bodies of her son and of his bodyguards, but later told a fireman who took her to hospital that she hadn't seen them. She had seen nothing of the carnage at all.

Borsellino's daughter Lucia, who had been studying at a friend's house, heard the sound of the explosion some distance away. She soon reached Via d'Amelio. A sheet covering her father's body was raised for her to see it; Lucia cradled his head in her arms. Afterwards, Lucia went back home and found the strength to tell her mother: 'You should have seen how serene Daddy's expression was.'

On the floor by the back seat of Borsellino's car lay his leather briefcase; it was intact. Inside, police found his home keys, a pack of cigarettes and a white swimming costume which was still damp. But there was no sign of a large diary bound in red leather, in which he regularly took notes and which he never let anyone else read. His wife Agnese had seen him busy writing in it that afternoon, shortly before leaving their villa by the sea.

Borsellino died at the age of fifty-two, as he had predicted, just like his father and his grandfather before him. Later, Agnese confided: 'Paolo started to die when Giovanni [Falcone] died.'

That evening police bodyguards, many of them friends of the latest victims, voiced their frustration at the powerlessness of the Italian state just as they had done after Falcone's murder. They kicked the car of the chief prosecutor Piero Giammanco, shouting 'Pig!' and called for the death penalty to be introduced for Mafiosi. 'Either war is declared on the Mafia or we set up "secret sects" to sort things out ourselves,' one bodyguard protested. Demonstrators spat at Giammanco and the national police chief Parisi, and threw coins at the justice minister Martelli and the interior minister Mancino.

Reflecting the widespread anger and dismay across Italy, Borsellino's family refused the offer of a state funeral. A separate funeral service was held for the bodyguards, and again the protesters turned on senior political leaders. They insulted, kicked and slapped the police chief Parisi, and got close enough to shove against the president, Oscar Luigi Scalfaro, who was quickly hustled out.

The prosecutor's coffin was placed in the church opposite his home, Santa Luisa di Marillac. His family wanted to wait for his daughter Fiammetta to come back from her holiday in Bali before burying him. The priest gave the family a key to the small chapel where the coffin was placed, fanned by ventilators.

Three days after her father's death, Fiammetta called from Bali to ask: 'How's Daddy?' She had heard nothing about the car bomb.

Fiammetta took a twelve-hour flight, in tears, and returned to embrace the coffin before the burial. Afterwards, she insisted on going to their villa with her mother, and her brother and sister. She climbed the stairs to her parents' bedroom and sat on their bed. Then, she curled up on the still-crumpled sheet where her father had lain for his last siesta.

A few days after Borsellino's death, his former colleague Ayala was summoned by the prime minister Giuliano Amato. When he walked into the premier's opulent office in the sixteenth-century Palazzo Chigi in the centre of Rome, Ayala found waiting for him not only Amato but also the chiefs of the police, the *carabinieri* and the secret service.

'We've assessed the situation,' Ayala was told. 'We believe that if they continue, you'll be the next one. What do you think?'

'I understand,' Ayala managed to say.

The security chiefs told Ayala that from now on he should travel to Sicily as rarely as possible. They talked of buying a French-made car that had an electronic system capable of preventing signals from a remote control detonating bombs, but the problem was that it also deactivated any pacemakers in the vicinity. Ayala refused the offer.

From then on, on the few occasions Ayala did land on official flights at the airport outside Palermo, he found two *carabinieri* helicopters waiting for him. He decided which one to board, and then both the helicopters would take off bound for Palermo – one flew along the coast, while the other flew further inland.

Ayala couldn't help himself recalling what he'd told Falcone more than half a dozen years earlier – what was the point of their bodyguards changing the routes they took every day, if they always took the motorway to get to and from the airport?

The loss of their second top anti-Mafia fighter in just fifty-seven days left the Italian authorities reeling. For the prosecutor

Gian Carlo Caselli, who had successfully fought Red Brigade terrorism, the assassinations had brought Italy to its knees. It was in danger of becoming a Mafia state, a Colombia-style drug-nation dominated by a secret criminal society.

In the days that followed, the Rome government sent 7,000 troops to Sicily to guard the law courts, police stations and the homes of anti-Mafia prosecutors. Troops replaced police officers, freeing them up to dedicate more time to Mafia investigations.

The Rome parliament passed many laws that Falcone and Borsellino had themselves demanded to no avail: the first witness protection programme of the kind in Italy, with lower sentences, protection and other benefits for Mafia collaborators; faster trials and harsher prison regimes for Mafiosi, who were spirited away from the mainland to islands off the coast to stop them staying in contact with their crime families; police could now carry out house searches without warrants, a measure which had greatly bolstered the fight against the terrorist Red Brigades; and police were given extensive powers to infiltrate Mafia families in undercover 'sting' operations, and to bug private phone calls and conversations.

Antonino Calderone, a collaborator from eastern Sicily, was so elated by the state's reaction to the assassinations that he urged the anti-Mafia commission of the Rome parliament: 'Now is the best time to bring the Mafia to its knees. Even more must be done, a superhuman effort must be made because success is possible. Otherwise, they are capable of doing anything. They are like rats on a sinking ship who hang on to anything; they are capable of everything, and they have shown it.'

For once, The Executioner learnt about an assassination from the TV, as he watched the news of Borsellino's death at his coastal villa west of Palermo.

The news surprised Brusca. 'That was quick,' he said to La Barbera, one of Falcone's killers.

Brusca was reminded of the car bomb he had used to kill Falcone's boss Chinnici in 1983. 'They did it the old way,' he remarked – as a veteran of such assassinations, what interested him most was the method used.

Rita Atria, the Mafiosa in skirts

The shepherd's daughter Rita Atria, a slight, pretty brunette, was only eleven years old when the body of her father Vito was carried into her home, riddled with bullets. He had earned his living by working seventeen acres of vines and olive groves near the small town of Partanna in western Sicily; he was not a member of the local Mafia family but he had repeatedly done their bidding – until the bosses had decided to eliminate him, for a reason known only to them.

Rita's mother shed no tears but prayed, while her brother Nicola swore repeatedly and kicked everything within reach, shouting he would have revenge. One day the killers will be punished, the girl thought to herself as she witnessed his fury. As their father's coffin was lowered into the grave, Rita and Nicola held hands and swore to themselves they would take revenge.

To avenge his father, Nicola first had to establish who had killed him; he decided to infiltrate the local Mafia family to find out as much as he could. It was 'blind rage' which motivated his risky gambit, as an investigator put it. Working with the Mafiosi and their accomplices, he started to deal in cannabis, heroin and other drugs. Officially, Nicola made his living thanks to a bar he ran, but he took to driving expensive cars, and his wife, Piera Aiello, wore furs. Nicola always carried a gun in his belt.

But Piera came to fear for her husband, and the furs and racy cars soon lost their charm. In late 1990, the twenty-five-year-old Piera gave Nicola an ultimatum: she told him she was sick of his life of crime and would leave him if he didn't change. But her pleas fell on deaf ears. In the spring of the following year, his sister Rita also challenged Nicola, asking how he could trust the criminals he spent so much time with. Nicola retorted that he had to obtain revenge for his father's death, and so he needed allies and protectors.

A month later in June 1991, as Nicola sweated by the wood-burning oven of the Pizzeria Europa which he had taken over just three days earlier, Piera saw two gunmen burst in from a back entrance leading into the kitchen and rush towards him. Despite her horror at the sight, she remained lucid enough to notice that one of the gunmen was short and thin, and that he seemed very unsure of himself as he fired his sawn-off shotgun at her husband, standing with his legs wide apart.

Nicola's mother Giovanna, who had shed no tears for her husband's death, this time wept continuously. His widow Piera mourned for only part of the summer then, one August morning, she sought revenge; she went to the *carabinieri* police and started to tell them all she knew about the local Mafia family.

Soon Nicola's sister Rita decided to follow the example set by her sister-in-law. The teenager told the police that she wanted to reveal all she knew about the murders of her father and of her brother, and about the Mafia in her home town. But the police refused to see her; they didn't believe an adolescent could have anything useful to tell them.

The *carabinieri* had however underestimated the obstinate streak in Rita's character; as a child, she had clashed repeatedly with her parents when she set her heart on something, and not even her father screaming at her or slapping, kicking, or beating her would make her change her mind. More recently, her doggedness had finally persuaded her mother to allow her to put her name down for a hotel management school.

Rita had decided to talk to the police, and she would make them listen. She kept calling them, once or twice a week, until they finally relented. To investigators, Rita reeled off the names of dozens of Mafiosi; when the police didn't believe her, she would turn red with anger. Rita was so ruthless in describing the crimes they committed that the police jokingly nicknamed her 'the *Mafiosa* in skirts'.

Now at last, Rita's testimony was taken seriously and she was passed on to a prosecutor in Borsellino's office, who at the time was still based in Marsala, responsible for Mafia investigations in western Sicily. At her meetings with Borsellino and a colleague, Rita gradually realised her father wasn't as she had imagined him until then, a kind figure who was generous towards the poor, but instead an accomplice of the Mafiosi. She grew close to Borsellino, and called him 'Uncle Paolo'. He in turn felt responsible for her, and was impressed by her determination. 'This girl's got balls; if she was a man she'd be a Mafia boss,' he joked.

Together with Piera's account, Rita's evidence prompted the arrests of twenty-six suspects, including several members of the ruling Accardo family, accused of Mafia membership, drug dealing and illegal possession of weapons. The two women also testified against the Christian Democrat MP Vincenzo Culicchia. Rita accused Culicchia, a former gym teacher who never missed Sunday Mass, of ordering the death of Stefanino Nastasi, a deputy mayor whose only crime was having obtained more votes than him in mayoral elections. Culicchia denied the accusation.

Word of Rita's collaboration with the police soon leaked out and one night in November 1991 a young man who used to work for her father rang the buzzer at her home shortly before midnight. The man claimed he wanted to express his condolences for the murder of her brother, and kept insisting he be allowed in – a full six months after the killing.

Borsellino realised that Rita's life was in danger, and from then on he took her under his wing. The prosecutor managed to persuade Rita's mother to agree to him finding a secret refuge for the teenager, and guaranteeing her protection. Borsellino worried that Rita's mother, who always wore dark clothes in mourning, would do everything in her power to stop her daughter collaborating with his office. So the police lied to Rita's mother, telling her that the Mafia was after her daughter because they couldn't reach Piera, who was already on the witness protection programme.

Borsellino felt responsible for Rita and arranged for her to leave home at short notice, under armed escort. Rita was flown to Rome and joined Piera at the flat where she lived with her young daughter. The flat, the telephone and all other services were registered under a false name. Rita told her neighbours her name was 'Vanessa' and that she worked as a secretary at the interior ministry; she also lied about her age, saying she was twenty. Although they were banned from going to crowded places such as cinemas and the theatre, the two women couldn't resist going out and enjoying Rome. They went to see films together and Rita visited museums. They never spoke about why they lived in hiding.

Slowly, Rita appeared to find new reasons for hope. She wrote with delight in her diary about the beauty of Rome, and the sense of freedom which living in the city gave her – something which had been foreign to her in Partanna. She sometimes stayed up all night, doing things she would never have thought of doing back in Sicily; she liked to play cards with Piera until dawn. The two women talked vaguely about their future; Rita thought they could open a bar in northern Italy, and Piera dreamt of becoming a police officer one day.

In Rome, Rita met and fell in love with Gabriele, a southerner like her who was doing his military service in the Navy; they decided to get married one day. But to her diary, Rita confided her fear that the Mafia would murder her. '*I'm sure I won't have a long life if I'm killed by the people I'm going to accuse during the trial. I would have been happy living together with Nicola and my father,*' she wrote in late December. She made plans not for her wedding but for her funeral. She wanted very few people to attend the service: '*my mother must absolutely not come to my funeral or see me after my death.*' She wanted to be dressed in black, and when her coffin was carried into the church, the organist should play Franz Schubert's *Ave Maria*.

Rita's mother could not accept her daughter's departure. Far from helping the police, she refused to give them the teenager's clothes which they wanted to take to Rome. A judge had to give the police a warrant to go and fetch them instead. The mother suspected that her daughter was collaborating, and pleaded again and again with Borsellino, his colleagues and the police.

'Rita has to come back to Partanna. She's a little girl, she doesn't know anything, she doesn't understand anything. When her dad died she was just eleven years old. She says things people have told her to say,' the mother insisted.

Borsellino tried to reason with her. 'Rita can't live in Partanna. She's doing something which is very dangerous. She has to be protected . . .' he said.

The mother interrupted him with a chilling remark: 'All things come in threes. She might as well come home, to me.'

Over and over again, Rita's mother repeated: 'We're women. We don't know anything. You can't change your destiny. Just like you can't do anything against an earthquake.'

But when Rita said she never wanted to see her mother again, Borsellino urged the young woman: 'She's still your mother. She's got rights. She's suffering; try again.'

Rita agreed to go back home for a short visit when her mother invited her to celebrate New Year's Eve with her. Rita hoped that they could be reconciled but her hopes were swiftly dashed. When Rita's bodyguards left the two women alone for a few moments when it was nearly time for Rita to leave, her mother threatened her. If ever she found out that Rita was collaborating with the police, she said, 'I'll make sure you come to the same end as your brother.' She told her she knew people who would kill Rita if she asked them. Rita had little choice but to lie, and promise that she would never collaborate.

And yet Rita missed her family. In her diary, she wrote of her loneliness in Rome, cut off from family and friends. She wrote on 12 January 1992: *'It's almost nine o'clock in the evening, I feel sad and demoralized maybe because I'm unable to dream any more, I see only so much darkness. What worries me isn't the fact that I will have to die, but that I'll never manage to be loved by anyone. I'll never manage to be happy and fulfil my dreams ... I can't distinguish anymore between good and evil, everything has become so dark and squalid. I thought that time could heal all wounds, but it's not true, time opens them wider and wider, killing you slowly. When will this nightmare end?'*

Rita met Borsellino at least once a month in Rome and she embraced 'Uncle Paolo' affectionately every time, grateful for the fact that he took care of her everyday needs. In tears, she talked to Borsellino about her mother's attitude. He tried to reassure her: 'Who cares, Rita? One day she'll understand. And in the meantime you're not alone, you've got me.'

When Rita was particularly worried about her fate, he would cup her face in his hands. 'Calm down, don't do this, don't worry,' he'd say and pat her gently on the back. He gave her a piece of paper on which he had written his office and home numbers. 'Call me whenever you want, when you need something, when you're feeling lonely,' the prosecutor told her. Back home, Borsellino told his eldest daughter Lucia that Rita reminded him of her.

In early 1992, Rita asked the witness protection service for a flat of her own, together with the living allowance she was entitled to. She wanted to live with her boyfriend before they got married. But in early June, Gabriele was transferred to an Italian Navy outpost in Albania. He called her at least twice a week to tell her how much he missed her. Rita concentrated on her studies. She travelled to a hotel management school in eastern Sicily to take an examination to qualify for a third year of studying.

As her bodyguards watched over her, she chose one of the three essay subjects set by examiners; the topic was the fight against the Mafia after the assassination of Falcone the previous month. Rita wrote: '*The only way of eliminating this evil is to make young people who live in Cosa Nostra realise that outside it, there's another world made of simple but beautiful things, of purity, a world where you're treated with respect because of who you are, not because you're the son of this or that person, or because you paid extortion money to obtain a favour. Maybe the world will never be honest, but who's to stop us dreaming? Maybe if each of us tries to change, maybe we'll succeed.*' Rita passed the exam.

On the day the TV broke the news of Borsellino's murder – her 'Uncle Paolo' – Rita refused to watch. She shed no tears and told Piera: 'My destiny is awful: every time I become close to someone who's like a father to me, the Mafia kills him.' Looking bewildered, Rita repeated again and again: 'We've had it now, there's no one protecting us anymore.'

She kept toying with the piece of paper which Borsellino had given her with his phone numbers – 'Call me whenever you want, when you need something, when you're feeling lonely,' he'd told her. Rita always had that piece of paper on her. But despite everything, neither Rita nor Piera thought of going back on their decision to collaborate.

Over the next few days, Rita talked to Piera about the arrangements for her own funeral, telling her what she would wear and that she wanted a cushion of red roses, with a white lily in the middle – the lily would be the only white flower at her funeral. Piera thought Rita was being bizarre; she didn't understand why Rita liked to talk about her own funeral arrangements.

'What the hell do I care how I'm dressed, when I'm dead?' Piera said with a laugh.

Rita wrote in her diary: '*Now that Borsellino is dead, no one can understand the emptiness he has left in my life. Everybody's scared but the only thing I'm scared of is that the Mafia state will win and these poor idiots who fight against windmills will be killed.*

'*Before fighting the Mafia you have to examine your own conscience and then, after having defeated the Mafia inside you, you can fight the Mafia which is among your friends. The Mafia is us and our wrong way of behaving. Borsellino, you died for what you believed in but without you I'm dead.*'

It was the last page she ever wrote.

Five days after Borsellino's death, Rita decided to move into a small, seventh-floor flat of her own on Rome's south-eastern outskirts. Before she left the flat she shared with Piera, the latter asked if she was sure she wanted to go and live alone after what had happened – meaning Borsellino's murder. Rita replied that she had dreamt of having her own home ever since she had arrived in Rome; she was no longer a little girl. The new home might stop her feeling so empty inside; it might help her feel happier, she said.

Piera helped Rita carry her things into the new flat. There was a false name by the Entryphone. An officer of the witness protection service told Rita that a phone, also registered under a false name, would be installed soon; he warned her not to give the number to too many people.

That evening, after they had finished the move, Piera saw she was sitting silently on her balcony, staring up at the stars. Rita had a home of her own at last, but she was still depressed – she had been due to go to Sicily with Piera the next day, but she told Piera she wasn't feeling well and would stay in Rome.

A concerned Piera insisted that Rita come back to her flat for the night. Rita refused, and the two women ended up staying on the balcony all night. If I was to die, Rita whispered to her sister-in-law at one point, you mustn't cry; you must celebrate instead because at last I'll have joined the only people I really loved, my father and my brother. I've taken a big decision, Rita added, but I can't tell you anything. I'll tell you when you come back from Sicily. Piera tried to comfort Rita, telling her that things weren't going badly as she now lived in Rome, and Gabriele was hugely fond of her.

The next morning, Rita said goodbye to Piera at the airport, wishing her a good trip and asking her to say hello to Sicily for her. Stop feeling sad, Piera told her, life is beautiful.

At about 4 p.m. the next day, 26 July, a stiflingly hot Sunday on which most Romans had deserted their city to flee to the seaside, Rita threw herself from the balcony of her seventh-floor flat. As she fell to her death, dressed in her pink pyjamas, her hair ribbon became caught on the balustrade of a fourth-floor balcony.

On the wall of her new flat, written in pencil and in big block capitals were the words: '*I LOVE YOU. DON'T LEAVE ME. MY HEART WON'T LIVE WITHOUT YOU.*' A note on the chest of drawers read: '*Now the one who protected me is no more, I've lost heart, I can't bear it any more . . .*'

Rita Atria – 'the girl courage' as the newspapers called her after her story became known – was buried in the cemetery at Partanna, next to her brother. The epitaph on Rita's grave read: '*Truth lives.*'

Rita's mother stayed away from the funeral. But five months later, in November, she went into the cemetery and found her daughter's grave. She pulled out a hammer and started striking at the tombstone. As it broke, Rita's photograph fell from its place in a little marble bas-relief in the shape of an open Bible. The cemetery's caretaker came running, and then called the police who took Rita's mother in for questioning.

She told them that she couldn't bear that the photograph had been put there by Piera. 'I'm not a monster,' she told them. 'I'm a woman who has lost everything. I love my daughter Rita.'

Part 3

Hunt:

July 1992–2012

Don Vito's 'delicate' mission

Several days after Borsellino's murder, Gioè and La Barbera – two of the Mafiosi who had killed Falcone – drove to the Palermo harbour to join a queue of cars waiting to board the night ferry to Naples. The ferry, which left every evening at 8 p.m., was popular with newly married couples who, after a noisy send-off and lewd jokes about their wedding night from dozens of well-wishers gathered on the quayside, left the Sicilian capital for a honeymoon on the island of Capri in the Gulf of Naples, or on the Amalfi Coast.

There was nothing romantic about Gioè and La Barbera's trip. The pair were on their way to Teramo near the Adriatic Coast to buy weapons and order false identity papers and driving licences for the fugitive Corleonesi boss Bagarella whose men had shot Boris Giuliano, the head of Palermo's flying squad, in the back and had carried out many other murders. In the car was a bag stuffed with 100 million lire in cash to pay for their purchases, and photocopies of documents belonging to Bagarella for the forger to work from.

The number of police officers patrolling Palermo had risen sharply since the assassination of the two prosecutors and a patrol checking on the queue at the harbour stopped Gioè and La Barbera's car, a Nissan Patrol. The officers asked the two Mafiosi for their identity papers and boarding passes for the ferry.

The boarding pass Gioè handed over was not in his name. Gioè tried to explain: 'I sent the boy who works with me to buy the tickets, perhaps he got confused and gave his name instead.'

The officers believed him. 'Well then, go and get the ticket changed,' one of them said.

Gioè sent La Barbera to the ticket office and managed – without any of the officers noticing – to pull the bag with the cash and papers out of the car. Gioè placed it on the ground a few yards away from him, far enough to claim it wasn't his if he was challenged about it.

La Barbera returned from the ticket office. It was closed, he told the officers, and he hadn't been able to change the name on the boarding pass.

'Alright, get on board, but explain the situation to the officer in charge,' one of the policemen said.

Gioè, still unnoticed, recovered the bag and placed it back in the car.

Then, two of Falcone's assassins slipped away.

A few weeks later, Brusca ordered Gioè and La Barbera to escort him to the town of Mazara del Vallo on the west coast of Sicily, where Bagarella was hiding in a villa for the summer. At the villa, Gioè and La Barbera went up to a bedroom where they stretched out for an afternoon siesta.

Suddenly, Bagarella opened the door and told Gioè: 'There's someone who'd like to say hello to you.'

In the sitting-room, Gioè immediately recognised the godfather Riina. '*Buongiorno*,' Gioè greeted him respectfully.

The godfather stared at him, a look of surprise on his lined face. 'Just "*buongiorno*"? Is that all you say to me? Well, it's true we haven't seen each other for a long time.'

Gioè corrected himself swiftly. '*Zu* [Uncle] Totò!' he exclaimed, using a term which indicated both respect and affection.

Later, Riina talked of a plan to kill a Mafioso who refused to obey the orders of the Corleonesi family. But the rebel was taking his precautions: he always wore a bullet-proof jacket and used an armour-plated car.

'There's no problem. All you need is a bang,' Riina said. He wanted to blow up the victim in the centre of the town where he lived.

Gioè and several other Mafiosi dared to disagree, warning that the blast risked claiming innocent bystanders, perhaps women and children.

'So what? So many children die in Sarajevo and nobody worries about it,' Riina said – the Bosnian capital was then under merciless siege by Serbian forces.

Gioè insisted, arguing that if a car bomb was used, police would be quick to link the blast to Borsellino's assassination. His argument apparently helped to save the Mafioso's life, because Riina eventually called off the murder.

The godfather may have spared one rebel Mafioso's life, but he had no intention of halting his strategy of terror. Riina, according to the son of the ex-mayor Don Vito, was becoming impatient at the lack of response to the demands he had made of the Italian state in early July – from a revision of the maxi-trial to the abolition of life sentences.

'The Tractor' Provenzano, Riina's second-in-command, sent Don Vito a message: '*I believe it's time we all made an effort, as we'd already discussed at our last meeting, our friend*' – the godfather Riina – '*is very hurried, let's hope we get the reply in time, if there was the time for us to talk about it together. I know that you have the good habit of going to the cemetery for your father's birthday, do you remember, you mentioned it to me . . . we could see each other to pray together to God . . . We need to know, because we need time to get organised.*' In his account, Massimo, Don Vito's son, failed to identify who was putting pressure on Riina to continue the wave of terror; but he called this person 'the great architect'.

Soon afterwards, Provenzano sent another message with a word of warning: thanks to the Mafia's unrivalled network of informers, he had apparently found out that a team – perhaps sent by the *carabinieri* officers who had established contact with Don Vito – was now watching the flat that the ex-mayor rented for his visits to Palermo. Provenzano wrote: '*Very dear Engineer, I've been told that the same people we are talking to have now rented a flat in front of your home, they put an office there to hear and to watch . . . we have to be careful also on the day of our next meeting, I'll let [Massimo] know.*' Don Vito took to staying in a hotel instead.

Provenzano himself became increasingly cautious after his informers tipped him off that Massimo was being followed when he came to Palermo. The boss sent Don Vito another message: '*Very dear Engineer, . . . it isn't prudent to meet on Thursday 23rd as we'd agreed the last time we saw each other. I've spoken to mutual friends and they told me that when [Massimo] comes to Palermo he isn't alone. I know the boy is careful. In my opinion there's something not right and if you continue to talk to these people, let me know. Let the Good Lord protect us.*'

Don Vito met '*these people*' that summer. On a hot afternoon, Massimo greeted Colonel Mori and Captain De Donno of the *carabinieri*'s elite anti-Mafia unit – neither was in uniform, for the sake of discretion – as they walked across Rome's Piazza di Spagna to the ex-mayor's home.

Mori, wearing a red Lacoste polo shirt because of the heat, was friendly to Massimo and thanked him for making the talks possible. He asked whether doing so was risky for Massimo, and advised him to be careful and avoid going to Palermo. If he did go to Sicily, Mori said, he shouldn't make the flight booking in his own name, nor should he mention the trip on the phone.

Massimo escorted the two officers up to the flat and showed them into the sitting-room. Following his father's orders, he had previously turned on the air-conditioning and put on some music – Don Vito worried about hidden microphones.

'Good afternoon, Colonel,' Don Vito greeted Mori.

'It's a great pleasure; thank you for seeing us,' Mori said.

'I'd like to be able to share your pleasure, but perhaps it's somewhat premature,' Don Vito retorted, as caustic as ever.

They began talking but soon Don Vito demanded bluntly: 'Let's be clear, Colonel ... I'd like to know who's sending you, and how far you both have credibility because, as you can well imagine, this isn't the first initiative of this kind I've conducted, but it could be the last, seeing the delicate nature of what's on the table.' The two officers assured him that a senior commander of theirs was also involved.

The talks lasted a couple of hours; Mori later described them as 'a simple first contact'. Afterwards, Don Vito was so doubtful about the officers' credibility that he sought the advice of both 'The Tractor' Provenzano and a mysterious Italian intelligence officer whom Massimo identified only as 'Franco'. He described 'Franco' as a friend of his father from the 1960s, with glasses and greying hair, well mannered and always smartly dressed.

'Franco' reported back that the talks were known not only to the *carabinieri*'s commanding officer, but also to two government ministers – the interior minister Mancino and the defence minister Virginio Rognoni. The ministers have denied knowing anything about the talks. Both Provenzano and 'Franco' encouraged Don Vito to continue the talks.

At his next meeting with Mori and De Donno a few weeks later, Don Vito asked them what precisely they wanted from him.

Mori expressed his concern at the assassinations of Falcone and Borsellino. '*Signor* Ciancimino, what's all this about?'

Mori asked. 'Now it's a dialogue of the deaf. On one side there's Cosa Nostra, and on the other there's the state. But isn't it possible to talk to these people?'

To the colonel's surprise, Don Vito immediately agreed to act as a mediator – implicitly admitting that he knew members of the Mafia.

Afterwards, Don Vito told his first-born son Giovanni that he'd been entrusted with the task of negotiating with the Mafia to put an end to outrages like the assassinations of Falcone and Borsellino.

'Are you crazy?' Giovanni exclaimed. He worried that such a negotiation would only worsen his father's judicial problems.

'It's something which can benefit everyone,' Don Vito insisted.

Giovanni protested again, and his father shot back: 'What do you want? You want me to spend another ten years in prison? If I go back to jail, I'll die.'

At their third – and final – meeting, in October 1992, Don Vito told Mori that he had contacted what he called 'the other side'; he clearly meant the Mafia. Don Vito said he had been asked who the two *carabinieri* officers represented. Mori told him not to worry about this and to continue their talks. Don Vito appeared to be satisfied with Mori's answer.

The ex-mayor then announced that the two officers could meet 'the other side', but only on condition that this took place abroad; that Don Vito acted as the mediator; and that something was done about the investigations into his own past. Don Vito asked Mori: 'What are you offering?'

'Here's what we offer: the various Riinas, Provenzanos and their friends give themselves up and the state will treat them and their families well.'

Don Vito, who was sitting down, slapped his knees with his hands and then jumped to his feet. 'You want me dead, or rather you want to die too! I can't say that kind of thing to anyone.'

It was out of the question, he insisted, that he could pass on such a message. Don Vito said he would tell his contact that they had decided on a pause for thought. He frostily escorted Mori and De Donno to the door.

The attempt by the two officers to find a mole who could lead them to the godfather of the Mafia and his lieutenants had failed – after five wasted months.

Almost two decades later, after Don Vito died, both Mori and De Donno paid an unexpected price for their efforts. Prosecutors in Palermo placed both of them under investigation – Mori, who was by now promoted to the rank of general, was accused of complicity with Cosa Nostra, and De Donno of posing a threat to the state, together with Don Vito's son Massimo and the two former godfathers Riina and Provenzano and others. The suspects all denied wrongdoing.

Massimo offered investigators a reconstruction of the talks that contrasted sharply with that of the two officers. According to Massimo, the key meetings had taken place before Borsellino's death, not afterwards; prosecutors theorised that Borsellino had been killed because he had found out about the negotiations, and had opposed them.

Massimo also alleged that his father had handed the officers the list of demands drawn up by the godfather Riina. Ten years later, Massimo claimed, he came across that piece of paper again as he helped his father write his memoirs. Stuck to it was a Post-it note with the words: '*Personally handed to the carabiniere Colonel Mario Mori.*' The note was allegedly in Don Vito's handwriting.

But Mori denied ever receiving a list of demands, and alleged the Post-it note was fake. If he had ever been given such a list, he insisted, he would have seized it immediately as concrete evidence that Don Vito was in contact with Mafiosi;

he would then have used it to pressure him to collaborate. Mori denied he had launched negotiations, describing his contacts with Don Vito as 'relations of a confidential nature'. He had never intended to seal a pact with Cosa Nostra.

Giuseppe Marchese betrays the law of silence

When the jailed soldier Giuseppe Marchese watched Rosaria Schifani, whose husband Vito had been killed with Falcone, appeal to Mafiosi to 'get down on your knees . . . and change your plans of death radically' if they wanted forgiveness, he felt tears coming to his eyes. Watching the funeral on TV with fellow prisoners in the maximum-security, nineteenth-century jail on the otherwise blessed Tuscan island of Pianosa, he pretended he needed to go to the bathroom in order to hide his tears.

Killing and creating mayhem had rarely, if ever, troubled Marchese, a twenty-eight-year-old car mechanic serving life sentences for murder and membership of the Mafia – the latter imposed by Falcone's maxi-trial. His sister was married to Riina's brother-in-law and, despite his youth, the other Mafiosi treated him with respect.

Bolstering his criminal pedigree, Marchese's uncle Filippo was the head of the powerful Corso dei Mille family in Palermo. Just before executing a victim, his uncle liked to call out their name and surname and add the words: 'Your story ends here.' Both Marchese's grandfathers were Mafiosi, and during his childhood the police had raided his home repeatedly searching for his father, a cattle breeder wanted for his ties with the society.

From adolescence, Marchese had been forced to follow the Mafia's 'code of honour'. When he was sixteen, his elders disapproved of his relationship with Rosaria, a girl whose parents were separated. Separation, let alone divorce, wasn't tolerated by the Mafia and Marchese's brother told him to 'clean up the family mess'. For the Mafia, the only solution was to kill Rosaria's father; if the girl were an orphan, she would be acceptable, his brother told him. 'You are going to ruin yourself and ruin your family with this marriage. If you won't kill him, we shall,' Marchese's brother said. Trapped, Marchese and the girl stopped seeing each other. 'I broke off our relationship, because if I had accepted I would no longer have been able to look Rosaria in the eye,' Marchese explained later.

It was Riina himself who decided that Marchese should be initiated into the Mafia, at the age of seventeen. He decreed that Marchese's membership of the Mafia should be a secret even within the organisation, and that he should take orders only from Riina himself and his uncle. Marchese was still a teenager when, together with his uncle and another accomplice, he shot dead three Mafiosi and a bystander in 1981, on Christmas Day in the afternoon – the newspapers called it 'The Christmas Massacre'.

Police arrested Marchese only three weeks later. His uncle ordered him to fake madness so that he would be sent to a mental hospital. Marchese did his best, but failed to convince the psychiatrists that he was insane. Soon afterwards, Riina made his uncle 'disappear'; the uncle had broken the rule that Mafiosi must bear imprisonment without complaint – a rule that many others failed to respect. Two years later, the boss Bagarella, Marchese's brother-in-law, revealed that the uncle had been killed.

For years, Marchese had trusted Riina blindly, convinced that the Mafia's 'code of honour' was its foundation stone; but now he began to doubt the godfather. And yet he remained loyal. In his seventh year in jail, at Palermo's Ucciardone prison, he and his brother killed a fellow convict, the Palermitan boss Vincenzo Puccio, in his sleep – by beating him with a cast-iron steak pan. According to Riina, Puccio was conspiring against him. Again, the godfather betrayed Marchese: Riina had Puccio's brother killed that same day, which destroyed the Marchese brothers' alibi that they had quarrelled with Puccio over what to watch on TV.

Finally, the scales began to drop from Marchese's eyes. 'I gradually realised that, for Riina and other Mafiosi very close to him, these rules were a sham and all that mattered to them was power,' Marchese explained later. He came to see the Mafia as 'only masks of hypocrisy and power, a never-ending spiral of lies.'

The assassinations of Falcone and Borsellino, whom he had considered his enemies for most of his life, shocked him greatly. He was particularly struck by the way Falcone was killed; many more victims could have been killed in the explosion – including his own family, who were at Palermo's airport that day.

Watching the funerals of Falcone, Borsellino and those who died with them – and, in particular, hearing the widow Rosaria's appeal – finally made him decide to collaborate. With both Falcone and Borsellino dead, he resolved to turn to their former chief investigator, Italy's 'Supercop' Gianni De Gennaro. Through a guard he trusted, Marchese sent a written message to the governor of the prison, asking to meet De Gennaro.

In his office in the former convent of Santa Priscilla in Rome, De Gennaro hesitated when the governor passed on Marchese's message. The prospect of Marchese betraying the Mafia – why else would he contact him? – could prove an extraordinary opportunity. Marchese would be the first collaborator from Riina's Corleonesi family, the first breach in the Mafia's most powerful clan. Previous supergrasses, most famously Buscetta, 'The Godfather of Two Worlds' whom De Gennaro himself had investigated together with Falcone, had all been from the society's losing side, the defeated enemies of the Corleonesi.

But De Gennaro suspected a trap. Did Marchese want to kill him? He knew he was an obvious target for the Mafia: he was the only survivor of the four-man team – Falcone, Borsellino and De Gennaro's police colleague Cassarà and himself – that had fathered the maxi-trial. And murder in a prison would be no novelty for Marchese; a steak pan had been enough to eliminate Puccio.

De Gennaro, however, had sworn he would catch Falcone's killers 'if it's the last thing I do in my life'. With no leads whatsoever to follow up, he decided he couldn't afford to miss what Marchese had to say to him. De Gennaro took only one precaution for his own personal safety. A fully armed ex-paratrooper, whom he knew well, escorted him when he left Rome by helicopter, bound for the prison island of Pianosa. They flew out on 23 August 1992 – precisely three months after Falcone's murder.

Precautions were also taken to guarantee Marchese's safety. If word of Marchese's meeting with De Gennaro were to leak out, the Mafia would swiftly order his death – in jail, at the hands of another prisoner. To ensure secrecy, De Gennaro and the prison governor crafted a stratagem. All the convicts in Marchese's wing of the jail were summoned, in turn, to the prison administrators' offices, on the pretext of having new photographs taken. They were then escorted back to their cell after only a few minutes.

When Marchese's turn came, he was escorted to a visiting room – bare save for a table and two chairs – where he found De Gennaro waiting for him. The former paratrooper stood just outside, ready to burst in at any moment.

'Here I am, I'm De Gennaro,' the veteran police chief said.

'Sir, you're f—ed,' Marchese greeted him bluntly.

'In what sense?' De Gennaro shot back.

'In the sense that they've got to get you. There's an order from Riina to kill you: he's asked people in Rome to check on your movements and any habits you've got. Then the Corleonesi will handle it.'

'Do you know anything else about this?'

'No. But I know that a few years ago they also asked a guy from the Magliana gang,' Marchese replied – the Magliana were a Roman underworld gang. 'We gave him some drugs and he was supposed to kill you.'

De Gennaro thought Marchese was telling him the truth; he had already heard from a trusted source that the gang were plotting to kill him.

'Do you intend to collaborate?' De Gennaro asked.

'Yes, and I've got many things to tell you. But you've got to get me out of here without anyone suspecting anything.'

'What's the situation inside Cosa Nostra now?'

'Riina is still in command, and now there's the problem of these special prisons. Cosa Nostra isn't happy about the new rules, and it's already started making friends with prison guards, trying to threaten them or win them over.'

Marchese added: 'I heard another thing, sir; there may be an attack in a plane or in an airport in September, because Riina has told his closest lieutenants not to travel to Milan during that whole month.'

With the time available to them running out – Marchese had to be led back to his cell before the length of his absence alerted his fellow prisoners – De Gennaro had one more thing to ask: 'The guard you spoke to last time will tell you when we're going to come and fetch you; you'll have to pretend you're ill. But now tell me one thing: what do you know about Falcone's assassination?'

'I don't know much, even though I've been inside for ages. But I think it was people close to Riina and my brother-in-law, Bagarella. You've got to get onto Nino Gioè and a certain Santino, known as "Half Nose". They're both from Altofonte.'

'Alright Marchese, be ready when the guard tells you.'

One morning a few days later, a helicopter landed in the main yard of the prison. An ambulance drove an apparently sick Marchese, lying on a stretcher, to the helicopter and he was lifted into it. The helicopter left immediately. As it soared above the island and headed down Italy's west coast, Marchese pulled the messages he had received from the prison guard out of the pocket of his jeans and ripped them to pieces.

Escorting Marchese was the DIA force's Francesco Gratteri, a bearded, dark-skinned deputy police chief in his late thirties from southern Calabria who was to head the investigation into the new collaborator's testimony. Over the clatter of the helicopter's rotor, Gratteri asked him for any leads which would help find Riina or Bagarella.

But Gratteri got only a little more out of him than De Gennaro had: 'Half Nose' Santino owned a big villa which bosses sometimes used for their meetings. Marchese had found that out from chatting to prisoners and to his own relatives.

The DIA swiftly hid Marchese away in a safe house near the coast, a few miles outside Rome. To two prosecutors from Palermo who came to question him, he explained that he had decided to turn his back on the Mafia because it no longer respected the rules he had long believed in. 'I want to start a new life; I want to get rid of everything that made me responsible for serious crimes,' Marchese said. In time, he confessed to more than twenty murders.

A week into his life in hiding, Marchese's handlers worried that his disappearance would soon make his family suspicious. Marchese's brothers, Mafiosi like him, were in the habit of visiting him often in prison and always filled him in on the Mafia's affairs. The DIA decided to stage another cover up.

One morning in early September, armed bodyguards drove Marchese to a hospital in Livorno on the coast of Tuscany where, in a wing sealed off for the purpose, he was watched around the clock. The collaborator's brother Gregorio was told he could see him in the hospital.

'Pino, why are you here?' Gregorio asked the next day when he walked into Marchese's hospital room.

'I pretended to be mad again. I swallowed a spoon and they brought me here,' Marchese replied.

'Why?'

'To get out of Pianosa; life is hell in there. How are things?'

'Everything's fine.'

Marchese asked about his sister: 'How's Vincenzina?'

'Fine.'

'And Luchino?' Marchese asked. The DIA officers had instructed him to try to find out about the whereabouts of Riina's brother-in-law Bagarella.

'We meet up there,' his brother replied.

It was all Marchese could get out of his brother.

When Gregorio left, he seemed unconvinced by his brother's explanation of his move. The Mafia dictated that its members must serve their time in prison, and only the society itself could decide on exceptions to this rule. A decade earlier, Riina had eliminated Marchese's own uncle for breaking that rule and now Marchese had infringed it too.

DIA officers in plain clothes followed Gregorio when his plane landed at Palermo airport, hoping that he would lead them to Bagarella. But the collaborator's brother was clearly wary. He drove off in a car, stopped to swap it for a scooter, and then abandoned the scooter to get into another car. Gregorio kept checking if he was being followed, and the officers had to drop their surveillance. When the society found out about Marchese, 'The Executioner' Brusca said his betrayal of both his Mafia family and his blood family 'stained the whole of Cosa Nostra with dishonour'.

But the DIA's investigators now had a new trail to go on – Nino Gioè and the mysterious 'Santino Half Nose'.

Case closed?

The hunt for Falcone's killers had only just begun when the Palermo police suddenly claimed they had virtually solved Borsellino's murder. On the day after Borsellino's death, a police officer had found the engine unit of a small car in Via d'Amelio. It didn't appear to belong to any of the wrecked cars in the street and the investigators presumed the engine belonged to the car in which the bomb had been placed. Using simply some cotton wool and some acetone, an expert consultant revealed the serial number and the type of car – a purplish red Fiat 126 which had been stolen on 10 July 1992, nine days before the blast.

Two months later police arrested Vincenzo Scarantino, a petty drug trafficker, accused of ordering the theft and of passing on the Fiat to Cosa Nostra. But the twenty-seven-year-old Scarantino did not fit the usual profile of a Mafia killer entrusted with claiming a 'distinguished cadaver' such as Borsellino's. His only previous crimes were drug dealing and cigarette smuggling, for which he had served a year in prison.

Scarantino's only link to Cosa Nostra was his sister, who was married to Salvatore Profeta, a Mafioso from Palermo's Guadagna family. His personality did not sit easily with the society's strict 'code of honour'. A member of a religious confraternity, he was also a regular client of transsexuals. Doctors had declared him unfit for military service, saying he suffered from neuropathy, a disease of the nerves.

But the police were convinced Scarantino had helped to murder Borsellino. Arrested alongside him were his Mafioso brother-in-law Profeta, Giuseppe Orofino, owner of the garage where the Fiat had been parked for a time, and Pietro Scotto, a telecommunications technician suspected of bugging Borsellino's mother's phone to find out his movements.

Defence lawyers picked large holes in the police's investigation. They pointed out that the engine unit at the origin of the investigation was nowhere to be seen in films of Via d'Amelio taken by the fire brigade on the afternoon of the explosion. None of the suspects knew where the men who had blown up the bomb were stationed, nor who they were. Nor did they know where the explosives came from.

The police brushed aside such doubts, and held firm to their reconstruction.

The police became even more convinced they had a watertight case when Scarantino confessed in 1994 that he had helped to carry out Borsellino's murder. He described himself as a Mafioso, confessing to several murders and claiming to know Cosa Nostra's secrets.

Scarantino said that he had accompanied several bosses to a meeting with the godfather Riina in a Palermo suburb, just a month after Falcone's murder. He had waited outside the room where Riina and the bosses talked, only going in to get a glass of water. At that precise moment, he had heard Riina, who was sitting at the head of a table, condemn Borsellino to death: 'This bastard has to be blown up like that neuter who'd stayed alive' – meaning Falcone, who had survived until he reached hospital. 'Borsellino is causing more trouble than Falcone,' Riina added.

Scarantino also described how he had stolen the Fiat and loaded it with explosives, how Borsellino's mother's phone had been bugged, and how he had handed over the car to accomplices in a Palermo square at dawn on the morning of the explosion.

But four collaborators whom Scarantino claimed were present later denied the meeting with Riina ever took place. They had never seen Scarantino, they said, and ridiculed his 'revelations'. One collaborator, when confronted with Scarantino, challenged his claim that he was a member of Cosa Nostra. 'You're a liar, who put you up to this? Who coached you? Tell us the truth; you have to say the truth. No one knows you. Who are you?' the collaborator charged, before turning to investigators: 'But do you really believe this person? This man is offending Italy!' Other collaborators accused Scarantino of lying – 'You're talking a load of bullshit,' one told him to his face, saying he was play-acting.

Several of Scarantino's claims alarmed investigators. He named the Catania boss as Aldo Forliti – the boss's name was in fact Alfio Ferlito. He claimed the boss Stefano 'The Prince' Bontate had been killed because he had failed to pay back a debt – Bontate had in fact been killed by the Corleonesi family in order to rid itself of a rival. Most outrageously, Scarantino claimed he had beheaded a victim with a box cutter.

One prosecutor who questioned Scarantino about the murders he claimed to have committed, aside from Borsellino's, dismissed him as a completely unreliable witness and 'phoney from head to toe'. Ilda Boccassini, another leading prosecutor who had been a close friend of Falcone's, resigned from her job in protest at the way Borsellino's murder was being investigated, ripping to shreds Scarantino's credibility.

Scarantino's family accused the police of beating him up and claimed he had made a false confession under duress. At the Pianosa prison, he was given very little food and that had worms in it; he was given injections of a liquid which, he was told, contained the HIV virus; he was threatened with death by hanging; he was not allowed to wash himself, and buck-ets of ice-cold water were thrown over him when he tried to sleep. He was even promised 200 million lire in exchange for a confession, they said.

The first time Scarantino's wife saw him in prison after his arrest, she almost failed to recognise him – he had lost 50 kilos and looked like a tramp. In the last months before deciding to collaborate, he had tried to commit suicide by striking repeat-edly at his left wrist with a fork. When he 'confessed', his wife accused the police of giving him written notes on what he should say and making him learn them by heart.

After he was given the status of collaborator and released, Scarantino repeatedly went back on his testimony, admitting to having made a false confession. He presented himself no fewer than ten times at the gates of jails across Italy asking to be taken prisoner. He also sent judges and prosecutors a flurry of letters demanding to have his status as a collaborator revoked, and went on a hunger strike to press his case.

But the judicial machine pressed on regardless. On the basis of Scarantino's false confession, and on evidence from a genuine collaborator concerning those who had commis-sioned Borsellino's murder, prosecutors issued eighteen arrest warrants for suspects. They included the bosses Filippo and Giuseppe Graviano, of Palermo's Brancaccio family, and Pietro Aglieri, who was passionate about philosophy and theology.

When the case came to court a lawyer for Scarantino's brother-in-law, the Mafioso Profeta, summoned a transsexual who described her erotic relationship with Scarantino. The lawyer argued it was impossible for someone who had had such relations with a transsexual to be trusted by Cosa Nostra, let alone become a member of the society.

In court, Scarantino formally withdrew his confession: 'God forgive me, I committed perjury . . . I know nothing about Cosa Nostra.' He added: 'All lies. I invented every-thing, together with the police and based on what I read in the newspapers.'

He had lied, he said, to obtain better treatment in prison. He had been manipulated and given testimony suggested to him by investigators. He had learnt the names of Cosa Nostra's bosses from a book written by the supergrass Buscetta – which the police detectives had given him – in order to make himself seem knowledgeable about the society. He had described the Fiat's route to Via d'Amelio, but the truth was he had no idea of the whereabouts of the street where Borsellino died. A collaborator told him he'd got the route wrong, and he corrected it.

Bursting into tears repeatedly, he told the court: 'I was used like a teddy bear with batteries, and forced with threats to take the state for a ride. I ate worms in prison. The guards told me that while I was in jail my wife was prostituting herself in the street.'

But judges took no account of his retraction and many of his fellow accused were given life sentences, only some of which were reduced on appeal. Scarantino himself was sentenced to eighteen years in prison. Then he again changed his story, this time claiming that his confession had been genuine. 'I went back on my confession because they threatened me,' he said. Cosa Nostra had sent him messages telling him that 'collabo-rators are walking corpses'.

It was only many years later that the case built on Scarantino finally unravelled.

The hunt for Antonino Gioè's 'den'

Unknown to the DIA officers, two of those whom the collaborator Marchese had named as Falcone's killers killed again just over two weeks after he first betrayed them. On 17 September 1992, Bagarella and Gioè – flanked by 'The Executioner' Brusca and La Barbera – murdered Ignazio Salvo, Sicily's leading tax collector who was himself a Mafioso.

The team shot dead Salvo, heir to a dynasty whose yachts had paintings by Monet and Van Gogh hanging on their walls, as he accompanied a dinner guest back to her car in the garden of his villa. Salvo's only sin was that he had been a financier for the former prime minister Giulio Andreotti, who was now on Riina's blacklist.

The godfather then demanded yet another 'distinguished cadaver' – he ordered Brusca to kill Judge Pietro Grasso, who had served in the maxi-trial and now worked for an agency co-ordinating anti-Mafia prosecutions across Italy. The murder, Riina hoped, would help force the state to yield to his demands.

'They've stopped [talking], we need another little jolt to make them start negotiating again,' Riina said.

Brusca replied that he knew Grasso's habits; he was 'an easy target, who could be hit straight away'.

Brusca knew that Grasso regularly went to Monreale near Palermo to have dinner with his mother-in-law, who was seriously ill. Brusca's lieutenants, Gioè and La Barbera, inspected the area repeatedly and suggested burying explosives in a manhole. They planned to make a large hole in the bottom of a van, park the van over the manhole, and lower the bomb into it.

The killers got as far as obtaining the special key needed to open the manhole cover, and a remote-control device similar to the one used to murder Falcone. But they feared that interference from a nearby bank's alarm system risked detonating the bomb at any moment. The plot to kill Judge Grasso was dropped.

The DIA had no clue as to the identity of the 'Santino Half Nose' whom Marchese had mentioned, but Gioè was no stranger to them. He had been on the police's books for the past thirteen years.

The son of an ex-railway worker born in Altofonte near Palermo, Gioè had first been jailed in his early thirties for drug trafficking. His criminal record quickly blossomed when he was first accused of kidnapping, murdering and concealing the bodies of two brothers; and then of carrying out three more murders, which included that of Boris Giuliano, the head of Palermo's flying squad. Gioè had served only eight years in prison before a judge sent him into internal exile in northern Italy. For the past three years he had been a free man and was back in Altofonte.

For the DIA, the town of Altofonte was almost off-limits. Virtually hemmed in by mountains, Altofonte was so small, and its residents so wary of outsiders, that they would immediately spot plain-clothed officers who started asking questions.

The DIA set up a new force to follow up Marchese's testimony. It was led from Rome by Gratteri, the officer who had escorted the collaborator from prison, and on the ground in Sicily by the chief superintendent Maria Luisa Pellizzari, a thirty-three-year-old from the Venice region whose previous

quarries included members of Rome's Magliana gang. Twelve
officers were assigned to the new team, which set up a logistics base in a converted residential complex near Palermo's
sprawling Favorita park. A mixed bunch of officers from three
separate forces – the police, the *carabinieri* and the finance
police who specialised in financial fraud and tax evasion – the
team had little knowledge of the Mafia, and even less of the
clans outside Palermo.

Gratteri sent four officers on a brief, discreet mission to
Altofonte to find out what they could about the forty-four-
year-old Gioè. They reported back that he lived with his wife
Luisa in a house very close to the main square; that he worked
in a petrol station just outside the town; and that he used at
least three phones – one at his home, one at the petrol station,
and also a mobile phone which was in Luisa's name and registered at an address which turned out to be uninhabited.

From an office in the law courts in Rome far to the north
of Sicily, the DIA started to listen in to the calls he made from
his home and from the petrol station. The technology available at the time didn't allow them to listen in on the calls he
made on his mobile; they could only monitor them. All the
officers could establish was who Gioè called, and who called
him. To their frustration, they quickly found out that Gioè
often asked people to call him back on his mobile – he clearly
knew it was safe.

Gratteri ruled out trying to watch Gioè at his home as it was
so close to the main square. But the petrol station a couple of
miles downhill, where he spent much of his days, was easier.
When Gioè was known to be in the petrol station, two officers
would park an unmarked car by the edge of the road a short
distance away uphill. While one officer pretended the car had
broken down, or had a flat tyre, the other would climb up a
tree and watch Gioè through a pair of binoculars, occasionally
taking photographs.

But the risk of being spotted meant the team watched him for no more than half an hour a day. They managed to find out that the owner of a Nissan Patrol who stopped to talk with Gioè almost every day was Gioacchino La Barbera, a thirty-two-year-old who was also from Altofonte. A quick check established that La Barbera ran a small earthmoving business and had a clean record. But his father had once been involved in a Mafia investigation. Phone taps revealed that Gioè and La Barbera called each other often, but their conversations on the phones the officers could intercept were brief and suspiciously cryptic. In one exchange, Gioè told La Barbera to bring him 'those things'; in another, La Barbera mentioned 'that business'. They used only first names, or pseudonyms, on the phone – one acquaintance was simply 'the pensioner'.

At about noon on 13 October 1992, the team had a lucky break. An officer was watching as a 4x4 car with three men inside stopped at the petrol station. One of the men was La Barbera. The men talked to Gioè for some time. Later, a check on the car's Palermo registration number established that it belonged to Enzo Brusca – the younger brother of Giovanni 'The Executioner' Brusca.

'Boys, this is getting serious,' Gratteri burst out. 'If these people are seeing Enzo, it means that through them we can get to Giovanni.'

From the phone intercepts, Gratteri discovered that Gioè rarely spent the night at the home he shared with his wife near the main square of Altofonte. He often called her at 7.30 a.m. to tell her he was coming to her 'for some coffee'. He also regularly told her to do some food shopping for him to pick up. For Gratteri, the priority was to find Gioè's other home – he apparently considered it a safe house, which intrigued the officers as he was a free man and had settled his scores with the Italian justice system.

Within a few weeks, Gratteri found out that Gioè was still a ladies' man, despite his marriage. He had a mistress – Giovanna, a twenty-six-year-old post-office worker who was also a friend of his wife, who knew nothing about the relationship. But Giovanna's strict father did find out about it. Incensed, he had tried to put a stop to the affair by appealing to the boss Brusca to make Gioè leave his daughter – or, if that didn't work, to kill him. Brusca did nothing, and the relationship endured.

The DIA tapped the phones both at Giovanna's home and at the post office where she worked. Shortly after 10 p.m. on 1 December 1992, Gioè called his mistress.

'My little hen,' he greeted Giovanna cheerfully.

'You're smiling . . . Where are you?' she asked, sounding suspicious.

'I said to myself: who knows whether the hen has gone out.'

'Yeah . . . as if I go out . . . Where are you going?'

'I'm going to the den. I'm going to bed.'

Moments later, Giovanna complained bitterly to her lover: 'Your hen is always at home. You're always out, while I'm sitting on my f—ing arse at home!'

'As long as no one is breaking it for you . . .' Gioè joked. His brand of humour only upset Giovanna further, and it took him several minutes to pacify her; she was clearly feeling neglected by him.

Where was 'the den', the officers wondered. And why did Gioè need it? The intercepts yielded a clue. In one conversation, La Barbera explained to Gioè: 'I'm at the end of the expressway. Come there, then we'll go to the den.'

From then on, officers took turns to keep watch on the expressway that cuts through Palermo's Golden Shell valley, near the turn-off for the Altofonte ring road to find out where Gioè spent his nights – perhaps together with La Barbera. An officer would park his car along the road and try to spot La Barbera's Nissan, or Gioè's green Renault Clio – whose left rear headlight was broken, making it easily recognisable. If Gioè's car was spotted, another officer would be stationed a few hundred years further on the following evening. The method was agonisingly slow, but following Gioè was out of the question as there was too little traffic on the road and anyone tailing him would have been spotted immediately.

Just after 8 a.m. on 3 December, Gioè called his mistress.

'Hello?' Giovanna said.

'Hello,' said Gioè, who didn't sound keen to talk.

'Where are you?'

'Well . . .'

'At the den?'

'Yes . . .'

'With his mobile phone?' The officers listening in had no idea who Giovanna was referring to.

'Yes . . .'

'You said the calls remain listed!' Giovanna objected.

'Well . . . um . . .' Gioè said.

'And doesn't that worry you?' Giovanna asked.

'I'll delete them now.'

'So why did you tell me it was a problem, and now you tell me you can delete them?' Giovanna insisted, her tone angry.

'I can delete them when I've got the time, because I've got to make another five calls,' Gioè replied weakly.

'And who are you calling, are you calling her too?' Giovanna asked, apparently suspecting that she and Gioè's wife were not the only women in his life.

Gioè tried to calm her down. He explained that he had arrived at 'the den' at 11.20 p.m. the previous evening, had gone to bed at midnight and had slept only until 5 a.m. But that wasn't good enough for Giovanna; she kept asking what he had done in the forty minutes between arriving at 'the den' and going to bed.

The bickering went on for some time, but it revealed nothing about the safe house.

That evening, the luck of the deputy police chief Gratteri changed. Two officers parked on the expressway spotted Gioè's Renault Clio and decided – despite orders to the contrary – to risk following it. Keeping a safe distance, they tailed him all the way to Palermo's western outskirts and to a private dead-end street, Via Ignazio Gioè, lined with elegant villas protected by high walls and CCTV cameras. They saw him use a remote control to open a big gate at Number 40, and drive inside. The officers drove back to the DIA's Palermo base, where no one worried about flouted orders. The investigators toasted each other, raising paper glasses under the office's raw neon light.

Late on each of the next few evenings, both Gioè and La Barbera were seen arriving at the spot. There were fourteen flats in the residence which the pair had entered, but Gratteri had yet to find out which one was theirs. He flew from Rome to Palermo to see the place for himself. One evening, he and his female deputy Pellizzari posed as an elegantly dressed couple looking for an acquaintance. They spent some time staring at the names on the Entryphone by the gate. They also scanned the block of flats, hoping for any clues, then turned away, pretending they had the wrong address.

'You've got to dye your hair; you're so blonde you stand out a mile away,' Gratteri muttered to his colleague.

'Don't worry about me,' Pellizzari replied in her strong Venetian accent, which regularly caused raised eyebrows among Palermitans.

'And don't say anything. You're making things worse with that accent,' Gratteri retorted.

*   *   *

On 17 December, Gioè called his mistress. He sounded worried. Gioè was careful not to name names but he was apparently aware that the Mafioso Giovanni Drago, a cousin of the collaborator Marchese, had decided to turn state's evidence.

'Aren't you going to the office tomorrow?' Gioè asked Giovanna.

'Of course I'm going.'

'Ah . . . I'll call you tomorrow . . . Also because there's another little bird . . .'

'Ah!!! . . . What is it, a canary?' Giovanna asked.

'Well . . .'

'Or a nightingale, maybe a nightingale.'

Gioè burst out laughing. 'A cuckold! . . . He knows my name, but I'm not in touch with him.' He was presumably referring to a new collaborator.

Soon afterwards, two officers managed to hide a small camera in a tree, in a big field only thirty yards away from the gate on Via Ignazio Gioè that Gioè and La Barbera had driven through. The camera was powered by a car battery buried under the tree which had to be replaced every night. Apart from the cows grazing in the field during the day, it was deserted.

The camera worked perfectly, but there was no sign of either Gioè or La Barbera.

'They've gone,' the Palermo officers told Gratteri.

'What do you mean, they've gone?'

'Yes, they've abandoned "the den". We've lost them.'

Unknown to his hunters, Gioè had guessed the police were on his tracks. He had long been obsessive about being trailed. Before getting into his car, he would look around to check if he was being followed. He always wore his seat belt – a rarity in Sicily. He varied his speed, sometimes driving fast and sometimes slowly, checking his rear-view mirror constantly. He carried no weapons – unless he had a murder to carry out – had fake identity and car papers on him, and kept his car in perfect condition, all to avoid any problems should police stop him at a roadblock. He was so cautious that La Barbera often mocked him, telling him he was paranoid.

Gioè had started renting a two-bedroom flat in Via Ignazio Gioè – the street's name amused him – before Falcone's assassination. He had shown the owner a fake identity document. Both Gioè and La Barbera had keys to the flat, and took turns bringing women to it – the other would discreetly stay away on those nights.

But Gioè had recently become increasingly worried about the police, because there were rumours in Cosa Nostra of new collaborators close to the Corleonesi family. Gioè believed his fears had been realised when Riina's driver told him that the police had asked the local water authority for a lorry together with overalls, boots and protective helmets to monitor the area around Via Ignazio Gioè.

'F—, so that's it!' Gioè exclaimed when he was told – only a few days earlier, he had spotted one of the water authority's trucks parked near the hideout. It had in fact been requested not by the DIA team but by another police force, and not for the purpose of monitoring Gioè and La Barbera.

But from now on the pair stayed away from the flat. Guessing that his phones were being tapped, Gioè changed the pseudonyms he used for his Mafiosi friends to try and confuse any officers listening in. Then, he and La Barbera started to use a series of cloned mobile phone numbers. They changed numbers so frequently it proved impossible for the investigators to keep track of them, and the intercepts ground to a halt – as did surveillance of both Gioè and La Barbera. Yet another promising trail seemed to be leading nowhere. But that was all about to change.

The godfather's downfall

'What's the problem?' 'The Beast' Riina asked on the morning of 15 January 1993 when *carabiniere* Captain Sergio De Caprio, better known by his codename '*Ultimo*' (Last), stopped his car, an unpretentious Citroën. A maverick, ponytailed officer who smoked cigars, De Caprio responded by briskly opening the front passenger door, catching hold of the godfather by the throat, and stretching him out face down on the tarmac as his colleagues took care of the driver, Biondino.

Riina refused to admit who he was. 'You're making a mistake. I'm not this Riina. I don't understand what you're saying,' he insisted. At breakneck speed through the morning traffic, De Caprio escorted his quarry to barracks opposite Palermo's medieval Norman Palace, holding him firmly with a scarf tied around the godfather's neck – so firmly that Riina had difficulty breathing and started to cough.

On the way, clearly terrified that his captors were rival Mafiosi who would now execute him, Riina asked: 'But who are you?'

De Caprio, who thought of the late Falcone as both his mentor and his friend after working together on several investigations, took his time before replying: 'We're *carabinieri* officers. You're under arrest.'

The latest collaborator to betray the Mafia, Baldassare Di Maggio, a shepherd's son, had led the police to Riina. The godfather had been on the run for twenty-three years. From the same town as Brusca – San Giuseppe Jato – Di Maggio was a zealous murderer, drug trafficker and arms buyer who had hoped to head the local Mafia family. But Brusca had dashed those hopes and made himself the local boss. Di Maggio had realised his life was in danger when Riina reprimanded him for leaving his wife and two young children to start a new family with his mistress, telling him that because of the affair he would never become a boss.

Di Maggio fled to northern Italy with his pregnant mistress. He started wearing a bullet-proof vest, and kept a gun with a hundred or so bullets at his new home. But when the *carabinieri*, aware of his heavy record, called to search his flat, he jumped at the opportunity to betray the Mafia.

'I can show you how to capture Riina,' he told the amazed officers who questioned him. Soon afterwards in Palermo, debriefed by De Caprio, he led the captain to a complex of villas on Via Bernini in north-west Palermo, where he knew the Sansone brothers – two big Palermo builders – had a home. He also knew that one of the brothers occasionally acted as a driver for Riina. For hours on end, De Caprio's men secretly filmed the entrance to the complex from a parked van, until the collaborator exclaimed: 'Stop, stop. That's Ninetta' – Riina's wife.

De Caprio caught Riina the next morning. Dressed in a rust-coloured check jacket, brown corduroy trousers, green polo shirt and a matching cashmere scarf, the godfather stared with damp eyes at his captors. They had made him sit in front of a photograph of the slain General Dalla Chiesa which hung on the wall.

Only then did the godfather admit who he was. 'Yes, it's me. Call my lawyer,' he said.

Earlier that morning at about 9 a.m., under a leaden grey sky, 'The Executioner' Brusca and Gioè and several other bosses waited for Riina near a shopping centre in northern Palermo. They were due to meet him there and then drive on to another spot where he was to brief them about the next targets in his strategy of terror. The bosses waited for a quarter of an hour, but still there was no sign of him.

A worried-looking Biondo – the soldier who had helped watch out for Falcone at Palermo airport – suddenly arrived. 'Get away from here; get away from here. Something's happened,' he told them.

The bosses fled. Brusca called a news service and found out that Riina and his driver Biondino had been arrested only two miles away as they made their way to that morning's meeting. Brusca felt shocked, disappointed and furious. But he also felt relief. 'If they'd waited a few minutes longer, they could have got all of us,' he reflected.

A tearful Biondo related the news to the butchers Ganci and Cancemi: 'The cop grabbed *Zu* [Uncle] Totuccio by the hair, he pointed his gun at him and threw him into the car. I felt sorry for him.'

To Brusca's surprise, there was no news over the next few hours of Riina's wife Ninetta – a former primary school-teacher who the newspapers dubbed the First Lady of Cosa Nostra – or of their three children. Perhaps the police didn't know the godfather's address, he thought. Riina had lived in the villa since 1987; he employed a trusted architect to build his homes, which usually boasted a safe hidden behind a painting, and an airtight vault in which his wife kept her fur coats. Riina passed himself off as an entrepreneur, and none of his neighbours suspected he was anything else. He used forged identity papers and a forged driving licence, although usually he had a driver.

There was no phone at the villa, so Brusca ordered the boss La Barbera and another Mafioso to go and see what had happened to them. They saw no police in the area whatsoever, so they gave Ninetta and her three children time to pack a few suitcases, and then drove them to the railway station in a small, cramped car.

Ninetta and the children walked into the station, carrying their luggage, and then walked out again a few moments later – she wanted to give the impression they had just arrived by train. They then took a taxi to the house they still had in the godfather's stronghold, Corleone.

A couple of days later, Brusca sent La Barbera and several soldiers to the villa with orders to 'take away everything that can be taken away' after the family's hurried departure. La Barbera recovered paintings and silverware among other items. But he made a bonfire in the garden of Ninetta's fur coats – found in a specially built airtight room – and her dowry, even the fine table and bed linen her mother had embroidered by hand. He preferred to dispose of it all on the spot, because he was worried he could be seen driving a large truck out of the residential complex.

Before leaving, the Mafiosi cleaned and vacuumed the villa thoroughly, then painted the inside walls to eliminate any trace of the godfather and his family.

The bonfire infuriated Ninetta's brother Bagarella. 'La Barbera even burnt her treasured mementoes. He deserves to be killed,' Bagarella fumed.

A few days later, Ninetta went to the *carabinieri* police station in Corleone to ask them to leave her and her family in peace from now on. 'I've always been with my husband and my children these past years. I educated them myself. I've come back because this is where they should grow up,' she said.

Ninetta brushed off an officer's questions about the godfather's crimes, telling him: 'My husband isn't the person you describe. He's an exquisite man. I wish all men could be like him, an exemplary father. He's too good; he's a victim of circumstances.'

At DIA headquarters in the ex-convent in Rome, De Gennaro put on a brave face after being beaten by the *carabinieri*, the police's eternal rivals, in the hunt for Riina.

'It's the *carabinieri* who caught the big fish,' a friend teased him.

'Today I'm a happy man,' De Gennaro retorted.

But on the day of the godfather's capture, he sent an order to the DIA team in Palermo urging them to step up their efforts to find the two bosses named by the collaborator Marchese as two of Falcone's killers, Gioè and La Barbera.

From his refuge in the United States, the supergrass Buscetta who had revealed all he knew about Cosa Nostra to Falcone, rejoiced at the capture of the enemy who had ordered the executions of his children: 'The arrest of the boss of bosses is the first miracle of 1993. It's a beautiful thing . . . I have lived with hatred for Riina. God is great, and today Riina will pay.'

In mid February, more than a month after the DIA had lost track of Gioè and La Barbera, two of its officers were driving down the street on which its Palermo base was located when they noticed a blue Nissan Terrano parked in front of a pizzeria. The two investigators remembered that before La Barbera had vanished, he had ordered a brand-new Terrano model from the city's LP Auto car dealership. They went up to the car to check – and on the back was an LP Auto sticker.

They knew the pizzeria well; it was conveniently close to their offices and they had eaten there several times. One of them walked in and headed for the bathroom. On his way through the room, he recognised Gioè and La Barbera sitting at a table with two other people. The officer walked out again. He and his colleague alerted their base, marvelling at their luck.

Two hours later, the Mafiosi finished their meal and left. La Barbera and one of the unknown men drove off in the Terrano, followed by three unmarked DIA cars; Gioè and the other man drove off in another car, followed by two more of the team's cars. The officers kept relaying each other to avoid being noticed. There were two officers in each car but they made sure that only the driver was visible. The other officer was stretched out on the back seat, communicating via radio with the others. Police officers usually drove around in pairs, so a lone driver would be less likely to raise suspicion. Each officer also took turns to drive.

The officers following Gioè saw him dropped off at the petrol station outside Altofonte, but failed to see where he went that night. The officers tailing La Barbera managed to stick to him. He led them to a street behind the Civic Hospital – where doctors had struggled to keep Falcone alive – and close to the Cemetery of the Holy Spirit. With a remote control, La Barbera opened the gate of Number 17, Via Giovan Battista Ughetti, and parked near two anonymous, nine-storey blocks of flats where washing was hanging out to dry on the tiny terraces. Anxious not to get too close, they called off the surveillance. But they were back shortly before dawn the next morning, and spotted Gioè's Renault parked there – the team had apparently stumbled on Gioè and La Barbera's new 'den'.

The hideout was in the block of flats furthest from the street, which was lined with modern blocks and shops. From Rome, the chief De Gennaro pressed his men to find out urgently which flat was the 'den' – he was keen to hide a microphone inside.

A search at the land registry office revealed there were four small one-bedroom flats, on each floor – a total of forty including the ground floor one. The flats were mostly rented out to university students for short lets, through a local estate agent. The officers ruled out approaching the estate agent as being too risky. They also ruled out following Gioè and La Barbera into the block. One investigator suggested they could pretend that a shopping bag had split open spilling flour on the floor by the lift just before the pair arrived – that way, their white shoeprints would lead to the right flat. But this idea was also rejected.

'Let's watch out for them switching on the lights after we've seen them go upstairs,' another officer suggested. But the block of flats could hardly be seen from the road; it could be watched from the car park, but the latter was small and anyone in it would be spotted easily.

The team had to do something. They decided to make enquiries about the residents who lived in the block. Did they have links to Gioè and La Barbera? Did they have links to Cosa Nostra? Would they raise the alarm if they spotted the undercover officers?

The team resorted to a well-tried stratagem. One morning one of the officers, disguised as a priest – complete with dog-collar, missal and a pack of holy images – took the lift to the top floor. He then slowly worked his way down the block, knocking on all doors with a polite smile and greeting those who opened with the words '*Buongiorno*, do you know our parish?' Palermitans were well used to priests calling on them to try to attract the faithful to their church. But all the officer managed to establish was that most of the flats were empty during the day; he saw only a couple of families, and a few students.

After sunset one evening in late February, two officers let themselves into the block opposite Gioè and La Barbera's, and waited. Tipped off via radio that the two Mafiosi were returning, they raced up to the top floor only to find that the door leading out onto the communal terrace was locked. They hurriedly broke the lock, rushed out onto the terrace and started to scrutinise the opposite block of flats through binoculars.

They saw a light shining behind a big window in the slope of the roof opposite them. Someone passed behind the window of the ninth-floor apartment. A few seconds later, a man the two officers both recognised as Gioè opened the window, looked down at the car park, and then closed it again.

The next morning, after Gioè and La Barbera had gone, another officer placed a toothpick in the doorjamb a few inches from the floor to make sure the ninth-floor flat was the right one. After the pair returned later that day, the team found the toothpick on the floor. The team had found the new hideout at last.

In Rome, the team's leader Gratteri hired a new recruit for a brief mission – Riccardo, a short, white-haired *carabinieri* warrant officer with a bad leg. More than a decade earlier, he had become an expert at opening the locks of hideouts used by terrorists of the Red Brigades without leaving trace of his handiwork. Over the past few years, he had gained access to the homes of Muslim terrorists and planted microphones in them, but now he was close to retirement.

Riccardo immediately agreed to help Gratteri. But before flying to Palermo, he asked for as much information about the door, the lock and the block of flats as possible. He wanted photographs, and technical data including the thickness of floors and ceilings, and how much iron there was in the walls – this was necessary to ensure the listening device would work.

The photograph of the lock reassured Riccardo. It was a common type, which he had dealt with many times. At DIA headquarters in Rome, he demonstrated with an identical model and a series of hooks and tiny iron rods that he could open and close the lock in under three and a half minutes – the maximum time allotted for entering and leaving the flat.

Riccardo flew to Palermo the next day. He brought with him a microphone and transmitter the size of a matchbox, and four batteries which could last three to four months.

As rare sleet fell on Palermo one evening in early March, Riccardo and a colleague sat in a parked car, briefcase in lap, waiting for Gioè and La Barbera to leave their flat. The officers knew they would not have to wait long. Surveillance had shown that the Mafiosi both went out almost every evening; Gioè would go to his wife or his mistress, while La Barbera would meet one of his many girlfriends.

Once Gioè and La Barbera had gone, tailed by other officers, Riccardo and his colleague walked up to the gate. The officer climbed over it and then opened it from inside for Riccardo. They went up to the top-floor flat and Riccardo got to work.

Less than 500 yards away, La Barbera stopped his car outside a bar and walked in. An officer following him raised the alarm, worried that he might return to the flat within minutes.

Riccardo had almost finished opening the lock when his colleague received a warning on his radio: 'Careful, perhaps La Barbera is coming back. Get out of there.'

Riccardo and the officer stared at each other in silence. Then Riccardo started closing the lock as fast as he could, while the officer pointed his gun at the staircase and at the door of the lift. A minute later, they were back in the street, hiding in their car.

A short distance away, La Barbera walked out of the bar carrying a small packet – perhaps a pack of cigarettes – got into his car and drove off, away from the hideout. 'The target has come out and is going away in the expected direction,' the officer following him reported.

Moments later Riccardo and his colleague were back on the landing of the ninth floor. Working faster than before,

Riccardo opened the lock easily. With an electric torch, the two men made a quick tour of the flat: a small sitting-room with a table, two chairs and a sofa with a flowered pattern, as well as a small kitchen and a bathroom. Up a few steps in an attic was the bedroom, with twin beds separated by a small bedside table, a cupboard, and a small TV set resting on a chair. Touching as few objects as possible, they searched for weapons but found none.

The team had decided the microphone should be placed in the bedroom, as Gioè and La Barbera went to the flat mainly at night. Riccardo opened the drawer of the bedside table, took out a screw designed to stop the drawer falling out, and exulted in a low voice: 'There's a fair bit of space; it's just what we needed.'

Riccardo quickly positioned the microphone, wires and batteries. After less than ten minutes in the flat, the two officers walked out. Riccardo closed the lock and dusted around it. 'Done, we can leave,' he said.

Soon afterwards, a senior DIA officer called De Gennaro and, in the style of statements made by the terrorist Red Brigades, reported: 'Today an armed cell of our organisation made an incursion into an enemy hideout . . .'

In a more informal tone, the officer added: 'Gianni, we've completed the first, real operation by the DIA. You'll see that it will produce results beyond your wildest dreams.'

The bugging was the first police operation to penetrate Cosa Nostra without the help of collaborators. Never before had investigators managed to listen in on Mafiosi talking freely – and for hours at a time – in a refuge they believed was completely safe.

The Mafia on tape

On the evening of 6 March, an old, battered Ford Transit van parked in a street near Gioè and La Barbera's hideout. In the van sat two DIA officers with headphones who started listening to the two Mafiosi. As they chatted in the bedroom, Gioè and La Barbera talked about drug deals and other Cosa Nostra business; they mentioned tension between Brusca and Bagarella, which the officers took to mean they were in contact with the two fugitives.

From then on, six officers took turns to spend stretches of twenty-four hours in the van, from 10 p.m. to 10 p.m. the following evening; the van also had a camp bed for them to snatch some sleep on. Much of what the Mafiosi said was difficult to understand. They talked in Italian, or in the Sicilian dialect, or even in the dialect of their hometown Altofonte, with sentences that were often interrupted, and made sense only to them.

To make things even more complicated, Gioè and La Barbera often watched TV while they talked, sitting or lying on their beds. One of their favourite programmes was *Colpo Grosso*, a striptease competition for housewives, and the officers had to endure the pair's bawdy comments on the contestants' looks.

In order not to jeopardise the operation, the officers on duty left the van as rarely as they could. They went outside to buy food, or to throw away plastic bottles in which they had relieved themselves. One evening when both Gioè and La Barbera were out, an officer left the van to throw away a bagful of rubbish. Suddenly he saw Gioè, and the latter's mistress Giovanna, walking towards him; they carried two pizzas and were heading for the flat. Apparently in a good mood because of the evening that awaited him, Gioè greeted the officer: '*Buonasera.*'

The officer, worried that Gioè would notice his Roman accent, smiled and nodded, saying nothing. That night, the tapes recorded not only the couple's comments on the pizzas, but also the sounds of their lovemaking.

Shortly before 1 a.m. on 9 March, Gioè and La Barbera discussed a plan for ferrying drugs from Palermo to Milan. Part of their conversation was in code:

> La Barbera: 'I said to him: "*Signor* Roberto, any news?" You know what Roberto's like . . . I told him I'd come up with someone, and he said to me: "Come on your own first, because there's some news or some other noise." Roberto doesn't talk at all, it's impossible to get a reply out of him on the phone.'
>
> Gioè: 'But do you think he's got the stuff?'
>
> La Barbera: '. . . I think he's got a bit of other stuff.'
>
> Gioè: 'To sell?'
>
> La Barbera: 'Cocaine.'
>
> Gioè: 'What are we supposed to do with cocaine, we don't have any . . .'
>
> La Barbera: '. . . But what the f— is going on, I don't understand Roberto . . .'
>
> Gioè: 'What does Roberto want? Doesn't he know what we want? We want "the black one" . . . he goes away, he comes back, he doesn't know what to do. We've got to do the business with the things we can sell, right?'
>
> La Barbera: 'Right, we've got to take . . .'

Gioè: 'If we take ten kilos of "the black one" and there are ten kilos of "the black one" and five kilos of cocaine for . . .'

La Barbera: 'F— that! We can't do anymore than that.'

Later that day, in the port of Sciacca on Sicily's south coast, police seized five tonnes of hashish aboard a fishing boat. The hashish had been packed into plastic drums and was due to be loaded onto a waiting truck.

The two Mafiosi commented bitterly on the news:

La Barbera: 'F—'

Gioè: 'F— . . . 5,000 kilos of stuff.'

La Barbera: '5,000 kilos of hashish.'

Gioè: 'Ah, f—!'

La Barbera: 'It was supposed to be for us . . . Right, 5,000 kilos of hashish, you know how much you could have made with that? About a hundred million.'

The pair switched from drugs to another lucrative source of profits for Cosa Nostra – public works contracts. Gioè and La Barbera had chosen a company they wanted the town hall in Altofonte to award a public works contract to – but some officials apparently needed to be intimidated:

Gioè: 'The first firm which puts itself forward, we place a big bomb, a bomb of 20, 30 kilos of stuff and we make the whole town shake, that way they'll ask themselves: "F—, is it worth it or not?" (*he laughs*) . . . As soon as Totò leaves the town hall . . . At two o'clock, as soon as he's finished work, he arrives home; as soon as he arrives inside his home we point at him what we've got to point at him, we show him our shotguns trained on him and we say to him: "Don't talk bullshit to me, for this job, the important thing is that I do it . . . How many times are you going to make me come up here? The next time I come, I'll come to shoot you, so bear that in mind, and don't start talking bullshit to me, because the next time I come up here, I'll come to shoot you . . ." '

La Barbera: 'F— me! That's right! That would be good, it's not as if we're doing anything to him, who says this f—er should always win?'

Gioè and La Barbera spent part of that evening handling their guns – the officers listening in could hear metallic clicks as they cradled them:

La Barbera: 'How long is this one?'

Gioè: 'Four inches.'

La Barbera: 'You should oil it a bit.'

Gioè: 'No, you just put a detergent and you dry it . . . you mix it with grease . . . The grip's small, never mind . . . F—, two bifilars, 7.65 . . . two and a half million, two and a half million, two 7.65 pistols. Two and a half million, that's for sure.'

La Barbera: 'Two and a half million, well . . . It's a good price!'

Gioè: 'You should have seen what shape it was in when they gave it to me, I had to cut it up.'

That afternoon, on 10 March, Gioè and La Barbera talked about a pursuit which had nothing to do with Cosa Nostra. With them was a friend, Salvatore 'Totò' Bentivegna.

Gioè: 'What should we do? . . . We have to find her . . .'

La Barbera: 'Yeah . . .'

Bentivegna: 'If we could get the address, she lives in a villa in Mondello . . . She lives there with her father.'

Gioè: 'Do you want to see to it . . . that girl with the boy . . . ?'

Bentivegna: 'Yeah, the one with the red thing, I know the one you mean, that girl . . .'

La Barbera: 'The face isn't anything much . . . But I like the rest . . . Forget it.'

Gioè: 'But really, how come you didn't get the address?'

La Barbera: 'There were two of them and I went after one of them, the other one is . . . I think she's got a boyfriend, so I tried it on with this one . . .'

Bentivegna: 'Did she make eye contact?'

La Barbera: 'We started chatting . . . She told me: "I live at Mondello, I'm in an attic." '

Gioè: 'F—!'

La Barbera: 'I don't like the face, but she'll be a . . .'

Bentivegna: 'You're interested . . . Forty . . .'

La Barbera: 'She's thirty-seven or thirty-eight . . . We might have coffee together.'

Bentivegna: 'Ah!'

Gioè: 'Of course, if she's got a friend I'll go for it . . .'

Five days later, Gioè watched the news with a friend identified only as Vito. They talked about a murder described in the broadcast:

Vito: 'He says one guy died in the car.'

Gioè: '. . . the car . . .'

Vito: 'F— . . . so it's true!'

Gioè: 'He jumped . . . with the pistol in one hand . . . then he shot him in the head . . . they got him . . . and it jammed . . . he jumped, f— he was alive . . .'

Vito: 'They arrested him for aiding and abetting . . .'

Gioè: 'If you have to die . . . boom . . . boom . . . He got a deadly blow . . . It's better to shoot him in the head . . . You shoot him then you . . .'

Vito: 'But it might also be something . . . Shooting him when he's moving, it's possible that a shot . . .'

Gioè: 'But it's better, the head's easier . . . tan . . . tan . . .'

Vito: 'The guy shot him when he was in front of him and the teeth jumped out . . . Well, the things that happen sometimes . . .'

A few days later, 'Supercop' De Gennaro reluctantly ordered the arrests of Gioè and La Barbera. They had made vague references to planned attacks believed to target rival Mafiosi near the law courts in Palermo and prison guards on the Tuscan island of Pianosa. 'Prepare the ground,' Gioè told La Barbera. 'Get things ready before the bomb blows up.'

De Gennaro's order was a huge disappointment for the Palermo team – it meant ending an unprecedented operation which they were convinced would lead them to Brusca and Bagarella. But De Gennaro felt he had no choice.

Shortly before 9 a.m. on 19 March, a car pulled up alongside Gioè's as he drove away from the hideout. A DIA officer ordered him to stop. Gioè, who was unarmed, betrayed no reaction and did as he was told. Asked for his driving licence, he showed the officer a fake document. 'You must come with us,' the officer said simply.

Escorted to the DIA's offices, Gioè refused to answer questions and prosecutors ordered him jailed as a suspected member of Cosa Nostra. That evening, the police handed him the prosecutors' four-page arrest warrant; Gioè found out from it that his conversations at the hideout had been taped.

A search of the hideout that day found many false identity papers and driving licences, as well as 4.3 million lire in cash, and a hair dye spray. The biggest surprise – and a source of bitter disappointment for those who had argued against ending the operation – was an identity card in the name of Francesco Guida. The photograph was missing but the officers recognised Bagarella in a picture they found next to it. One of Cosa Nostra's most wanted fugitives had just escaped them.

Bagarella was not the only one who had slipped away. Among the papers was a photocopy of a driving licence, also with a photograph next to it – that of Mario Santo Di Matteo. The investigators discovered that he was also known as 'Santino Half Nose' – named by the collaborator Marchese as one of Falcone's killers, in his first conversation with De Gennaro eight months earlier.

La Barbera had left Palermo and all the DIA had to go on were signals showing his mobile phone was somewhere in the centre of Milan, Italy's business and fashion capital. But only three days after Gioè's arrest, officers who had been scouring the city spotted La Barbera drinking coffee as he sat in a smart bar near Milan's cathedral.

Soon after his arrest, his captors tried to persuade him to collaborate.

'Leave me alone,' was his only reply.

Among the items found on La Barbera were three credit cards, receipts from restaurants and pizzerias in the Milan area, notes with the names and phone numbers of several women – and two images of the Immaculate Conception, apparently his good luck charms.

The DIA saw this as a meagre harvest for such an unprecedented operation. With the pressure off – and with more time on their hands now – the investigators started taking turns to go through the many hours of tapes, to see if anyone had missed anything. It was slow, frustrating work – the tapes often had to be laboriously cleaned to make the Mafiosi's conversations comprehensible.

But in among the banter about girls and guns, the officers had let something slip – something game-changing.

Gioè's last letter

The DIA officers realised they had missed a vital exchange between Gioè and La Barbera a full two months after it took place. It was only in mid May that the investigators noticed what had been said on 9 March, between 00.40 a.m. and 1.55 a.m., when the two friends had been watching the striptease programme *Colpo Grosso*, making lewd comments as usual.

La Barbera was trying to explain to Gioè, in dialect, where a new collaborator lived in Capaci, the town closest to the stretch of motorway where Falcone had been blown up.

Gioè: '. . . there must have been someone else . . .'

La Barbera: 'And so?'

Gioè: 'Well . . .'

La Barbera: 'That's possible . . . Once Santinu made me remember . . .'

Gioè: 'Yeah . . .'

La Barbera: 'In a nutshell . . . Do you remember the car repairer's, close to where I waited there, there at Capaci where we did the *attentatuni* [the big attack], by the car repairer's . . . ?'

For the officers, it was as if they had La Barbera in front of them, confessing to assassinating Falcone. And Gioè had understood what his friend was referring to immediately – showing that he knew all about it and could well have been involved in the assassination, the investigators thought.

Records for Gioè's mobile phone on the day of the assassination, 23 May 1992, revealed nothing. He had activated it only ten days later. But La Barbera's calls were intriguing. At 5.48 p.m., eight minutes before the bomb blew up, he had received a call from the soldier Giovan Battista Ferrante, lasting ten seconds. He had then called a phone in the name of 'Half Nose' Di Matteo at 5.49 p.m., a conversation lasting just over five minutes. Between 6.39 p.m. and 9.03 p.m. that evening, La Barbera had made and received at least seven calls to and from the phone in Di Matteo's name. More checks revealed that Gioè, and not Di Matteo, had been using the latter's phone at the time.

When he pored through the DIA's thick report on the phone records that he had requested, shivers ran down the spine of the prosecutor Lo Voi – who was a close friend of Falcone's and now led the investigation into Gioè and La Barbera. He realised the timings and the areas of the calls pointed inevitably to Falcone's murder.

'It's them,' Lo Voi thought to himself. 'They're the ones who did it.'

As he languished in the G7 wing of Rome's Rebibbia jail, reserved for Mafiosi held under the harshest prison regime, Gioè had no idea what his captors had stumbled across – as they had missed the exchange before his arrest, it didn't feature in the arrest warrant he'd been given.

Gioè had always been a neat, clean-shaven man who dressed smartly. But in prison he began to grow a beard and stopped combing his hair. La Barbera, held a couple of cells away from his friend, caught a glimpse of Gioè as he was led down the corridor for his daily hour of exercise – La Barbera was struck by how unkempt he looked, and by the dazed expression in his eyes.

'Why don't you tidy yourself up a bit?' La Barbera asked Gioè in a message through a neighbour.

Gioè replied that he wanted to make it harder for anyone to recognise him if a collaborator betrayed him. He was particularly worried about Marchese, he said, even though they hadn't met for ten years.

Gioè's spirits lifted when Cosa Nostra almost managed to kill Maurizio Costanzo, a popular TV chat-show host who had repeatedly denounced the society during his programmes. On the evening of Riina's arrest, the presenter had quipped: 'If I was in the habit of drinking, this evening I'd get drunk I'm so happy.' A car bomb almost blew up Costanzo and his girlfriend as they drove down a Rome street on 14 May; twenty-three people were injured but the couple was unhurt.

Gioè sent a message to La Barbera: 'Now I feel better.'

The attempt to kill Costanzo was the prelude to a new season of Cosa Nostra bombings across Italy as Riina's strategy of terror continued, despite his arrest. That spring and summer, the targets were not prosecutors, judges or police chiefs but the country's cultural and religious heritage – and anyone who happened to be nearby at the time of the blasts.

On the night of 26 May, a bomb near the Uffizi Gallery in Florence killed five people and wounded twenty-nine. The explosion destroyed or damaged works by the masters Giotto, Titian, Bernini and Rubens among others. On 27 July, another bomb destroyed a modern art museum in Milan, killing five people and wounding a dozen. And that night a bomb in Rome wounded seventeen people and damaged the basilica of St John Lateran and the church of San Giorgio al Velabro.

Unlike Riina, the new godfather, 'The Tractor' Provenzano, believed the strategy of terror would backfire on Cosa Nostra, making the state crack down on the society in retaliation. He complained to Bagarella, Riina's brother-in-law, about the bombings. But Bagarella retorted arrogantly: 'If you don't agree with them, why don't you walk around with a big sign around your neck with "I don't have anything to do with the massacres" written on it?'

But Gioè and La Barbera's arrest, and the revelation that their conversations had been taped, prompted Cosa Nostra to drop a plan entailing yet more attacks. It had intended to blow up the Leaning Tower of Pisa, to place poisoned snacks on supermarket shelves, and to scatter syringes containing blood contaminated by the HIV virus on beaches. The aim was to create widespread panic and put pressure on the state to treat Cosa Nostra with more leniency. In order to avoid causing casualties, bosses would notify the authorities in advance.

Riina's bloodthirstiness was to prove too much for one of Falcone's assassins. The butcher Cancemi – who had shouted about 'that f—er' at the TV screen when first reports said Falcone had been injured but not killed in the motorway bombing, and then ordered champagne when he died – drew a line at the godfather's next tactic.

At a meeting with several bosses, Cancemi heard Riina rail against the growing number of collaborators. 'The evil is these supergrasses, because if it wasn't for them, even if the whole world united against us it would be no skin off our noses. So we have to kill them all ... starting with their children, six years old. That way we'll give these supergrasses a good lesson!' Riina had said.

For Cancemi, who played with his six grandchildren for hours on end, this was too much. The only time he had felt any emotion when killing someone was when he helped to strangle a man who was carrying a shopping bag with meat he had just bought for his children. Today, after a couple of decades in Cosa Nostra, he had no intention of becoming a child murderer.

Cancemi had good reason to feel estranged from the society – he feared for his life. A friend who had just seen

'The Tractor' Provenzano, now Riina's successor as godfather of Cosa Nostra, warned Cancemi not to answer any summons from him. He gave no explanation – Cancemi thought his misgivings about the strategy of terror had been noticed. When the summons came in late July, he decided to betray Cosa Nostra and seek the state's protection.

After a sleepless night, Cancemi left his home and walked through Palermo's deserted streets – it was 5.30 a.m., on 22 July – to the *carabinieri* police barracks in the city centre. A young orderly stood guard in a sentry-box outside the barracks. Cancemi went up to him.

'Good morning, I'd like to speak to one of your superiors,' Cancemi said.

'At this time in the morning?' the orderly asked him.

'Yes, I have to speak with one of your superiors.'

'Look, it's impossible. Who are you looking for at this time in the morning?'

Cancemi stared hard at the orderly. 'Look, I'm a fugitive. Now what do you reckon?'

The young man rushed out of the sentry-box. He was so flustered Cancemi felt sorry for him. The orderly called a junior officer who escorted Cancemi into the barracks to meet a captain. Cancemi explained that he wanted to collaborate because he believed that Riina had trampled over the principles of Cosa Nostra.

Cancemi's first revelation was that the society wanted to avenge the capture of the godfather Riina seven months earlier by seizing his captor, Captain 'Ultimo'. 'First of all,' Cancemi said, 'I want to know who this Captain "Ultimo" is, because he's got to be warned that Provenzano wants to kill him. He wants to kidnap him,' Cancemi said.

That spring, Cancemi explained, the new godfather Provenzano had announced that he had found a way of kidnapping 'Ultimo'. Provenzano said he wanted to interrogate him and then murder him. If the plan failed, Cosa Nostra would simply murder him directly.

Cancemi then offered his stunned listeners a chance to catch Provenzano himself. 'If you want to arrest Provenzano, I've got an appointment with him this morning,' Cancemi said. But the officers had to hurry, he added: Cancemi was due to meet the boss Carlo Greco near the Baby Luna bar at 7 a.m., and Greco would drive him to meet the godfather. Cancemi offered to go to the appointment, with the *carabinieri* tailing him.

At first, the officers listening to Cancemi didn't believe him. They feared it might be a trap, and besides their own intelligence said that Provenzano was probably dead – they'd heard that he'd been shot by a sniper with a precision rifle. The fact that Provenzano's family had returned to Corleone after years in hiding was seen as proof of his death.

Cancemi told them it was absurd to think Provenzano was dead. Only two months earlier he'd seen the godfather himself – Provenzano was alive, although he was thin and suffered from problems with his prostate, which meant he kept going to the bathroom.

The officers' attitude got on Cancemi's already frayed nerves and he lost his temper. 'I've told you that I have to meet Carlo Greco, if you don't want to catch Provenzano, at least arrest Greco!' he shouted.

Cancemi thought he had managed to convince the officers he was telling the truth when they finally decided to conceal a microphone in a pocket of his trousers to record the meeting with Provenzano. But the officers spent so much time arguing – whether to use an armoured van to follow him, or helicopters – that the time for the appointment came and went. The Italian state lost its chance to capture the new godfather.

'They didn't have the guts,' a disappointed Cancemi commented later.

For the time being, a cautious Cancemi – the only member of the *Cupola* executive governing Cosa Nostra ever to give himself up – kept quiet about Falcone's murder. When asked about it, he lied – he knew nothing, he claimed.

He admitted that as a member of the *Cupola*, he had ordered an unspecified number of murders. But he confessed to carrying out only 'a few' himself – 'my role wasn't that of a hit man, I had responsibilities,' he explained. He said that it could take up to seven Mafiosi to strangle a victim. 'There are those who react violently, they fight, they shout: "F—ers!" There are others who ask for forgiveness; they try to save their lives,' Cancemi said.

At the Rebibbia prison in Rome one evening, six days after Cancemi's betrayal, Gioè sat down to write a long letter. He was forty-five years old and it was the last he ever wrote. His taped conversations had implicated his relatives and he now insisted they were innocent:

> *This evening I'm recovering the peace and the serenity which I'd lost about seventeen years ago. Having lost these two things I became a monster and I've been a monster up to the moment I took the pen to write these few lines.*
>
> *... These few lines which I only hope can serve to save innocents ... who just because of my monstrosity have found themselves subject to legal proceedings.*
>
> *... Now, my first moment of lucidity, I'm trying to remember all the lies I said in Via Ughetti and on the phone.*

His brother Giuseppe had '*never shared my life*'; his other brother, Mario, had always criticised him more than anyone else, '*but unfortunately after my arrest he had to intervene to recover a credit from dirty dealings.*' He dedicated only a couple of lines to the spouse he had been unfaithful to: '*My wife has been the victim of my monstrosity only as far as married life is concerned.'*

Gioè blamed himself for betraying Cosa Nostra's secrets – albeit unwittingly – *'with my chattering and lies'*. He added: *'I represent the end of everything and I believe that from tomorrow, or soon, the supergrasses can go back home with much more honour than me – I don't have any honour.'*

He ends: *'Before going, I ask my mother and God for forgiveness, because their love cannot have obstacles. All the rest of the world will never be able to forgive me.'*

Signed: *'Gioè Antonino.'*

He then made a noose using his trainers' shoelaces.

At 11.50 p.m. that night, Gianni Mosetti, a prison guard, found Gioè's body hanging by the neck from the metal grating on his cell window. It was the first Mafioso suicide in living memory, and it testified to the crisis within Cosa Nostra, as did the collaborators who were turning against it.

Gioè had talked of hanging when he voiced his frustration at Cosa Nostra's strategy of terror, just after Falcone's assassination. 'What can we do? Either we get a life sentence, or the Corleonesi shoot us. Or we slip a rope around our necks and we kill ourselves,' he had told La Barbera.

When Gioè hung himself, the godfather responsible for that strategy – Riina himself – was sleeping, no doubt soundly, in a cell a short distance away.

A plotter turns collaborator

True to Cosa Nostra's tradition of slipping into bed with political leaders, 'The Tractor' Provenzano offered to end the strategy of terror in exchange for better treatment by the state. According to Giuffrè, Provenzano's former right-hand man, the godfather sealed a pact in the summer of 1993 with the future senator Dell'Utri.

Under the alleged deal, Cosa Nostra pledged to halt its wave of terror in exchange for an easing of the pressure from police and judiciary, fewer seizures of the society's assets, and fewer benefits for collaborators. After consulting Cosa Nostra bosses, Provenzano threw the organisation's weight behind the new Forza Italia party led by media mogul Silvio Berlusconi.

'We're in good hands with Dell'Utri,' Provenzano reported. Giuffrè added: 'And we all started to work for Forza Italia.'

That autumn, and apparently in ignorance of Provenzano's alleged dealings, 'The Executioner' Brusca attempted to launch a negotiation of his own. According to his own later account, he read in a magazine that Vittorio Mangano, a Palermo Mafioso, had worked for Berlusconi as a bailiff, stableman and bodyguard at his eighteenth-century villa near Milan.

Brusca summoned Mangano and, in the presence of Riina's brother-in-law, Bagarella, asked him if he knew Berlusconi. Mangano replied that he did, and that it would be possible to reach him through Dell'Utri. Brusca asked him to go to Milan and pass on a warning to Berlusconi and Dell'Utri: either they made a deal with Cosa Nostra and pledged to review the maxi-trial and ease prison conditions for Mafiosi, or 'the massacres would continue'.

According to Mangano, Dell'Utri responded to the message with a 'Thank you, thank you, at your service.' But Brusca's initiative was to be wrecked when Mangano was arrested some time later.

Berlusconi branded Brusca's account a 'folly'. Both Dell'Utri and Berlusconi have denied any links to Cosa Nostra. Berlusconi has said he sacked Mangano as soon as he found out about the man's Mafia ties. Dell'Utri has also said he knew nothing of Mangano's Mafia links at first and got rid of him as soon as he did.

Cosa Nostra punctuated its negotiations with violence. After partially blowing up two of Rome's churches in the spring, it turned against a shy but brave parish priest in Palermo's Brancaccio neighbourhood. The fifty-five-year-old Father Giuseppe Puglisi, a shoemaker's son, dedicated himself to supporting young drug addicts and misfits in the area, and campaigning against Cosa Nostra, especially among teenagers. In church, he denounced Mafiosi as 'beasts' and 'animals', offering to meet them in a local square. 'Let us talk together. I would like to meet you and understand why you stand in the way of those who try to help your children and teach them to be law-abiding and show mutual respect,' he said.

Father Puglisi's activism was not to the liking of the bosses Filippo and Giuseppe Graviano, who suspected that he passed information to the police about Cosa Nostra's local affairs. The society decided to give Father Puglisi two warnings; it set fire to the door of his church and then set fire to a van belonging to a firm which was restoring the building.

Father Puglisi talked about the threats in his homily at a Mass held to commemorate Borsellino's murder. He named the Graviano brothers and accused them of being behind the threats. And at the 'Our Father' community centre next to the church, the priest put up a big poster of Falcone and Borsellino.

Incensed, the Graviano brothers resolved to kill Father Puglisi, but they wanted to ensure that the murder would not be attributed to Cosa Nostra. They entrusted the task to Gaspare 'Baldy' Spatuzza, a whitewasher who had carried out dozens of murders for Cosa Nostra but was not yet a member. He had helped up to blow up the bomb near the Uffizi Gallery in Florence that spring. Dissolving his victims in acid was routine for Spatuzza. On one occasion, he held a sandwich in one hand while stirring a drum full of acid with the handle of a broom. Inside was the body of a young thief.

At first, Spatuzza thought of murdering Father Puglisi in a fake car accident. Then he decided on a fake robbery. Shortly after 10 p.m. on 15 September 1993, which happened to be Father Puglisi's fifty-sixth birthday, Spatuzza and Salvatore Grigoli, an accomplice, followed the priest as he walked from his church to his home only a few hundred yards away. Just after Father Puglisi had inserted his key in the lock of his front door, Spatuzza walked up and announced: 'This is a robbery.'

'I was expecting this,' Father Puglisi replied.

Grigoli fired one bullet into the back of the priest's neck. Spatuzza picked up his briefcase but, finding only personal documents in it, all he stole were the stamps on the driving licence. The body lay for a full half hour on the pavement before the neighbours finally decided to call the police. A few days later, Giuseppe Graviano ordered Spatuzza to kill a notorious robber and to abandon the latter's burnt body near the church, so that locals would think Cosa Nostra had executed the priest's killer. But Spatuzza found it impossible to leave it there so the plan failed.

It was the first time that Cosa Nostra had killed a member of the clergy.

The investigators into Falcone's assassination, who had made little progress over the past year and a half, finally got their breakthrough when Mario Santo Di Matteo decided to collaborate. Arrested in June 1993, Di Matteo agonised until October before deciding to talk. He said the violence unleashed by Riina sickened him. 'The things that were done were not right, like Falcone's murder, like the murders of so many people who were killed without reason. It was enough for someone to take a bit of a dislike to a guy, and he'd bite the dust. That was the teaching of *Signor* Riina . . .' Di Matteo said.

Falcone's murder was the first crime he confessed to. He revealed the names of the other conspirators and their role. After Di Matteo's testimony, the butcher Cancemi had little choice but to confess to Falcone's killing too. When he had started to collaborate that summer, he had insisted he knew nothing about it.

The investigators could now put a face on Falcone's assassins. They issued warrants for their arrest. Ferrante was caught in November, bringing to four the number of Falcone's assassins behind bars, alongside Cancemi, Di Matteo and La Barbera.

The cigarette ends left at the vantage point on the hillside above the motorway had been damaged by rain after Falcone's murder. With the help of the FBI, which offered its co-operation partly because of the respect it had for Falcone, analysis of DNA traces revealed only that they had probably been smoked by at least three different individuals. An expert found that traces on three of the cigarette ends were compatible with the DNA of La Barbera and of Di Matteo, with a certainty of 91.2 per cent; none were compatible with the chain-smoking Gioè.

Now only thirty-four, La Barbera had no intention of committing suicide like Gioè, nor of spending the rest of his life in prison. He too confessed to his role in Falcone's assassination, and described the roles played by the other assassins. He was the first to tell investigators that it was Brusca who had flicked the lever that blew up the motorway.

The collaborators' betrayals undermined Brusca's authority within Cosa Nostra; never had his status within the society been so jeopardised. The two informers whose testimony was the most devastating for Cosa Nostra both came from the family he headed – Di Maggio, who led police to Riina, and now Di Matteo who, as the first to describe in detail the plot behind Falcone's murder, 'sent us all to Hell', as Brusca put it.

Riina's brother-in-law Bagarella and several other bosses summoned Brusca to a lime depot east of Palermo in mid-November and reprimanded him for failing to keep his underlings in line. The bosses deliberated for a couple of hours on how to fight back against the new wave of collaborators. They finally decided to kidnap Di Matteo's twelve-year-old son Giuseppe, to punish his father, hoping at the same time to discourage other Mafiosi from turning state's evidence.

Kidnapping the boy was, in Brusca's words, 'in the interest of Cosa Nostra as a whole'. The bosses were divided on what to do with Giuseppe once they had kidnapped him. Some wanted to kill the boy immediately; others including Brusca argued that he should be kept alive for a while. Brusca's camp won. He agreed to carry out the kidnapping and use it to try to make Di Matteo go back on his testimony.

Ten days later, on 23 November 1993, six Mafiosi recruited by Brusca and dressed as police officers approached Giuseppe at his riding school in the town of Altofonte. They told the boy they had come to take him to his father; Giuseppe beamed in delight, exclaiming, 'My father! Of course I'll come!' Later

Spatuzza, one of the kidnappers, commented: 'In the boy's eyes we were angels, but deep down we were wolves.'

The 'wolves' held Giuseppe for 779 days. As Brusca explained, there was nothing 'noble' about his preservation of Giuseppe's life for more than two years – it was 'a question of tactics'. He had to keep his hostage alive so that he could force Di Matteo to recant his testimony. But the kidnapping, and the threats which Brusca sent Di Matteo and his family, accomplished nothing. According to Brusca, Di Matteo made the mistake of underestimating his foes; he was convinced that they would not harm his son.

On 11 January 1996, Brusca's brother Enzo and two other kidnappers strangled the now fourteen-year-old Giuseppe. Enzo told the boy before killing him: 'I would have looked after you like the apple of my eye if your father hadn't been a bastard. I'm sorry . . .' They then stripped the body naked before dissolving it in a drum of acid.

In his memoirs, Brusca confessed his part in the boy's murder. 'I won't look for excuses. I had no hesitation in sending a boy to his death,' Brusca explained. But he quibbled callously: 'Giuseppe was twelve when he was kidnapped, but he was fourteen when he died. He wasn't a *bambino* [child] any more.'

The crime earned Brusca a new nickname – 'The Monster'. He reflected: 'Perhaps I wouldn't have become that if I'd killed only Judge Falcone and his wife.' But for Brusca, Giuseppe's kidnapping was 'the direct consequence' of Falcone's murder. 'It was the first symptom that we were losing control of the situation and that, in the attempt to get back in control, we became locked in a spiral and never got out.'

On the day Giuseppe was kidnapped, the bright, fast-talking thirty-one-year-old Alfonso Sabella joined the team of anti-Mafia prosecutors at the Palermo law courts as its youngest member. Born in the small mountain town of Bivona in western Sicily, Sabella had graduated in law studies with top marks before joining his parents' practice – both of them were lawyers. Although he himself was against hunting, Sabella found himself defending hunters and also poachers.

Sabella's defence tactics were unusual – he once managed to persuade a judge to agree to the autopsy of a dead rabbit. The aim was to establish whether three game wardens had caught the animal at night, using powerful torches to dazzle it – such torches were banned. But the autopsy failed to establish the time of the rabbit's death, and Sabella's clients were acquitted.

Sabella loved to listen to the stories the hunters told of tracking down rabbits, hares, partridges and skylarks. The key to their success, they told him, was to know the territory. They boasted that they knew every den, clearing and stream in the woods. They studied the traces their prey left and knew how the time of day, or the weather, could determine the routes hares or rabbits took. They spent hours waiting in the same place. Sooner or later, they knew, the prey would come their way. Later, Sabella acknowledged his debt to the hunters of Bivona. 'They taught me the techniques and the philosophy of hunting,' he said.

Married with a one-year-old daughter, Sabella had at first planned to work as a magistrate in the civil courts, but after meeting Falcone he was so impressed that he decided on a career as a prosecutor instead, and himself became a hunter – his quarry no longer rabbits and partridges, but the bosses and soldiers of Cosa Nostra. Like the hunters, he learnt to know the territory. He learnt that the society's lookouts could range from an eleven-year-old boy to an old peasant; they might be a barber or a cobbler – all of them would pass on news of any outsider spotted on their territory. 'And the game can become dangerous, because the hunters risk becoming the hunted,' Sabella explained. 'You have to be very cautious, taking one small, silent step at a time. Never show yourself. Work downwind from the prey so it doesn't smell the hunter.'

Sabella modelled himself on Falcone. Echoing his murdered colleague's remark that to fight Cosa Nostra, 'you have to learn to live and think like the Mafiosi', Sabella stressed the need 'to understand the way the fugitive moves, what his links are, his contacts; you have to think like him, put yourself in his place, and almost identify with him.' This meant understanding not only the Sicilian dialect but also how it varied from one town to the next.

Shortly after his arrival at the Palermo law courts, Sabella wrote a list of the most wanted Cosa Nostra bosses inside the cover of the desk diary used by his boss, chief prosecutor Gian Carlo Caselli. Crossing them off was to become almost a game for the two prosecutors.

In the spring of 1995, the boss Leoluca Bagarella was near the top of Sabella's list. For the young prosecutor, the stocky but powerfully built Bagarella – not Provenzano – had become the true godfather of Cosa Nostra after the arrest of his brother-in-law Riina. The key to Bagarella's power was the fact that he had taken command of Cosa Nostra's entire military wing, made up of the most efficient killers from families ranging from Palermo to Trapani in the west. Sabella believed that although Provenzano was formally the new godfather, he had no such private army at his disposal.

Bagarella, born to a family that had been in Cosa Nostra for six generations, was no easy prey, thanks to his constant fear of capture. He always worried that he would be caught, that undercover officers might be following him, or that the police were listening in on his conversations at his hideout or on his mobile phone. After Riina's arrest, he had become even more wary and now had a radio scanner and would spend whole days at home just monitoring the wavelengths used by the police. Whenever the police broadcast an alert, Bagarella worried they were coming to get him. Eventually his paranoia proved too much even for him: he grabbed the scanner and threw it against the wall, shattering it. 'F— it! When they want to get me, they'll get me!' he shouted.

His paranoia cost lives. Convinced that bosses who had been defeated by his Corleonesi family in the 1980s were plotting to kill him in revenge, Bagarella issued many death sentences. In April 1995, he sent a team to ambush Gateano Buscemi, a small property developer and Mafioso from Villabate south of Palermo. Bagarella had killed the man's uncle a month earlier.

The team drove Buscemi to Cosa Nostra's 'chamber of death' – a drab office the size of a keeper's lodge in a warehouse in the eastern outskirts of Palermo. On the walls hung the images of several saints: the Virgin Mary; Saint Rosalia, the patron saint of Palermo; Saint Rita, patron saint of desperate causes; and Saint Christopher, patron saint of drivers. But there was nothing holy about the objects that lay in a concealed niche in the wall: handcuffs, ropes, nooses, wire and latex gloves.

Bagarella arrived at the 'chamber of death' soon after Buscemi. The kidnappers forced the property developer Buscemi to sit in a chair; they tied him up and placed a rope around his neck. Bagarella started to question Buscemi about his Mafia family, slapping him again and again.

Buscemi realised he would never leave the room alive and suggested a deal; he would reveal everything he knew about his fellow Mafiosi, on condition that his body was not dissolved in acid. His wife and children must have a grave to mourn him, Buscemi pleaded.

Bagarella agreed to the pact and the 'interrogation', under the glare of a cheap neon light, lasted for more than eight hours. When Bagarella realised there was nothing more he could get out of Buscemi, he started to strangle his victim. With the job unfinished, Bagarella opened the door of the office and told a few henchmen waiting outside: 'If any of you want to say goodbye to him, you can do it now.' Several of them went in and finished the job. Buscemi's body was abandoned in a street in his home town, the rope still tied around his neck. Bagarella had kept his promise.

Bagarella fancied himself as the patriarch Don Vito Corleone in the classic film *The Godfather*, by Francis Ford Coppola. During his first years on the run, he liked to be called 'Don Vito' like the fictional character, and in the early 1990s he chose the music of the saga for the film of his wedding. He married the beautiful Vincenzina Marchese, niece of the Palermo boss Filippo Marchese, giving a reception for hundreds of guests at the luxurious Villa Igiea hotel outside Palermo.

One collaborator said that Bagarella was so much in love with Vincenzina that he would race home whenever she called him to say she had put pasta on to cook for them. Sometimes Vincenzina's call came when Bagarella was busy strangling his latest victim. He would leave the victim in the hands of his accomplices, dutifully return home for lunch, and then return to complete the job.

Vincenzina stayed loyally at Bagarella's side during his years on the run – the ideal companion for a Mafioso. She was the perfect Mafia spouse, as described by a collaborator: 'a wife, even knowing her own husband is a criminal and a murderer and seeing the kind of people he talks to, is ready to accept any sacrifice for the love of a man who is faithful and who loves her. There are women, wives or mothers of Mafiosi, who are worthy of admiration for the sacrifices they make.'

But Vincenzina eventually began to believe that the couple's inability to have children was God's punishment for the kidnapping of Giuseppe Di Matteo, carried out by her husband's men. She had become pregnant several times but always lost the child after two or three months. Loneliness and the shame of seeing her brother Giuseppe become a collaborator worsened her fits of depression. She tried to kill herself several times; on two occasions, friends stopped her jumping off a balcony.

One afternoon in mid May 1995, Bagarella returned home to find his wife's body hanging from a rope she had tied to a beam. Unable to give her a proper funeral because he was on the run, Bagarella called a friend and together they carried her out of the flat at night. They held her body up by the arms, pretending that she had fainted. No one saw them leave. Bagarella buried his wife in a secret grave dug on another Mafioso's land, near Palermo.

Bagarella started to dress in black, and stopped killing – it was his way of mourning. Among those who owed their lives to Vincenzina's suicide were several Mafiosi, a couple of lawyers, an MP and a wealthy businessman.

On Brusca's trail

Within a few days of Bagarella's wife hanging herself, another of the boss's relatives decided to collaborate. Emanuele Di Filippo, a soldier in his early forties with a vague resemblance to the French actor Alain Delon, had a sister whose husband was the brother of Bagarella's late wife. In prison, Di Filippo suffered from depression and had tried to hang himself with a sheet tied to the bars of his bed.

In Rome's Rebibbia prison, Di Filippo revealed to the young prosecutor Sabella that his younger brother Pasquale, nicknamed 'The Lady' because of his effeminate manner, was one of Bagarella's trusted lieutenants. Police from the DIA agency placed several bugs in Pasquale's house. One of them was discovered when a Mafioso at the house heard the voice of his wife, who was putting their son to bed next door, on the TV set as he watched the evening news. The bug was quickly spotted inside a light switch.

Sabella ordered Pasquale's arrest and accused him of belonging to Cosa Nostra. The prosecutor was waiting for Pasquale when he was escorted to the DIA's Palermo offices. Sabella couldn't help noticing that Pasquale, whose hair was ash blond, was in such a state that his face kept switching colour from deathly pale to crimson and back again. Sabella told him of the many years in prison that awaited him, and a sweating, tearful Pasquale swiftly decided to collaborate.

Pasquale's first revelation was about Bagarella. The key figure helping the boss stay on the run, he said, was a man he knew only as 'Tony', who had a clothes shop in Corso Tukory. It was a busy street of cheap shops and eateries near Palermo's Norman Palace. 'He's his driver, his factotum, his right-hand man. Look for him!' he said.

Sabella had already come across 'Tony', whose real name was Antonio Calvaruso. The prosecutor had arrested him four years earlier for alleged pimping at the nightclub Les Tours d'Orient outside the city. Calvaruso was expert at fleecing his clients. Customers were forced to order a drink every quarter of an hour; those who ordered champagne had no idea they were served common Asti Cinzano sparkling wine poured into empty bottles of 1962 vintage Dom Perignon. Nor did customers have any idea that the equally compulsory 'Mexican' drink they ordered for the Romanian, Latin American and African prostitutes at the nightclub to get them drunk was not alcoholic at all, but a mix of sugar, lemon juice and water.

DIA officers discovered that Calvaruso worked every day at the clothes shop, which sold casual menswear. They also discovered that he often entered a nearby block of flats opposite the building where two anti-Mafia prosecutors lived – one, Giuseppe Pignatone, was formally in charge of the hunt for Bagarella. The block where the prosecutors lived was protected by soldiers on a couple of army jeeps, so Sabella replaced two of the soldiers with DIA officers. From then on, they watched the building that Calvaruso kept visiting; Sabella suspected that Bagarella was hiding there.

Sabella had guessed right. Occasionally, Bagarella liked to watch the prosecutors through a pair of binoculars from the windows of his hideout, laughing to himself as they came and went with their armoured escorts.

* * *

For three days, officers kept a watch on the clothes shop. On the afternoon of 24 June, as the first warm sirocco wind of the summer blew through Palermo, two officers saw a man who looked vaguely like Bagarella – he had a black moustache and wore Ray-Ban sunglasses – walk into the shop. As they waited for him to come out again, the officers talked hurriedly and decided it must be Bagarella.

Soon afterwards, Bagarella walked out of the shop holding a bag – inside, they learnt later, was a pair of Levi's jeans that he had bought a few days earlier, and which had been shortened for him. The boss got into a blue Opel and drove off. Only a few yards down the street, two unmarked cars flanked him on either side and closed in, forcing him to stop.

Bagarella lied to the officers who asked him for his papers. 'There must be a mistake; I'm Franco Amato, a post-office worker,' he said as he handed over a false identity card.

But later, at the DIA offices, Bagarella admitted who he was, and congratulated the officers who had captured him.

Sabella's superior, the chief prosecutor Caselli, came to see Bagarella. 'Good evening. I'm the Palermo prosecutor and I'm here to ask you if you intend to say something; if you have some statements to make,' Caselli said.

'I know you well, sir. You just go on being the prosecutor, and I'll be the prisoner,' Bagarella replied.

Late that evening, the DIA's Captain Gigi Bruno phoned Bagarella's sister Ninetta – the wife of the jailed godfather Riina – to tell her about the arrest.

'Good evening, is this the Riina home? I'm Captain Bruno of the DIA. I'm sorry to bother you at home at this hour, but I wanted to inform you that we have arrested your brother Leoluca,' Bruno said.

Ninetta reacted with a stream of insults, mixed with cries of despair.

The phlegmatic Bruno added: 'Again I'm sorry I disturbed you. I wish you a good evening.'

In Bagarella's flat, the DIA found a handwritten note. '*My husband is the best man in the world and he deserves a statue of gold,*' it read. The note was in Bagarella's handwriting: Sabella discovered later that it was a copy of one his late wife Vincenzina had given her relatives. A vase of fresh flowers stood in front of a silver-framed photograph of a veiled Vincenzina on her wedding day. Bagarella obviously mourned his wife. He was wearing her wedding ring on the day of his arrest. In a cellar, the DIA found a few pistols and shotguns – a small, personal arsenal.

At the Palermo law courts the next day, with a grinning Sabella watching him, the chief prosecutor Caselli slowly opened his diary and turned to the list of wanted bosses. He took a green pen and drew a line over Bagarella's name. This was to become a ritual every time they caught a boss.

Sabella felt he still had unfinished business with Bagarella – or rather the latter's late wife Vincenzina. All Sabella knew of her grave was that it wasn't in a cemetery, and that bothered him. He felt sorry for Vincenzina – she had lived through a terrible ordeal, the wife of a boss, and the sister of a collaborator. He knew she had been a Catholic, and he wanted her buried on consecrated ground. It was a purely personal matter for Sabella; he had no intention of accusing Bagarella of concealing a body – an offence under Italian law. What was the point, given all the murders he was already accused of?

For Vincenzina's sake, Sabella made an exception. He never sought deals of any kind with Mafiosi or their lawyers, but on this occasion he approached Bagarella's lawyer and told him: 'If your client tells me where his wife's grave is, I promise I'll get her buried on consecrated ground. And I'll also get an escort for him to go and visit her grave.' Sabella never got an answer from Bagarella.

Sabella was far from satisfied with Bagarella's arrest. 'Bagarella's good, but Brusca would have been better,' he told his senior colleague Lo Voi, who headed the hunt for Brusca. For Sabella, Brusca would be a bigger prize even than the godfather 'The Tractor' Provenzano. For one thing, Brusca had murdered more people than Provenzano.

Brusca was no ordinary quarry; Sabella saw him as 'the icon of evil' – who had assassinated Falcone, and kidnapped and murdered the young Giuseppe Di Matteo. Sabella usually managed to be dispassionate about the Mafiosi he hunted, but he hated Brusca. It was because of Falcone that Sabella had chosen to become a prosecutor, and Brusca had killed Falcone. He also hated Brusca for killing Francesca, whom Sabella had met when she was a young, and beautiful, civil judge.

Brusca himself was more worried about 'The Tractor' Provenzano than investigators like Sabella. As Provenzano exploited Bagarella's arrest to conquer Palermo, Brusca felt the godfather might turn against him. When Provenzano summoned Brusca to a meeting at a concrete plant near Corleone, various bosses warned him to be careful, and he took several bodyguards with him. 'I got my driver to take me over there, and we arranged that if anything happened I would throw my mobile phone out of the window and that would be the signal: they would come in shooting, and do whatever they could,' Brusca recalled. 'I was armed, and so were they. But as it turned out there was no need. I could see there was no danger, so I came out again straight away and told him, "It's OK, you can go, it's fine".'

Eight months later, in January 1996, the former nightclub manager 'Tony' Calvaruso first set Sabella on the trail of

'The Executioner' Brusca. After deciding to join the growing ranks of collaborators, Calvaruso told a DIA officer in
a visiting room at Rome's Rebibbia prison: 'I can give you
some useful information: I know where Giovanni Brusca built
himself a house.'

Calvaruso, who impressed Sabella with his extraordinary
photographic memory of faces and places, led investigators
to a typically Sicilian, ancient fortified farmhouse with a vast
courtyard near Palermo. Within the complex was a luxurious,
three-storey building which boasted a beautiful garden with
exotic plants and an automatic irrigation system. Sabella and
his colleagues decided that raiding the building immediately
might be risky, as they had no idea who was living there –
Calvaruso's tip-off was based on information that was seven
months old, and Sabella worried that Brusca had long moved
on.

Surveillance teams started to keep watch. But despite their
precautions, their presence was noticed by the rival *carabinieri*
police, who dispatched a helicopter to scan the area on the
day after Calvaruso had led the DIA to it. To the exasperation
of the surveillance teams, the helicopter flew low over the area
and hovered over the farmhouse itself, its rotors raising clouds
of earth and dust.

After five days of fruitless watching, the DIA raided the
building at dawn on a Sunday. There was no one inside, but
the officers found plenty of signs that someone had lived
there until very recently – including a copy of the local newspaper, *Giornale di Sicilia*, dated 7 January, the very day the
police had first reached the area. In a drawer, they found a
passport belonging to Brusca's girlfriend Rosaria, and several
recent photographs of their five-year-old son Davide – the
first images of him to fall into police hands.

As he walked from room to room, Sabella marvelled at
Brusca's lavishness. The refuge boasted granite floors covered

with Persian rugs. The bathrooms had huge Jacuzzis, gold taps and so much multicoloured granite they felt like tombs to Sabella. There was air-conditioning throughout, and the freezers were filled with enough food to last the boss months.

What struck Sabella most were three walk-in wardrobes – one for Brusca, one for Rosaria and one for Davide. They were so big they were more like rooms than wardrobes, the prosecutor thought. Rosaria's was filled with clothes by Giorgio Armani and other Italian designers. 'The bitch,' Sabella thought to himself. 'She knows Brusca's money is dirty with blood, but here she is spending it on luxury clothes.' The women of the Mafia had always made Sabella see red.

Brusca's wardrobe boasted hundreds of shirts covering an entire wall. Perfectly ironed and starched, they were arranged on hangers and ordered strictly by colour from pink to yellow, blue, pale green and salmon. The collection included a long row of white silk and linen shirts. To Sabella, it all looked like 'a rainbow of shirts' – his own were all light blue. The contents of Brusca's wardrobe taught him something new about the boss's character – the man was vain, on a studied, almost manic quest for elegance.

Later, the prosecutor discovered that the rash of new collaborators had made Brusca more cautious, but done nothing to stop his extravagant spending. The boss had stopped going to luxury boutiques in Palermo himself, but sent his lieutenants instead to buy his clothes and watches.

As Sabella came across Brusca's slippers, pyjamas and shaving cream, he felt the boss's smell still lingered in his home. On the bedside table lay a paperback copy of *Men of Honour: The Truth about the Mafia* by Falcone and the French journalist Marcelle Padovani. Brusca was studying his enemy, wanting to understand what made him tick, Sabella thought – and in a way, Brusca must have admired Falcone. Perhaps Brusca had been reading the words of his most famous victim while Sabella was hunting him. Never before had Sabella felt so close to Brusca.

Later, Sabella found out that Rosaria and Davide had been on the terrace of the building when the helicopter arrived. She promptly decided to flee. The surveillance teams failed to see them go. Sabella guessed they had used an escape route found only later by the officers – an underground tunnel, no more than a giant steel tube, leading from the building to the bank of a nearby stream.

With hindsight, Sabella realised he should have raided Brusca's home on the day it was discovered. He bitterly regretted the mistake as Brusca might well have been there that day. He got no sleep the night after the raid as he kept turning it over in his mind. Later, Sabella was to agonise that he had missed a chance not only to catch Brusca, but also to save the life of the young hostage, Giuseppe Di Matteo – the teenager was killed on the night before the raid.

The thought that he could have saved Giuseppe became an obsession for Sabella. He told himself that, rationally, he couldn't have saved the boy as he would have had to find the spot where he was held, and Calvaruso didn't know where it was. Sabella could only have saved Giuseppe if he'd managed to arrest Brusca, and the latter had told him where the boy was – but that might have been too late as collaborators revealed that they were under orders to kill Giuseppe as soon as Brusca was arrested. Still Sabella always agonised over it, thinking that perhaps Brusca, to save the boy's life, would have told him where he was held.

Only a month later, Sabella got a new tip-off about Brusca – from Giuseppe Monticciolo, a building contractor who wore silk shirts and drove a Mercedes, but whose shoes were often streaked with lime dust. As Brusca's right-hand man, the short, dark-skinned Monticciolo had carried out the worst of jobs for him. He had also overseen the last year of Giuseppe Di Matteo's kidnapping.

Monticciolo had come to hate Brusca. He felt superior to him and hated being stuck in the position of second-in-command. When he was arrested in February – thanks to information from another collaborator – Monticciolo swiftly decided to collaborate and betray Brusca. Even before Monticciolo was taken to prison, he revealed that the two Brusca brothers, Giovanni and Enzo, were living in a flat in the town of Borgetto, west of Palermo.

This time, Sabella didn't hesitate and ordered an immediate raid. But he just missed both brothers; officers discovered that they had left only half an hour earlier. It was the second time that Sabella had drawn a blank. He thought to himself that Mafiosi had a sixth sense – it was as if they could smell police and prosecutors from a distance.

However, Sabella drew comfort from the fact that capturing Brusca's protectors and forcing him to abandon two hideouts amounted to a successful scorched-earth strategy. Surely the boss felt hounded, he thought.

That strategy was always the last card the prosecutor played when all other methods had failed. The technique, he cheerfully agreed, wasn't very sporting. The hunters he represented early in his career had told him about it repeatedly. They would set fire to parts of a wood to flush out boars and force them to race to the spot where they were waiting for them. Sabella played the scorched-earth card only when he had no alternative; arresting a contact of a fugitive boss could mean revealing months of surveillance, analysing phone taps and other bugged conversations.

Monticciolo's betrayal of Cosa Nostra prompted another of Brusca's henchmen to follow his example only a few days later. Vincenzo Chiodo had no information on Brusca's whereabouts, but together with Monticciolo he led Sabella to the spot where the teenage Giuseppe Di Matteo had spent his last weeks.

On a foggy morning in late February, the two collaborators escorted Sabella to a country cottage, half of it in a dilapidated state, near Brusca's fiefdom of San Giuseppe Jato. For the prosecutor, the cottage was 'a house of horrors' which concealed 'an underground refuge worthy of James Bond.'

In the cottage's filthy kitchen, a button on a remote-controlled device was supposed to lower part of the floor, allowing access to a small underground warren of three small rooms. The investigators couldn't find the remote control so officers forced their way through with a crowbar. One of the three windowless rooms, which had an iron door, had been Giuseppe's last prison – the boy had spent the last months of his life there and it was where he had been strangled. The room had been emptied since his death, but just looking into it made Sabella shudder. It smelt damp and musty; Sabella was surprised to find that it didn't smell of death. He walked away and wept; he didn't want the collaborators to see him crying.

In another of the rooms, Sabella saw the mouth of a narrow tunnel made out of steel tubing. Two officers squatted down and made their way down the muddy tunnel on hands and knees; the tunnel led to an underground tank a short distance away.

To their amazement, the officers discovered by torchlight that the tank contained the biggest arsenal ever found in Italy. It was made up of hundreds of weapons: ten Soviet-made RPG-18 rocket launchers, bazookas, more than four hundred pistols of various types and calibres, hundreds of Kalashnikov rifles, several dozen pump-action and semi-automatic shotguns, as well as machine-guns and dozens of grenades. Also in the tank were ammunition and drums containing three types of explosives – Semtex, plastic and TNT.

It took the police until well into the night to retrieve it all. Looking at the growing array of weapons in the glare of powerful lights of a generator, Sabella thought it was like the set of a film – a war film. A single missile from one of the RPGs, he reckoned, could pulverise an armour-plated car, or strike a plane as it took off or landed, killing hundreds of people. Cosa Nostra was well and truly 'at war' with the state.

A few days after showing Sabella the 'house of horrors', Monticciolo gave the prosecutor another, rather crude, lead. 'When his arse is on fire, Brusca runs to Agrigento,' Monticciolo told him. But he had no idea where precisely Brusca might be in Agrigento itself, a city on Sicily's southern coast, or somewhere near it. Neither did he know who was sheltering him.

Sabella felt more frustrated than ever. Seeing the arsenal that had been at Brusca's disposal made catching him even more urgent.

A Mafia code

When he first met Giovanni 'Shepherd Boy' Zerbo, a young cocaine and heroin dealer, in the offices of Palermo's flying squad, the prosecutor Sabella thought he would get nothing out of him. Shortly after his arrest in March 1996, the dealer had a dreamy, vaguely fearful look on his face – like a shepherd seeing a city for the first time, Sabella reflected. But soon afterwards Zerbo decided to collaborate and as Sabella listened, the prosecutor realised that he was much brighter – and much more helpful – than he had thought at first.

Sabella wanted help deciphering a pocket diary found on Salvatore Cucuzza, the boss of Palermo's Porta Nuova clan who had been arrested with Zerbo. Phone numbers in the diary were in code, letters replacing the numbers. To make things yet more difficult for Sabella, the real names of contacts were never used, only their nicknames or pseudonyms. One boss featured only as 'Long Death'.

Zerbo told Sabella that he knew the phone numbers of two brothers, drug traffickers who were nicknamed 'The Midgets' because of their size; they featured as such in the diary. Sabella learnt that Cucuzza, apparently thinking of his own family, had used the ten-letter phrase ''ntalè i soru' ('watch over the sisters', in Sicilian dialect) as a code, with each letter standing for a number.

Slowly, Sabella managed to decipher all the numbers in the diary – he felt as if he were 'reading Cosa Nostra's phonebook'.

He decided to focus on 'The Midgets' – otherwise known as the Adamo brothers – and ordered taps on their phones. Two phone numbers that the brothers contacted raised Sabella's suspicions; the numbers corresponded to two GSM mobile phones owned by a ninety-year-old woman in San Giuseppe Jato, Brusca's hometown. What was a woman of that age doing with two phones which boasted the most high-tech system on the market? Of all the prosecutors Sabella knew in Sicily, only Ilda Boccassini had a GSM phone, and that was because she'd recently been transferred from Milan.

Working with the flying squad, Sabella established that the ninety-year-old was the aunt of Santo Sottile, a butcher and one of Brusca's lieutenants. The prosecutor suspected that Sottile had registered the phones in her name but that he was in fact using them himself. Monitoring showed that every evening, between 8 and 8.30 p.m., one of the two phones was used to contact another GSM phone in the area of Agrigento. The discovery instantly reminded Sabella of the collaborator Monticciolo's remark: 'When his arse is on fire, Brusca runs to Agrigento.'

Intercepts established that the phones were being used by Brusca and Sottile – several collaborators recognised Brusca's voice. For Sabella, this was already a victory in itself. The scorched-earth strategy had robbed Brusca of practically all his protectors in his hometown of San Giuseppe Jato and he had fled to Agrigento, famous for the ancient Greek ruins in its Valley of the Temples, a couple of hours' drive to the south. A Cosa Nostra boss never left his territory because, as the boss Bagarella put it, 'presence is power'. Brusca's move underscored his weakness.

Unknown to Sabella, Brusca had moved into a two-storey villa outside Agrigento with his girlfriend Rosaria and their son Davide that April. He felt safe there as he'd used the villa in the past, and knew all the neighbours. Brusca used a false name; he had long lost faith in forgers and had made false documents himself, drawing on a stock of some 200 blank identity cards and many official stamps, as well as fake driving licences.

Brusca may have been forced to abandon his fiefdom but he remained jubilant. He had managed for the first time to set up a drug-trafficking deal with the blessing of Cosa Nostra. The society had invested two billion lire to bring cocaine, heroin and hashish from Colombia to Sicily. The cocaine and hashish would be sold in Italy, while the heroin would be sent on to New Jersey.

Brusca calculated that he was about to make a huge profit. A kilo of cocaine cost about $3,000 in Colombia. Importing it to Sicily, and buying off police and customs officers, added another $12,000 per kilo. But on the Italian market, the price jumped to $50,000 a kilo or more. The price rocketed even further once it reached North America.

The deal kept Brusca busy. He went back and forth between his villa and Palermo to meet accomplices, going for strolls along the city's broad avenues and stopping at a bar for a coffee or a pizzeria for a meal. But his eager anticipation of heavy profits was overshadowed by worries that the police might be on his trail. He knew that his accomplice Monticciolo and 'Shepherd Boy' Zerbo, whom he knew well, had turned state's evidence. He also suspected that the boss Cucuzza was starting to talk because police failed to parade him in front of the TV cameras as they usually did when they arrested Mafiosi.

Brusca always made a point of staying away from his relatives when he was on the run, but he decided to keep an eye on his brother Enzo, who was so angry about Monticciolo's betrayal that he had sworn to kill him in revenge. Brusca feared that Enzo would do something foolish and get himself

arrested if he let him out of his sight. He made Enzo move
into the villa with his wife and daughter.

After a month and a half at the villa, Brusca worried that he
had stayed there too long. He found another home, this time
in Palermo. The boss had new fake identity papers ready. He
thought of throwing his mobile phone away, but decided to
keep it as he needed to organise the drugs deal. For the same
reason, he stayed on at the villa. He had paid almost all the
two billion lire for the drugs consignment; only 400 million
lire were outstanding. He would wait to receive this sum to
complete the payment, and then move to Palermo.

The technology available at the time was powerless to give
Sabella a precise location for Brusca; all he learnt was that
Brusca was somewhere in an area of one and a half square
miles near the coast outside Agrigento. He tried to pinpoint
Brusca's phone more precisely by asking a mobile phone
operator to switch off nearby relay stations, but this resulted
only in furious protests from locals who were celebrating the
feast of their patron saint that day.

Soon afterwards, the police taped Brusca telling Sottile
that he was about to receive new phonecards from Belgium.
Sabella began to fret. If Brusca used those phonecards, they
would have to make a formal request to the Belgian authorities for permission to continue monitoring his calls – a slow
procedure which had little chance of success. Mindful of
previous missed opportunities, Sabella considered launching
a raid on the entire area with two or three hundred police
officers. But he dismissed the idea, as there was no guarantee
that Brusca would not slip through the net yet again.

The only alternative was old-fashioned surveillance. Sabella
sent some forty officers of the flying squad, both men and
women, to the area. Dressed in a tracksuit, one officer jogged
along the coast. A young female officer sunbathed on a beach.

Two others posed as a couple and enjoyed ice creams as they strolled past the shops. At night, whenever they encountered uniformed police or *carabinieri*, they would hide quickly, even throwing themselves into the ferns by the side of the road, as their presence had to remain secret.

On 16 May, the surveillance began to pay off. An officer reported seeing a little boy playing alone in a field. He was running after a brightly coloured ball. When the boy looked up, the officer had recognised him as Brusca's son Davide – he had been struck by the resemblance with the photographs seized at the earlier hideout. The officer saw the boy run towards a group of villas a few hundred yards from a beach, but was unable to establish which one he had entered.

Sabella felt he had too little to justify launching a raid. He had no idea whether Brusca was hiding in the same house as his girlfriend Rosaria and their son, and he still had no idea which house was Brusca's.

On 19 May 1996, a Sunday, two government ministers from Rome and many leading Sicilian politicians took part in a ceremony at the Norman Palace in Palermo four days ahead of the fourth anniversary of Falcone's murder.

As the politicians paid tribute to the victims of the motorway blast, Sabella and a handful of senior police officers sat pulling on cigarettes a few hundred yards away in the cramped listening room on the third floor of the flying squad's offices. Sabella smoked one Marlboro after another. Arnaldo La Barbera, the Palermo police chief, also smoked without a break, using the cigarette he had just finished to light his next one. Renato Cortese, a senior member of a special police unit dedicated to hunting bosses, puffed nervously on Tuscan cigars.

The air in the room stank so much that one detective from Rome walked out to get some fresh air. But no one else complained. They were listening in on 'The Executioner' who had blown up the victims being commemorated that day; Brusca was talking to the butcher Sottile. The pair chatted for a while. Sabella was one of the few investigators in the room who understood them perfectly. The dialect of his native town, Bivona, was very similar to that of San Giuseppe Jato where Brusca and Sottile came from.

For Sabella, hearing Brusca's voice was 'pure adrenalin, like foreplay with a beautiful woman', as he put it. He abruptly realised that 'Brusca' was no longer a name on a file, and that now he was just a few steps behind his quarry. He was struck by the high pitch of Brusca's voice – almost feminine, he thought – and how arrogant Brusca sounded; he didn't even bother to ask Sottile how he was.

Then Brusca said: 'Bring me a bit of good meat.' The words were not code: Brusca wanted the butcher to bring him a local delicacy, sausages with wild fennel seeds, and some steak.

The two agreed to meet in Agrigento. 'At the usual place,' they said before ending the call.

We've got him, Sabella thought silently to himself. The prosecutor and the police chiefs pored over maps of central Sicily to decide where their surveillance teams would start trailing Sottile. They decided it was too risky to start in his town of San Giuseppe Jato, and chose two spots along roads leading to Agrigento.

But somehow the butcher slipped through unseen. 'He hasn't come by, he hasn't come by,' the surveillance teams kept reporting. For some reason, investigators even lost track of Sottile's mobile phone. When contact was re-established, Sottile was already on his way back from Agrigento, having delivered his provisions. In the listening room, Sabella and his fellow investigators swore colourfully. Sabella cursed one saint after another.

The bells from the nearby cathedral enraged them even more. The faithful were celebrating the first mass by the new

bishop of Palermo and the pealing bells made it difficult to
hear Sottile's conversations. The room stank even more of
cigarette smoke as a result of the bells, because they had to
keep the windows closed.

'What bloody bad luck; it's as if Brusca had heard those
bells,' Sabella muttered.

'Well let's create a noise for him,' an officer said, thinking
aloud.

'That's right, we need to create some kind of noise near him
when he's on the phone, so we can find out precisely where he
is – an ambulance, or a street hawker or something,' Sabella
said.

The investigators thought an officer could pose as a hawker,
or as an ice-cream seller ringing a bell to attract customers. Or they could set off a car's anti-theft alarm. In the end,
the investigators decided an officer would ride a motorcycle
whose silencer had been removed, to make as much noise as
possible whenever Brusca was next on the phone to Sottile.

This time, they were determined, the prey would not slip
away.

Retribution for 'The Executioner'

The next morning, two officers hid at the end of the road which led to the villas near the spot where Brusca's girlfriend and son had been seen. If and when Brusca and Sottile called each other, the officers would ride through the area on the noisy motorcycle wearing crash helmets equipped with small headphones to keep in touch with flying squad headquarters in Palermo.

Some two hundred other officers waited nearby, also in hiding, and ready to rush to whichever villa was identified as Brusca's.

That same morning, Brusca enjoyed a leisurely breakfast in the small garden in front of a villa shaded by eucalyptus trees with his girlfriend and their son, together with his brother and his brother's family. The previous day, Brusca had seen a car drive past his villa with two people in it. He hadn't seen the pair before and had become suspicious, running to his car and following them for a while before deciding they weren't police.

Over breakfast, Brusca and his girlfriend Rosaria talked at length about finding a nursery school for their son in the area. They had decided it would be safest for Brusca if Rosaria stayed behind with the boy when the boss moved to Palermo.

The day went by uneventfully, with Brusca making a few phone calls to ask for the 400 million lire he needed to be brought to him quickly.

*   *   *

The officers on the ground nearby, and Sabella in the law courts in Palermo, had a long wait that day. Brusca and Sottile failed to call each other and Sabella spent most of the day smoking. At 7.30 p.m. he decided to go home because – a little superstitious – he remembered that he'd recently waited in his office for hours for another boss to be captured. He had left finally and got the call telling him the boss had been captured just after he arrived home. Perhaps leaving his office would bring him luck this time too?

Sabella arrived home half an hour later. He took off his jacket and tie and put some water on to boil for some pasta, but then turned the gas off again; he was too nervous to eat. He put the TV on. A trailer for a film about Falcone's assassination flashed up on the screen.

'Is that a good sign?' Sabella asked himself.

The film started shortly afterwards and Sabella watched it, although he couldn't concentrate.

At about 8.40 p.m., Sottile called Brusca. The officers stationed near the villas received the order to set off on their motorcycle. Soon afterwards, the racket made by the motorcycle reached the ears of the listeners at the flying squad in Palermo and Brusca's villa was immediately located.

Like Sabella, Brusca had started to watch the film about Falcone's assassination. The boss then walked outside to call his friend on his mobile phone, and saw a motorcycle pass in front of the villa with two men on it. Brusca became suspicious again; he prided himself on having a photographic memory, and he'd never seen a motorcycle go down his street. As he watched, the motorcycle turned round, came up to the villa, and stopped in front of the gate.

Brusca heard two loud bangs from the motorcycle's apparently faulty silencer. He guessed instantly that this must be a signal to help locate him.

'We've had it!' he shouted to his brother Enzo.

Apparently fearing it might be used against him if it was found, Brusca threw his mobile phone out of a window before racing out of the front door. He had not gone very far when he felt a huge mass of people jump on him – no fewer than fifteen officers had rushed at him. They slapped and punched him, which he thought was understandable. He had killed Falcone, and colleagues of the officers who were overpowering him. But the blows kept coming and Brusca pretended to faint, which calmed his captors down a little. For Brusca, it was the end of four and a half years on the run.

As stun grenades exploded around the villa, the officers stretched Brusca out on the ground on his stomach, and handcuffed him. The same fate befell his brother Enzo. Brusca's terrified son, Davide, ran out into the garden. A couple of officers caught him and took him to his mother.

Moments later, Brusca found himself on the back seat of a Fiat car, flanked on either side by two hooded officers. They insulted him, threatened him and kept pinching him so hard they bruised him. 'You're a bastard, you killed our men . . . You must die in prison. Don't you turn state's evidence or we'll kill you ourselves,' they told him.

The tormenting stopped when the officers' superior, Claudio Sanfilippo, head of the special unit hunting Cosa Nostra bosses, reprimanded them. He then introduced himself to the prisoner.

At home, as he watched the film about Falcone, Sabella couldn't stop thinking about the officers lying in wait for Brusca. It was getting late; the raid had been due to take place between 8 p.m. and 8.30 p.m. 'F—, the raid has failed,' Sabella thought.

Anxious for news, he called the commanding officer on the spot. The officer answered immediately. Sabella heard the sound of explosions, the officer cursing, and then a scream: 'We've got him! We've got him!'

He hung up, sank onto his sofa and started crying 'like a baby'. The screen in front of him displayed a graphic reconstruction of the motorway explosion which Brusca had engineered. Sabella called his bodyguards and within minutes they were rushing back to the law courts, charging down the motorway at 150 m.p.h. As his escort sped on, Sabella thought of Falcone, his wife Francesca and the boy Giuseppe Di Matteo.

Brusca stayed silent for the whole trip to Palermo. When the convoy escorting him reached the outskirts of the city, police officers who had been waiting by the roadside greeted his arrival by firing machine-guns into the air. Brusca's captors made a point of driving him past Falcone's former home, sirens blaring, before reaching police headquarters shortly before midnight where a waiting crowd jeered at him and applauded his captors. As he was lifted bodily and carried into the offices of the flying squad, Brusca noticed, despite his dazed state, that the film about Falcone was showing on a TV set.

Moments later, the relative of a bodyguard who had died with Falcone walked into the office where Brusca was held. The man grabbed a framed photograph of Falcone and Borsellino, and smashed it over Brusca's head, cutting his nose.

Sabella caught his first glimpse of Brusca shortly after midnight. The prosecutor couldn't meet Brusca, because the latter could only see him with a lawyer, but an officer accompanied Sabella to take a look at Brusca, through a door that was left ajar.

Brusca was alone. He sat staring at a wall, looking dazed and exhausted. He was bare-chested, his handcuffed hands clasped on his lap under his huge stomach; the paleness of his bare chest contrasting sharply with his thick black beard. Sabella was disgusted by the sight; his first impression was that Brusca really did look like 'The Pig' – one of his nicknames.

He cursed Brusca soundlessly: 'F— you, you f—ing bastard. Now you just stay there in chains; you'll die in prison. You have to die in prison. I'll make sure you do. You f—ing bastard.' Sabella didn't believe in the death penalty, but he would hardly have cared if Brusca had died in a shoot-out with the cops during that night's raid.

Sabella noticed Brusca's face was covered in cuts and bruises. That made the prosecutor angry, and he reprimanded a senior police officer. The order was given to remove Brusca's handcuffs, but the key was nowhere to be found – someone had thrown it away. The boss's captors were forced to call the fire brigade, which used an electric file to cut through the steel while the officer Sanfilippo splashed water onto Brusca's wrists as the file scorched his skin. After the handcuffs were finally taken off, Brusca had two long scars across his wrists.

In the early hours of the night, Sanfilippo escorted Brusca to the bathroom and allowed him to wash his face. Officers gave Brusca a clean shirt taken from his villa, a pair of trainers which belonged to the police, and a new pair of socks. The cuts to his nose and lips were cleaned up; he was still so stunned that he hadn't noticed blood was still trickling from them.

That night, after consulting Sabella, Sanfilippo and a colleague made a first attempt to persuade Brusca to collaborate. 'Listen, Brusca, let's be clear about this: you're in a hopeless situation. You're going to get an avalanche of life sentences. You're thirty-nine years old and what you're looking at is prison until the end of your days. Decide what you

want to do. The door of the state is open,' the officers told
him.

To their amazement, Brusca replied: 'I'll think about it and
let you know.'

At about 4 a.m., Brusca was led into a cell where he tried to
sleep, using a blanket as a pillow. But officers kept tormenting him, and Sanfilippo had to raise his voice several times to
order them to leave the prisoner alone.

A thousand thoughts went through Brusca's brain as he lay
in the cell: he'd been caught because of that damned mobile
phone; the police must have tinkered with the motorcycle's
catalyst to guide them to him. That night he cursed his mobile
phone, again and again. He agonised over who could have
tipped off the police about his hideout.

He thought about his life in Cosa Nostra, and asked himself:
'What made me do what I did?' He thought of his girlfriend
and his son, and started to worry that they might have been
hurt or killed in the explosions he'd heard at the time of the
arrest.

Later, Brusca became convinced that if his girlfriend and
their son hadn't been at the villa, the police might well have shot
him dead and claimed afterwards that he had died in a gunfight.
The boss also had what he quaintly called 'bad thoughts'. He
toyed with the idea of ordering the murders of all the officers
who had arrested him, but then gave up on the idea.

By his account, his Catholic faith helped him decide against
ordering another massacre. 'It may seem strange, but that's
how it is,' he explained.

Brusca managed to grab only a few hours sleep that night.
As soon as he woke up in the middle of the morning, officers
took his fingerprints and photographed him, before escorting
him into Sanfilippo's office.

The officer and the boss were left alone. Sanfilippo asked Brusca to consider becoming a collaborator. He also asked him about several bosses who were on the run.

To every question, Brusca replied: 'Could be.' But, as he recounted later, he began to think about the possibility of betraying Cosa Nostra.

Brusca interrupted Sanfilippo to ask a question himself. Could he see his son or his girlfriend? To his surprise, the request was granted. His son Davide – who had spent part of the night playing on a police computer – was shown in first, and Brusca sat him on his knees and talked to him. 'It was the most beautiful moment of my life,' Brusca recalled.

Brusca found himself being comforted by his son: 'Daddy, don't worry; Daddy, I'm here.' Davide saw the bruises on his father's face, and asked: 'Daddy, what did these bastards do to you? Did they hurt you?'

Brusca felt so weak and so useless that he could have cried with rage; he felt as if his son was a fifty-year-old reassuring him. His girlfriend Rosaria walked in and the three hugged each other. Soon afterwards, both Brusca's brother Enzo and his mother were shown in too. The boss was given ten minutes with them; ten minutes in which to reveal Davide's existence to his mother. Only Enzo had known about him.

The fact that the police had agreed to let Brusca see his girlfriend and his son so soon after his arrest made a huge impression on him. 'The enemy – the state – had granted his request, and Brusca suddenly discovered that there were things about the enemy that he didn't know. It was a small gesture for the police, but it was enormous for Brusca,' his lawyer Luigi Li Gotti explained.

Later that day, police led Brusca and Enzo outside – gaunt, unshaven and with bruises and scratches on their faces – to drive them to the Ucciardone prison. A small crowd clapped and cheered, shouting 'Monster!' and 'Assassin!' at Brusca.

Enzo stared wildly at the TV cameras and stuck his tongue out – an arrogant but childish gesture.

For Brusca, the reaction of the crowd was strange and humiliating. Its hostility 'massacred me morally . . . Everything I did in Cosa Nostra was in the belief that I was helping the weak and now I was being repaid with applause for the policemen who arrested me . . . I felt as if the world was upside down,' he explained.

On the way to the prison, officers in the convoy kept sounding their horns in triumph. In his car, Brusca thought about his prize victim. 'I killed Giovanni Falcone,' he thought. 'But why did I kill Giovanni Falcone?' He thought about all the times his father had met the godfather Riina behind closed doors, and how shortly after every meeting someone would die, someone would disappear.

'I raised Hell, but what was the point?' he asked himself.

The only weapon found by the officers who searched Brusca's villa was a toy pistol belonging to his son. They found two messages from the godfather Provenzano, which both ended with the words: '*May God help you and protect you.*'

On the first floor of the villa, the officers discovered what Sabella called 'the treasure room' – in one of several bags which had already been packed, perhaps in readiness for a fast departure, was a box containing Brusca's watch collection. Boasting more than fifty models, it was worthy of a fine connoisseur, Sabella thought, and included wrist and pocket watches by Rolex, Cartier, Vacheron Constantin and Baume & Mercier. Some were set with diamonds, others were made of gold and platinum.

Sabella saw the collection as a mark of a genuine passion, but also of something close to a disease. It was as if Brusca had a manic need to measure time, the time that passed between one crime and the next – but only with luxury watches. Sabella ordered all the watches seized. He returned only one, a Rolex, to Brusca because it was a birthday present to his son from the little boy's grandparents.

A few days later, Sabella deliberately neglected to stop a transcript of a phone intercept being leaked by a newspaper; an investigation was still under way, and the document was sub judice and therefore not meant to be available to the public. In the intercept, Brusca's girlfriend Rosaria asked the butcher Sottile to bring 30 million lire in cash because she wanted to spend it on a new collection by the fashion designer Moschino. Sabella was still angry about the luxurious clothes he had seen in Rosaria's wardrobe, and he did nothing to stop the newspaper running the story.

Brusca's secrets

On the fourth anniversary of Falcone's murder, 23 May 1996, members of local anti-Mafia associations – boys and girls from some of the most Mafia-infested neighbourhoods of Palermo, men and women, politicians and judges – marched through the city and stopped outside his home. They then continued on to the law courts.

From the window of his office, Sabella stared down at the crowd. As a rule, the prosecutor avoided commemorations of any kind; they depressed him and he preferred to just get on with his job. But he watched as the demonstrators clapped and cheered his boss Caselli, hailing the arrests his team had made – first and foremost, that of Brusca.

At 5 p.m. that afternoon, a senior guard at the Ucciardone prison called Sabella. 'Sir! The little boy needs some affection!' the guard exclaimed.

Sabella understood immediately – Brusca had decided to collaborate. Only three days after his arrest, 'The Executioner' of Falcone and so many others was ready to betray Cosa Nostra. And he was announcing his decision on the afternoon precisely four years after he had blown up the motorway.

Sabella sank back onto his chair and put his feet up on his desk; he lit a fresh cigarette. He remembered how the sight of Brusca half-naked at police headquarters had made his skin crawl. 'How the f— could I shake hands with him? He's disgusting!' Sabella thought to himself. If Brusca decided to collaborate, the task of questioning him would fall to Sabella.

It was too easy, Sabella reflected. Too easy for Brusca. The boss was one of Cosa Nostra's worst killers, and yet here he was already asking for the benefits that collaborators enjoyed – from a much-reduced prison sentence to protection and a monthly allowance granted by the state. What would Sabella tell the families of Brusca's victims? Didn't someone like Brusca deserve simply to serve a life sentence, to rot away and die? Shouldn't the state seek its own revenge to the very end? Deep down, Sabella didn't want Brusca to collaborate – he wanted to see him given a life sentence, locked up in jail and the key to his cell thrown away.

But then again, Sabella thought, didn't Brusca have the same legal rights as any other citizen – in this case those of a collaborator? And Brusca could guide investigators through the last two decades of Cosa Nostra's history, from the inside and at the top level. How could an investigator throw away such a gift?

But the question that most tormented Sabella was whether he could find the strength to shake Brusca's hand – the hand that had killed Falcone – when the time came to interrogate him. Sabella phoned his colleague Francesco Lo Voi, who had been a close friend of both Falcone and his wife Francesca.

'Franco, I'm shattered. I think that one wants to talk. What the f— do we do?' Sabella asked.

'What would Giovanni do if he was in our shoes?' Lo Voi replied. 'That's the only question we have to ask ourselves. And the answer is obvious: we've got to go ahead!'

To guarantee secrecy, Sabella met Brusca for the first time four days later not in the Ucciardone prison nor in the law courts, but in an office of Palermo's postal service. Guards escorted the boss there in a cramped prison van with tinted windows; the heat of the summer afternoon made Brusca sweat so much that he changed into a fresh shirt, which he had prudently brought with him, before he was led into the room where Sabella and several colleagues awaited him.

Sabella saw that Brusca had slightly trimmed his beard and his hair since his arrest, and then found himself shaking the boss's hand – as did the other investigators present. Brusca's handshake was limp, Sabella noticed. 'Good afternoon, pleased to meet you,' Sabella said mechanically. Brusca said nothing and kept his eyes down.

Sabella was struck by Brusca's manner. Far from appearing nervous or embarrassed as collaborators usually were when they began to testify, Brusca was arrogant and disdainful of the investigators seated opposite him. It was as if the boss felt he was doing the investigators a favour, against his will, Sabella thought.

As with every new collaborator, the priority for Sabella was to find out how the boss he considered to be the head of Cosa Nostra's military wing could help them prevent any impending murders, capture leading fugitives, seize any stocks of weapons, and neutralise any possible 'moles' in the police or the judiciary. But Brusca refused to answer such questions. Instead, he insisted on talking about another collaborator, Balduccio Di Maggio, insisting he had lied in accusing the former prime minister Andreotti of links to Cosa Nostra.

Brusca further irritated Sabella by asking, at the end of the meeting, for the return of the jewellery that had been seized from his girlfriend Rosaria after his arrest. 'Who the hell do you think you are?' Sabella thought. 'You should be in prison for life and have everything you ever owned seized by police, and you're complaining about some jewellery?'

That summer, Brusca again angered Sabella by asking, at the end of a meeting with four prosecutors in Rome's Rebibbia prison: 'But when will I get out?'

Sabella felt like getting up and throwing his chair at Brusca – how dare he ask such a question, when the prosecutors had yet to find out what he was up to?

'Ask me that question in ten years' time,' Sabella's boss Caselli replied. Sabella smiled at the remark.

Brusca had decided to collaborate with the state because he realised that the Cosa Nostra he had worshipped for so many years was nowhere near as powerful as he had believed. 'Brusca realised after the maxi-trial that the godfather Riina was no longer able to help him. He saw that it was "every man for himself" in Cosa Nostra, so where was the power, the omnipotence he'd thought it enjoyed?' his lawyer Li Gotti explained.

Brusca's faith in Cosa Nostra was also badly dented when the collaborator Cancemi testified in court that Riina had threatened to have Brusca eliminated for hatching a plan to deal in drugs, without first seeking his approval, and in another Mafia family's territory. The godfather simply told a henchman: 'Brusca deserves to get killed for doing that.' Riina spared Brusca, but the remark made Brusca 'more angry than if he'd killed me'.

Brusca was shocked that Riina could have made such a threat behind his back, rather than first approach his father, who had cared for the godfather for years when he was in hiding. 'The right thing would have been for Riina to complain to my father, who'd looked after him for so long. Riina's threat meant my father wasn't worth anything anymore,' Brusca protested to his lawyer. Brusca himself had risked his life for Riina, and he felt betrayed.

But initially, at least, Brusca was not the collaborator he claimed to be. Over the next months he lied repeatedly in an attempt to undermine the credibility of other collaborators and save several of his friends from jail. At the same time, to avoid a life sentence for himself, the boss gave investigators genuine evidence which allowed them to arrest several lieutenants of the godfather Provenzano.

It was only when Brusca was unmasked – his brother Enzo had betrayed him – that he finally started to tell Sabella what he wanted to know. Over the next three years, Sabella interrogated him eighty times, and Brusca was eventually granted the status of collaborator – the first boss from the ruling Corleonesi faction to betray Cosa Nostra.

One day, after he had talked for hours to Sabella about strangling victims and dissolving their bodies in acid without a trace of regret, Brusca described how he had killed a group of people – 'we cleaned our shoes a bit', he recalled, comparing the victims to dog excrement. The boss then apologised; he apparently thought the phrase was offensive. But he never apologised for any of the killings.

For years after he first began to collaborate, Brusca's reasoning was that of Cosa Nostra. Again and again he insisted: 'I never killed anyone for personal reasons. Whenever I had a personal problem with someone, I resolved it without resorting to murder. I was a soldier.' His lawyer Li Gotti explained to him that such a statement didn't make him any less guilty in the eyes of judges – to the contrary, it worsened his case – and he stopped saying it.

Two more of Falcone's killers turned state's evidence that summer – Calogero Ganci and Giovan Battista Ferrante, who had both spotted his convoy at Palermo's airport. Falcone's murder was the first crime Calogero Ganci confessed to. He said Cosa Nostra no longer respected values such as respect for the life of women and children, pointing to the 'horrible death' inflicted on the teenage hostage Giuseppe Di Matteo.

'I don't see myself as capable of committing that kind of crime in Cosa Nostra because to carry out a murder like that you need a cruelty that I'm not capable of. That's not me,' he said. His children had been due to join Cosa Nostra soon but he wanted them to have a better future outside its ranks. 'Cosa Nostra means death, obviously,' he remarked.

Collaborators were still only a minority in Cosa Nostra. Asked by Brusca's brother Enzo during one court hearing why he didn't turn state's evidence, the former godfather Riina – who is serving no fewer than thirteen life sentences – snapped: 'I'll be damned if I'll ever do anything like that. It's out of the question.'

Virtually buried alive in a cell of 65 square feet, the elderly Riina had lost none of his disdain when questioned by a prosecutor. 'I'm under no obligation to tell you or anyone else whether I'm a member of Cosa Nostra or whether I'm the boss of bosses or the under-boss of under-bosses. I ask you not to ask me that question, because I look after my interests and you look after yours. You're the prosecutor of Caltanissetta and I'm Salvatore Riina from Corleone,' he said.

But he was more forthcoming about his prison conditions: 'I feel as if people are taking the mickey out of me from morning until night because I've been held in isolation for seventeen years, always in isolation, video cameras in the rooms . . . and I'm supposed to be the godfather . . . video cameras in the cell, in the bathroom. I can't use the bidet, I can't have a shower,' he complained.

Despite such privations, he was unbowed: 'I'm eighty years old . . . At eighty, there's death. Age is age. But as you can't see I'm not at all debilitated . . . I think I'll carry on for another bit.'

On 26 September 1997, after a trial lasting two and a half years which ended with the judges and jury deliberating their verdict for a total of 600 hours, a court in the central Sicilian city of Caltanissetta condemned Brusca to twenty-six years in prison for Falcone's murder, and inflicted another twenty-four life sentences on other Mafiosi. Three years later, an appeal court confirmed the earlier verdict, and handed down another five more life sentences. Because of his collaboration, Brusca escaped a life sentence.

One of Italy's most notorious prisoners, Brusca today lives in solitary confinement in Rome's Rebibbia prison. Alone in a square cell measuring 10x10ft, he cooks his own food in a small kitchenette – for fear of being poisoned and to help pass the time. He spends his monthly state allowance of 250 euros on a strict diet, based on rice rather than pasta, and exercises often. According to one acquaintance, he is neat and tidy with small glasses, and looks like a calm, well-educated accountant. Gone is the paunch which had earned him the nickname 'The Pig'.

Apart from his lawyer, the only visitors he sees are Rosaria, whom he married in prison, and their son Davide, now a teenager. Brusca is allowed an hour a week with his wife and son, who are on the state's witness protection programme. He is also allowed out for brief periods with them every forty-five days. The boss has welcomed loneliness; it helps him to think things out and 'become lucid again'.

Brusca could write only in block capitals before his arrest, but has learnt joined up writing since. He reads widely, and follows criminal cases and trials on the radio. According to his former lawyer Luigi Li Gotti, a frequent visitor, 'Brusca believes he ruined twenty years of his life. He had a sense almost of omnipotence when he was in Cosa Nostra, but when that world collapsed he gradually started to free himself of his Mafioso mentality. Today he's completely detached himself from it.'

Occasionally, Brusca voices an opinion on the state of Italy's battle against Cosa Nostra. In a letter to the Sicilian journalist Saverio Lodato, with whom he wrote his memoirs, Brusca confided: *'Unfortunately, people talk about the mafia only when important people get killed; otherwise the subject doesn't interest anyone. That's been said several times in the past. And I'm sorry that I'm the one who has to repeat it.'*

In 2010, prosecutors launched an investigation into Brusca's assets after police searching the secret home of his wife and son found 188,000 euros in cash hidden under a mattress and in a cavity wall, as well as bank receipts. At a warehouse in Brusca's home town of San Giuseppe Jato, police seized some twenty paintings by modern artists.

Brusca and his wife told prosecutors that the money represented savings accumulated by putting aside the state allowance paid to collaborators and rent from a warehouse they owned.

According to investigators, Brusca also sent threatening letters from his prison cell. To the wife of an associate who refused to hand over earnings from a property in Palermo, Brusca wrote: 'I'll become more of a beast than I've ever been in my life.' He continued: 'I'm ready to get to the bottom of this, whatever it costs, and I'm not talking about legal steps . . . As soon as I can manage it, your husband will be the first person I go to see and then we'll see if he's worthy of a boss . . .'

Brusca begins his memoirs, written in prison, by saying that he wants to describe 'how Giovanni Brusca could have become what he became . . . I thought some people might be interested in finding out how you could become a "monster". Because you *become* a "monster".'

But there is little or no self-analysis in the book: Brusca limits himself to a precise, clinical account of his years in Cosa Nostra. He describes himself as 'a criminal who had been stopped in time; given how things were going, I wouldn't have stopped at anything to keep our organisation alive.' He adds: 'But I'm also a criminal who was stopped very late.'

He speaks only briefly of repentance: 'Everything I've done in my life I've done with strength, conviction and pride. That's my only justification,' he writes. 'I have long asked God for forgiveness. I have never asked for forgiveness from the relatives of the victims because I didn't want to revive their pain.' Testifying in court is his way of seeking their forgiveness.

But years after writing this, according to his lawyer, Brusca requested and obtained meetings with several relatives of victims of the Falcone and Borsellino murders. With the help of members of the clergy, Brusca and these relatives talked at length, in secret; the lawyer Li Gotti declined to identify them. 'Brusca wanted to meet them, to ask for their forgiveness,' was all Li Gotti would say.

'Baldy' chooses between God and Cosa Nostra

Sixteen years after Borsellino's murder, in the summer of 2008, the unconvincing reconstruction put together by the Palermo police was shaken to its foundations by a new collaborator, Gaspare 'Baldy' Spatuzza – who confessed to his role in the killing. Police had had no idea of his involvement.

The Palermo whitewasher with dozens of victims to his name had been arrested a year earlier at a hospital in the city, by a police officer who pretended to be a patient being rushed to the casualty department. When he turned state's evidence, Spatuzza explained he had joined Cosa Nostra because he wanted to avenge his brother, who had been killed when Spatuzza was only eleven. 'If I'd forgiven his killers at the time, I wouldn't have destroyed my life and that of my family,' the boss said years later.

Spatuzza took command of Palermo's Brancaccio clan after the arrests of both its rulers, the brothers Filippo and Giuseppe Graviano. Keen to enforce Cosa Nostra's twisted 'code of honour', he had once burst into the home of a woman student who was pregnant by a married Palermo boss. With several accomplices, Spatuzza forced her to take an abortion drug – supplied by a doctor close to Cosa Nostra – and she lost the baby. The boss's 'honour' was safe.

Spatuzza was serving life sentences for the murder of the priest Father Puglisi – in addition to the 1993 bombings in Milan, Florence and Rome – but he told investigators he had

decided to collaborate for religious reasons after spending
many hours with his prison chaplain. The chaplain prompted
him to study theology and what followed, the convict said,
was 'a beautiful spiritual journey'. Spatuzza explained: 'I
found myself at a crossroads: I had to choose between God
and Cosa Nostra.' He said he chose God.

In Caltanissetta, Spatuzza confessed to the prosecutor Sergio
Lari that he was the one who had stolen the purplish-red Fiat
126 in which the bomb meant for Borsellino had been placed.
He sketched the precise spot in southern Palermo where he
had stolen the car. Spatuzza had carried out the theft on the
orders of his boss Giuseppe Graviano – whom he revered
as 'Mother Nature' in recognition of his power over people's
destinies.

When he was given the order, Spatuzza recalled, 'I thought
straight away of Rocco Chinnici' – Falcone's former boss –
'who'd also been blown up by a Fiat 126 . . . but I didn't yet
know what I was getting involved in.'

He testified that he stole the car with his accomplice Fifetto
Cannella on the night of 8 July, ten days before Borsellino's
murder. There could hardly have been a less auspicious start
to the plot: Cannella took so long fumbling around in the Fiat
that Spatuzza, who had been waiting in another car, went to
see what was the matter.

'What are you doing?' Spatuzza asked.

'I'm having problems breaking the steering lock,' Cannella
replied.

The pair managed to break the lock in the end, but they
were unable to start the engine because Cannella 'had broken
all the wires'. The pair was reduced to pushing the car away.
They then hid it in a lock-up garage.

Shortly afterwards, 'Mother Nature' Graviano fired questions at Spatuzza. Where had he stolen it from? Did it belong

to anyone they knew? Was someone looking for it already? Spatuzza told him the clutch didn't work properly, and that he was sure the car belonged to a woman because women wore heels, and that meant they had difficulty with the clutch pedal. The brakes didn't work properly either, Spatuzza told the boss.

Graviano told him: 'Clean it all up and get rid of all the holy images and also the image of Saint Rosalia' – the patron saint of Palermo which many drivers stuck on their windscreens. Spatuzza did as he was told, burning all the papers he found in the car.

Two days later, Spatuzza moved the car to another lock-up garage and asked a mechanic to repair the brakes. 'I didn't tell him anything else,' Spatuzza related, 'I made him understand that the car belonged to a fugitive and that he mustn't talk.' (When police checked the burnt wreck of the Fiat, they found that the brakes were indeed almost new.)

Later, Spatuzza was given two batteries and a small aerial which were placed in the car. Then Graviano asked him to steal two number plates from two other Fiat 126s, telling him to do so on the morning of Saturday 18 July so that the theft would probably not be reported until the following Monday – the day after the murder.

On the afternoon of Friday 17 July, according to Spatuzza, he and Cannella drove the stolen Fiat 126 to another lock-up garage where it was packed with explosives. The next day, Spatuzza stole the two number plates he had been asked for and handed them over to Graviano – when they met, the boss advised him to spend the next day, Sunday, as far away from Palermo as he could. Police learnt from mobile phone records that Graviano had been in the area of Via d'Amelio at the time of the explosion.

According to the prosecution's reconstruction, Graviano and an accomplice had surveyed Via d'Amelio twice since the

first week of July. The boss had at first thought of renting a
flat there but had then decided to wait for Borsellino, with the
remote-controlled device that would blow up the car bomb, in
a garden behind his mother's flat. On Sunday 18 July, Mafiosi
started to keep watch at 7 a.m.

According to the prosecution, Salvatore Vitale, who was the
manager of a local horse-riding club and a Mafioso close to
Graviano, acted as a lookout for Cosa Nostra from a flat on
the ground floor of the block in which Borsellino's mother
lived. Vitale has already been given a life sentence for playing
a role in the kidnapping of the young Di Matteo, and a ten-
year sentence for Mafia links. According to the collaborator
Fabio Tranchina, Graviano's former driver, the boss blew up
the bomb from where he was hiding behind a wall in a nearby
garden.

Spatuzza insisted that Vincenzo Scarantino, the drug trafficker who had accused himself of ordering the Fiat's theft,
had lied about that and many other aspects of the case. But the
collaborator added that there was some truth to Scarantino's
account – they had both agreed on which car was used as the
car bomb, and that a garage owner and two other Palermo
Mafiosi were involved.

Scarantino had yet to explain how he knew this. But when
he was confronted by Spatuzza, he asked for the meeting
to be halted. Later, Scarantino recanted – again – his original confession, admitting that he had nothing to do with
Borsellino's murder. 'I've always lied,' he said. Two other
suspects who had been accepted as credible by the Supreme
Court also recanted their confessions, claiming they had lied
under police pressure.

For the first time in the history of Italy's fight against Cosa
Nostra, the testimony of a collaborator had shot to pieces an
investigation which had been validated by no fewer than nine

different trials and appeals, and resulted in the conviction of no fewer than forty-seven people.

On the eighteenth anniversary of Borsellino's murder in July 2010, the prosecutor Lari, who had questioned Spatuzza, acknowledged that the first investigation now appeared to be baseless. 'We're trying to establish the reasons for this colossal smokescreen operation. We have to verify whether it was with or without malice,' Lari said.

Lari and his colleagues launched a new investigation, this time into three detectives – all of them experienced investigators with solid reputations – suspected of using threats to obtain false confessions. The detectives' superior, Arnaldo La Barbera, had died of illness a decade after Borsellino's murder. Had La Barbera, prosecutors wondered, felt under so much pressure given the violence of Cosa Nostra's attacks, and the weakness of the state's response, that he had fed Scarantino evidence to bolster his testimony?

Or had La Barbera deliberately derailed the investigation, targeting petty criminals to avoid searching for powerful instigators, who were perhaps at the heart of the Italian state? For some investigators, this theory was bolstered by the discovery that La Barbera had worked with the SISDE secret service in the late 1980s, and by the testimony of several collaborators who spoke of a shadowy organisation, close to the state, that suggested objectives and strategies to Cosa Nostra.

Before he was put in charge of the police investigation into Borsellino's murder, La Barbera had forged himself a reputation as a 'tough cop' for his past shoot-outs with bandits. He had shot dead a bank robber during a chase along canals in Venice when he was based in the city, and in Palermo he also killed one thief and wounded another in the face and lower stomach as, armed only with a toy pistol, they tried to steal his wallet while he was having a facial in a beauty salon.

The strain of the Borsellino investigation had weighed on him, according to Gioacchino Genchi, who was an expert consultant on telecommunications working for prosecutors across Italy. Genchi reported that one night in May 1993, he and La Barbera rowed for hours as Genchi struggled to persuade him not to arrest the phone technician Pietro Scotto, suspected of having tapped the phone belonging to Borsellino's mother. Genchi argued that continuing to monitor Scotto would be far more useful than arresting him.

During the confrontation, La Barbera burst into tears. Genchi said he wept for three hours, telling him repeatedly that promotion for both of them was on the cards. La Barbera overruled Genchi, who was so disgusted by this and the investigation in general that he quit. Two months later, La Barbera was named head of the Rome criminal police.

In October 2011, an appeal court in Catania in eastern Sicily ordered the release of six convicts serving life sentences for Borsellino's death, pending a retrial. They included the Mafioso Salvatore Profeta, brother-in-law of the fake collaborator Scarantino. Scarantino himself and the phone technician Scotto remained in prison, however, because they were still serving other sentences for murder and drug trafficking.

In March 2012, the prosecutor Lari and his colleagues issued arrest warrants for the boss Salvatore Madonia, accused of ordering Borsellino's killing, and three other Mafiosi – the alleged lookout Vitale, Vittorio Tutino, accused of helping to steal the Fiat car which was then packed with explosives, and Calogero Pulci, suspected of giving false testimony. All denied wrongdoing.

For the prosecutor, Borsellino's murder was a 'terrorist' act because Cosa Nostra wanted to create panic among Italians and influence political leaders. The Mafia, the prosecutor argued, carried out the murder earlier than initially planned because Borsellino had found out about negotiations between the *carabiniere* Colonel Mori and the former Palermo mayor Ciancimino. The prosecutor was 'certain' that the Mafia saw Borsellino as objecting to the negotiations, prompting Riina to eliminate him 'as an obstacle to the success of the talks'. But so much remained a mystery to investigators that Lari himself described the arrest warrants as 'a starting point'.

Two decades after the murder of Borsellino and his body-guards, Italian justice had yet to establish once and for all why and how they died. And prosecutors in Caltanissetta are still investigating Falcone's assassination, following Spatuzza's disclosure that explosives used in the murder had been hidden underwater in casks tied to a fishing boat at Porticello, east of Palermo. They are trying to establish who was involved in this. Prosecutors are also seeking to establish who entered Falcone's office at the justice ministry in the days after the murder, when it had been sealed off by police. They believe someone destroyed several files on his computer.

Spatuzza confessed to many murders, including several that were unknown to investigators – a fact which boosted his cred-ibility in their eyes. But one of his crimes was all too familiar to them – the kidnapping of the young Giuseppe Di Matteo. Spatuzza had been one of the Mafiosi posing as police offic-ers who had tricked the boy into following them.

Influenced by his new religious faith, Spatuzza said: 'Even if I didn't kill him ... I'm guilty of the kidnapping and I'll account for that and the boy's death, not only in this life but also tomorrow, when there'll be someone waiting for me.'

Spatuzza was repentant: 'I ask for forgiveness from the family of the little Giuseppe Di Matteo and from all the civil society which we violated and offended. It's a millstone which we will carry for all eternity – we and all our future generations.'

But Giuseppe's mother, Francesca, rejected Spatuzza's

request. 'I refuse to forgive any of my son's assassins,' she said. 'He was an innocent boy who was kidnapped, tortured and abused even after his death. How can I forgive? I hope that all those who took part in the kidnapping and murder of my son will stay in prison for ever, starting with that monster Giovanni Brusca.'

The assassinations of Giovanni Falcone and Paolo Borsellino were 'Italy's September 11' – just as Americans can say where they were at the time of the terrorist attacks of September 2001 in New York and the Washington area, Italians remember where they were at the time of the murders. The prosecutor Luca Tescaroli, who investigated Falcone's murder, has called it 'the most despicable of the ambushes that the history of our country remembers'.

Since the assassinations, 'monsters' like Brusca and hundreds of other Mafiosi have been jailed. The sheer number of arrests is unprecedented – surpassed only by the crackdown launched by the Fascist dictator Benito Mussolini who refused to tolerate the challenge to his totalitarian rule that Cosa Nostra represented.

The wave of arrests culminated in April 2006 with the capture of Riina's successor as godfather, 'The Tractor' Provenzano, in a shack smelling of ricotta cheese and freshly made coffee outside his native Corleone. Few Mafiosi had become as fixated with police surveillance as Provenzano. A decade earlier, Giuffrè had given Provenzano an electronic device to search for detecting hidden bugs and Provenzano carried it in his jacket pocket at all times.

'As soon as he set foot indoors, he would go over the whole room, repeating "all right, all right, all right",' Giuffrè recalled, 'and he'd do the same thing with all our cars. He was increasingly fearful, during this period, and would never get in a car without first sweeping it for bugs with this machine. Honestly, his obsession with this thing was just crazy. And pointless, because even though he told the men hundreds of times, they just didn't take any notice and just carried on talking, and he'd end up shouting, "Would you just stop talking!" '

Despite years of such precautions, police discovered Provenzano's last refuge by tracking a bag containing his laundry. They used hidden video surveillance cameras, phone intercepts and old-fashioned surveillance. Finally, they found Provenzano dressed in loose-fitting, torn jeans and a blue jacket; a white scarf round his neck hid a scar left by a thyroid operation. A saucepan encrusted with remains of boiled chicory was on the stove. A spare set of false teeth lay next to his bed. On a table was a typewriter, some three hundred typed-up *pizzini* messages, many of them folded up and sealed with sticky tape, and a rosary made of wood. Also in the shack were a couple of open Bibles, with passages underlined by the godfather.

The murders of Falcone and Borsellino have also prompted an unprecedented wave of collaborators. This is in great part due to a witness protection programme which Falcone called for in vain during his lifetime – the law creating this programme was, according to Palermo's former chief prosecutor Caselli, 'literally soaked with his blood'.

Today, 284 ex-Mafiosi are part of the state's witness protection programme. The family of San Giuseppe Jato, a clan with a long history within Cosa Nostra and almost unique in its closeness to the godfather 'The Beast' Riina, saw five of its members betray the organisation's law of silence – the four perpetrators of Falcone's murder (Brusca, Di Maggio, Di Matteo and La Barbera) and the soldier Francesco Di Carlo. But the most potent sign of the crisis within Cosa Nostra was the collaboration of Giuseppe Marchese. Marchese was the first collaborator from the ranks of Riina's family, the

Corleonesi – the most powerful, and bloodthirsty, family in
the organisation.

However, in recent years, much of the ground gained against
Cosa Nostra has been lost. The fight against the Mafia has
long ceased to be a priority. This is in part the work of Cosa
Nostra itself, as under Provenzano's rule it abandoned the
strategy of terror which saw so many 'distinguished cadavers' in favour of the so-called 'submarine tactic'. The secret
society continues to make lucrative profits from extortion,
commissions on public works contracts and other criminal
enterprises, but strives to keep a low profile by keeping killings even of Mafiosi to a minimum.

Looking back on the arrests he had engineered – first and
foremost that of Brusca – the prosecutor Sabella has one
regret. 'I feel a bit bitter, because in a way I served as an instru-
ment to defeat a certain kind of Mafia – the most dangerous
one, the killer Mafia, the one that committed murders. But
that played into the hands of another Mafia, the "submarine
Mafia" – the one that mostly didn't kill but went about its
business and forged pacts with parts of the state,' Sabella says.
A string of recent investigations have shown that while one
part of the state arrests Mafiosi, another part – in the form of
corrupt politicians – seals pacts with them in return for votes.

Turning its back on the legacy of Falcone and Borsellino, the
state has gone so far as to discourage many potential collaborators from betraying Cosa Nostra. Under a law approved in
2001, a collaborator must reveal all he knows about the secret
society within six months of agreeing to talk, or face losing the
benefits he is entitled to – which include serving only a quarter of his prison sentence, a rent-free home and a monthly
allowance of a thousand pounds.

For Brusca's ex-lawyer Li Gotti, it would have been
impossible for The Executioner to comply with the new law.

'It takes a long time for a Mafioso like Brusca to free himself of his Mafioso mentality. It's not just a question of revealing things, it's a question of changing completely when you've been soaked in Cosa Nostra for a couple of decades,' Li Gotti said. 'Besides, it would have been physically impossible for Brusca, given he knew so much, to reveal everything within six months as he had to go up and down Italy to testify at dozens of different trials. The point isn't when a collaborator says something, but whether it's true or not,' Li Gotti added.

Fewer collaborators means a longer life on the run for Mafiosi. The boss believed to have succeeded Provenzano as godfather of Cosa Nostra, Matteo 'Diabolik' Messina Denaro – he owes his nickname to a cartoon criminal – has been a fugitive since 1993. Even greedier for luxury than Brusca, the drug trafficker Messina Denaro, from Trapani in western Sicily, spends his dirty money on Versace clothes, Rolex watches and Cristal champagne.

According to Salvatore Grigoli, a collaborator who spent two years helping Messina Denaro stay on the run, the 'boss of bosses' is now hiding in his fiefdom near Trapani. 'I remember he told me to flee to Venezuela; he said to me: "There are friends of the family there. I'd go myself if I didn't have responsibilities here." ' Grigoli said. 'He never left Italy. He never left Sicily. Because that's where those people who protect him are . . . no one will every betray him.'

Prosecutors, judges and police officers alone will never defeat Cosa Nostra. For too long, according to Falcone and Borsellino's friend and colleague Ayala, Italy has delegated the fight against the Mafia to the judiciary and the police alone. 'If we go on like this, we'll never beat the Mafia. Repression is necessary, but it's not enough. You have to teach the new generation a culture of respect for the law and for the state,'

said Ayala, who has toured schools across Sicily to talk about
the Mafia. When he was a child, he recalled, no one had ever
mentioned the Mafia at school. The Mafia will never be beaten
as long as the state remains all too often absent in Sicily, failing to guarantee Sicilians their rights as citizens. The state's
absence prompts Sicilians to turn to the Mafia for 'favours',
from security to a job or even a construction permit.

Ayala is optimistic, however. He hails the hundreds of busi-
nessmen and shopkeepers, especially in Palermo, who have
rebelled against the protection money levied by the Mafia,
known as '*ù pizzu*' after the word for a bird's beak. The
Addiopizzo association, created in 2004, has recruited more
than four hundred members who refuse to pay Cosa Nostra's
tax. Such a protest would have been unthinkable in Falcone
and Borsellino's lifetime – but some 80 per cent of businesses
in the Sicilian capital Palermo still pay the levy. For Ayala,
the two prosecutors' assassinations triggered a movement of
rebellion against Cosa Nostra which has taken solid root over
the years. He quotes the Chilean Nobel-Prize-winning poet
Pablo Neruda: '*You can cut all the flowers but you cannot keep
spring from coming.*'

Falcone himself would agree. Seven months before his
death, he wrote: 'There is no doubt we will have to fight the
Mafia for a long time to come. For a long time, but not for
eternity: because the Mafia is a human phenomenon, and like
all such human phenomena it has a beginning, an evolution,
and will also therefore have an end.'

But in the meantime, he argued, a maxim should be carved
on the chair of every magistrate and police officer: '*We can
always do something.*'

Acknowledgements

My warmest thanks to all those who helped with the research for this book. I would especially like to mention Giuseppe Ayala, Giovanni Bianconi, Renato Cortese, Anna Da Re, Roberto Della Monica, Martino Farneti, Riccardo Guido, Francesco La Licata, Sergio Lari, Luigi Li Gotti, Franco Lo Voi, Valeria Maffei, Colonel Pietro Oresta, Alfonso Sabella, Marco Sannella, Luca Tescaroli and Andrea Vogt.

Many thanks to Clare Alexander, my agent, for stimulating advice through the years. This includes first putting me in touch with Rupert Lancaster, my publisher at Hodder & Stoughton, to whom I am very grateful for championing this and previous books with enthusiasm and wisdom. Many thanks to the rest of the team at Hodder including Jason Bartholomew, Juliet Brightmore, Karen Geary, Tara Gladden, Ben Gutcher, Alice Howe and Kate Miles.

'La famiglia': I've been blessed with a family keen on both books and all things Italian, so thanks indeed to my sisters Martine and Katy, to Antony and to my parents for their constant encouragement. I'll always be hugely grateful to my mother for dropping everything to heavily improve not one but several drafts. And thanks to my wife's parents Giovanna and Antonio for their kindness in welcoming me during long stretches of writing.

Heartfelt thanks to my wife Rita for her ideas – she has herself worked with anti-Mafia associations in her homeland

– patience, and much more, and to our young son Sébastien for always knowing when to knock on the office door.

Picture Acknowledgements

Arma dei Carabinieri: 3 below. Giuseppe Ayala: 4. Nick Cornish: 2 above, 3 above. Olycom: 1, 5, 6, 7, 8. Guido Rossi/ SIPA: 2 below.

Notes on Sources

Prologue: March 1992

Arlacchi, Pino, *Gli uomini del disonore: La mafia siciliana nella vita del grande pentito Antonino Calderone*, Mondadori, 1992.

Bolzoni, Attilio and Giuseppe d'Avanzo, *Il capo dei capi: Vita e carriera criminale di Totò Riina*, Mondadori, 1993.

Caruso, Alfio, *Da cosa nasce cosa: Storia della mafia dal 1943 a oggi*, Longanesi, 2005.

Testimony of Gaspare Mutolo to the anti-Mafia commission of the Rome parliament, February 1993.

1. Plot: 1939–1992
Judge Falcone – Learning to live and think like Mafiosi

Ayala, Giuseppe, *Chi ha paura muore ogni giorno: I miei anni con Falcone e Borsellino*, Mondadori, 2008.

Falcone, Giovanni and Marcelle Padovani, *Men of Honour: The Truth about the Mafia*, Warner, 1993.

Galluzzo, Lucio, Franco Nicastro and Vincenzo Vasile, *Obiettivo Falcone*, Tullio Pironti, 1992.

La Licata, Francesco, *Storia di Giovanni Falcone*, Rizzoli, 1993.

Lodato, Saverio, *'Ho ucciso Giovanni Falcone': La confessione di Giovanni Brusca*, Mondadori, 2006.

Padovani, Marcelle, *Les dernières années de la mafia,* Gallimard, 1987.

Schifani, Rosaria and Felice Cavallaro, *Lettera ai mafiosi: Vi perdono ma inginocchiatevi,* Tullio Pironti, 1992.

Author interview with Giuseppe Ayala.

Falcone and 'The Godfather of Two Worlds'

Biagi, Enzo, *Il Boss è solo: Buscetta, la vera storia di un vero padrino,* Mondadori, 1986.

Buscetta, Tommaso, quoted in *Panorama* magazine, 28.02.93.

Caponnetto, Antonino, *I miei giorni a Palermo: Storie di mafia e di giustizia raccontate a Saverio Lodato,* Garzanti, 1992.

Commissione parlamentare di inchiesta sul fenomeno della Mafia e sulle associazioni criminali similari, Audizione del collaboratore di giustizia Tommaso Buscetta, 16.11.92.

Falcone, Giovanni and Marcelle Padovani, *ibid.*

Galluzzo, Lucio, Francesco La Licata and Saverio Lodato, eds., *Rapporto sulla Mafia degli anni '80,* S.F. Flaccovio, 1986, quoted in Claire Sterling, *The Mafia: The Long Reach of the International Sicilian Mafia,* Grafton, 1991.

Galluzzo, Lucio, *Tommaso Buscetta: L'uomo che tradì se stesso,* Musumeci, 1984, quoted in Sterling, *ibid.*

Grasso, Pietro and Alberto La Volpe, Alberto, *Per non morire di mafia,* Sperling & Kupfer, 2009.

Ingroia, Antonio, *Nel labirinto degli dèi: Storie di mafia e di antimafia,* il Saggiatore, 2010.

La Licata, Francesco, *ibid.*

Linares, *Racconti popolari,* quoted in Cesare Mori, *Con la Mafia ai ferri corti: Le memorie del 'Prefetto di Ferro',* Flavio Pagano, 1993.

Lodato, Saverio and Tommaso Buscetta, *La mafia ha vinto: Intervista con Tommaso Buscetta*, Mondadori, 2007.

Sterling, Claire, *ibid.*

Zingales, Leone, *Giovanni Falcone, un uomo normale*, Aliberti, 2007.

Author interview with Giuseppe Ayala.

Author interview with Francesco Lo Voi.

Giovanni Brusca, 'The Executioner'

Arnone, Giuseppe and Alfonso Galasso, *Mafia: Il processo di Agrigento*, La Zisa, 1988.

Falcone, Giovanni and Marcelle Padovani, *ibid.*

Lodato, Saverio, *'Ho ucciso Giovanni Falcone': La confessione di Giovanni Brusca*, Mondadori, 2006.

Sabella, Alfonso, *Cacciatore di mafiosi*, Mondadori, 2008.

Sterling, Claire, *ibid.*

Death as 'second nature'

Ayala, Giuseppe, *ibid.*

Capaci I grado, Corte di Assise, trial of Pietro Aglieri +40, Caltanissetta, testimony of Giuseppe Ayala on 08.01.96.

Capaci I grado, testimony of Mario Almerighi on 19.12.96.

Capaci I grado, testimony of Liliana Ferraro on 08.01.96.

Caponnetto, Antonino, *I miei giorni a Palermo: Storie di mafia e di giustizia raccontate a Saverio Lodato*, Garzanti, 1992.

Grasso, Pietro and Alberto La Volpe, *ibid.*

Falcone, Giovanni and Marcelle Padovani, *ibid.*

Lodato, Saverio and Tommaso Buscetta, *La mafia ha vinto: Intervista con Tommaso Buscetta*, Mondadori, 2007.

La Licata, Francesco, *ibid.*

Lucentini, Umberto, *Paolo Borsellino*, San Paolo, 2003.

Schifani, Rosaria and Felice Cavallaro, *Lettera ai mafiosi: Vi perdono ma inginocchiatevi*, Tullio Pironti, 1992.
Sterling, Claire, *ibid.*

Author interview with Giuseppe Ayala.
Author interview with Francesco La Licata.
Author interview with Francesco Lo Voi.

Dynamite and 'a walking corpse'

Addaura I grado, testimony of Maria Falcone on 29.11.99 (in Tescaroli, *Perchè fu ucciso Giovanni Falcone*)
Arlacchi, Pino, *Gli uomini del disonore: La mafia siciliana nella vita del grande pentito Antonino Calderone*, Mondadori, 1992.
Ayala, Giuseppe, *ibid.*
Bongiovanni, Giorgio and Lorenzo Baldo, *Gli ultimi giorni di Paolo Borsellino*, Aliberti, 2010.
Capaci I grado, testimony of Mario Almerighi on 19.12.96.
Capaci I grado, testimony of Giovanni Brusca on 27.03.97.
Capaci I grado, testimony of Vito D'Ambrosio on 20.12.96.
Galluzzo, Lucio, Franco Nicastro and Vincenzo Vasile, *Obiettivo Falcone*, Tullio Pironti, 1992.
La Licata, Francesco, *ibid.*
Lodato, Saverio, *'Ho ucciso Giovanni Falcone': La confessione di Giovanni Brusca*, Mondadori, 2006.
Schifani, Rosaria and Felice Cavallaro, *ibid.*
Tescaroli, Luca, *I misteri dell'Addaura … ma fu solo Cosa Nostra?*, Rubbettino, 2001.

Author interview with Francesco La Licata.

'They kill only in Palermo.'

Capaci I grado, testimony of Giuseppe Ayala on 08.01.96.
Capaci I grado, testimony of Liliana Ferraro on 08.01.96.
La Licata, Francesco, *ibid.*
Schifani, Rosaria and Felice Cavallaro, *ibid.*
Stille, Alexander, *Excellent Cadavers: The mafia and the death of the first Italian republic,* Vintage, 1996.
Testimony of Antonino Giuffrè at the Palermo 'Golden Market' assizes trial, 14.05.03, quoted in Clare Longrigg, *Boss of Bosses,* John Murray, 2008.

Author interview with Giuseppe Ayala.
Author interview with Giovanni Falcone.

'From now on, anything can happen.'

Borsellino bis, Corte d'assise di Caltanissetta, Testimony of Antonio Ingroia on 12.11.97.
Capaci I grado, testimony of Giovanni Brusca on 27.03.97, transcript p. 291 (in requisitoria Tescaroli, Part I, Vol III).
Capaci I grado, testimony of Giovanni Brusca on 28.03.97, transcript pp. 25–28 (in requisitoria Tescaroli, Part I, Vol III).
Capaci I grado, testimony of Calogero Ganci, 20.09.96, transcript p. 250 (in requisitoria Tescaroli, Part I, Vol II).
Capaci I grado, testimony of Claudio Martelli on 09.01.96.
Capaci I grado, testimony of Mario Santo Di Matteo on 15.04.96, transcript p.120 (in requisitoria Tescaroli, Part I, Vol I).
Falcone, Giovanni and Marcelle Padovani, *ibid.*
La Licata, Francesco, *ibid.*
Lodato, Saverio, *ibid.*
Lodato, Saverio and Pietro Grasso, *La mafia invisibile: La nuova strategia di Cosa Nostra,* Mondadori, 2001.

Author interview with Giuseppe Ayala.

A drainpipe, explosives and a skateboard

Bianconi, Giovanni and Gaetano Savatteri, *L'attentatuni: Storia di sbirri e mafiosi*, Baldini & Castoldi, 1998.
Capaci I grado, testimony of Giuseppe Ayala on 08.01.96.
Capaci I grado, testimony of Liliana Ferraro on 08.01.96.
Lodato, Saverio, *ibid*.
Schifani, Rosaria and Felice Cavallaro, *ibid*.

A Mafia vigil

Cancemi, Salvatore, *Riina mi fece i nomi di . . . : Confessioni di un ex boss della Cupola a Giorgio Bongiovanni*, Massari, 2002 (in requisitoria Capaci primo grado).
Capaci I grado, testimony of Calogero Ganci on 20.09.96, transcript pp. 209–10 (in requisitoria Tescaroli, Part I, Vol II).
Gruppo Abele, *Dalla mafia allo stato. I pentiti: Analisi e storie*, EGA, 2005.
Lodato, Saverio, *ibid*.

'This is the happiest period of my life.'

Ayala, Giuseppe, *ibid*.
Capaci I grado, testimony of Giuseppe Ayala on 08.01.96.
Capaci I grado, testimony of Francesca Carraturo on 21.09.95.
Capaci I grado, testimony of Vito D'Ambrosio on 20.12.96.
Capaci I grado, testimony of Mario Gralluzzo on 18.09.95.
Capaci I grado, testimony of Tommaso Staffoli on 18.09.95, quoted in Sentenza della Corte d'Assise di Caltanissetta (Aglieri + 36), 26.09.97.
Caponnetto, Antonino, *ibid*.
Ingroia, Antonio, *ibid*.
La Licata, Francesco, *ibid*.

Lodato, Saverio, *ibid.*
Schifani, Rosaria and Felice Cavallaro, *ibid.*

Author interview with Giuseppe Ayala.
Author interview with Francesco La Licata.

2. Ambush: 23 May 1992 – 26 July 1992
'The meat's arrived.'

Bianconi, Giovanni and Gaetano Savatteri, *ibid.*
Capaci I grado, testimony of Salvatore Cancemi on 18.09.96,
    transcript p. 250 (in requisitoria Tescaroli, Part I, Vol I).
Capaci I grado, testimony of Francesca Carraturo on
    21.09.95.
Capaci I grado, testimony of Gaspare Cervello on 19.09.95,
    quoted in Sentenza della Corte d'Assise di Caltanissetta
    (Aglieri +36), 26.09.97.
Capaci I grado, testimony of Giuseppe Costanza on
    19.09.95, quoted in Sentenza della Corte d'Assise di
    Caltanissetta (Aglieri +36), 26.09.97.
Capaci I grado, testimony of Calogero Ganci, 20.09.96 (in
    requisitoria Tescaroli, Part I, Vol II).
Capaci I grado, testimony of Gioacchino La Barbera on
    25.10.96 (in requisitoria Tescaroli, Part I, Vol II).
Schifani, Rosaria and Felice Cavallaro, *ibid.*

'The end of the world.'

Bongiovanni, Giorgio and Lorenzo Baldo, *ibid.*
Capaci I grado, testimony of Giovanni Brusca on 28.03.97
    (in requisitoria Tescaroli, Part I, Vol III).
Capaci I grado, testimony of Paolo Capuzza on 09.10.95,
    quoted in Sentenza della Corte d'Assise di Caltanissetta
    (Aglieri + 36), 26.09.97.

Capaci I grado, testimony of Gaspare Cervello on 19.09.95, quoted in Sentenza della Corte d'Assise di Caltanissetta (Aglieri + 36), 26.09.97.

Capaci I grado, testimony of Angelo Corbo on 19.09.95, quoted in Sentenza della Corte d'Assise di Caltanissetta (Aglieri +36), 26.09.97.

Lodato, Saverio, *ibid.*

Schifani, Rosaria and Felice Cavallaro, *ibid.*

Judge Borsellino loses his 'shield'

Bongiovanni, Giorgio and Lorenzo Baldo, *ibid.*

Caponnetto, Antonino, *ibid.*

Capaci I grado, testimony of Giovanni Brusca on 28.03.97 (in requisitoria Tescaroli, Part I, Vol III).

Capaci I grado, testimony of Carmelo Canale on 22.02.97.

Capaci I grado, testimony of Luigi Favuzza on 08.06.95.

Capaci I grado, testimony of Paolo Procaccianti on 08.06.95.

Ingroia, Antonio, *ibid.*

La Licata, Francesco, *ibid.*

Lo Bianco, Giuseppe and Sandra Rizza, *L'agenda rossa di Paolo Borsellino*, Chiarelettere, 2007.

Lucentini, Umberto, *Paolo Borsellino*, San Paolo, 2003.

Agnese Piraino, quoted in *Corriere della Sera*, 11.11.11.

Schifani, Rosaria and Felice Cavallaro, *ibid.*

A champagne toast

Bolzoni, Attilio and Giuseppe d'Avanzo, *Il capo dei capi: Vita e carriera criminale di Totò Riina*, Mondadori, 1993.

Bongiovanni, Giorgio and Lorenzo Baldo, *ibid.*

Capaci I grado, testimony of Giovann Battista Ferrante, 24.10.96 (in requisitoria Tescaroli, Part I, Vol II).

Commissione parlamentare di inchiesta sul fenomeno della

Mafia e sulle associazioni criminali similari, Audizione del collaboratore di giustizia Leonardo Messina, 4.12.92.

Lucentini, Umberto, *ibid.*

Schifani, Rosaria and Felice Cavallaro, *ibid.*

Author interview with Giuseppe Ayala.

Rosaria Schifani's plea for justice

Ayala, Giuseppe, *ibid.*

Bianconi, Giovanni and Gaetano Savatteri, *ibid.*

Bongiovanni, Giorgio and Lorenzo Baldo, *ibid.*

Capaci I grado, testimony of Salvatore Cancemi on 19.04.96 (in requisitoria Tescaroli, Part I, Vol I).

Caponnetto, Antonino, *ibid.*

Corriere della Sera, 27 May 1992, quoted in Alexander Stille, *Excellent Cadavers: The mafia and the death of the first Italian republic,* Vintage, 1996.

Gruppo Abele, *ibid.*

La Licata, Francesco, *ibid.*

Lodato, Saverio, *ibid.*

Lodato, Saverio and Tommaso Buscetta, *La mafia ha vinto: Intervista con Tommaso Buscetta,* Mondadori, 2007.

Lucentini, Umberto, *ibid.*

Schifani, Rosaria and Felice Cavallaro, *ibid.*

Tescaroli, Luca, *I misteri dell'Addaura ... ma fu solo Cosa Nostra?,* Rubbettino, 2001.

Zingales, Leone, *Giovanni Falcone, un uomo normale,* Aliberti, 2007.

Author interview with Francesco La Licata.

Judge Borsellino's race against time

Judge Salvatore Barresi, quoted in Stille, Alexander, *ibid*.

Borsellino bis, Corte d'assise di Caltanissetta, Testimony of Antonio Ingroia on 12.11.97.

Capaci I grado, testimony of Carmelo Canale on 22.02.97.

Caponnetto, Antonino, *ibid*.

Grasso, Pietro and Alberto La Volpe, *ibid*.

Lo Bianco, Giuseppe and Sandra Rizza, *L'agenda nera*, Chiarelettere, 2010.

Lo Bianco, Giuseppe and Sandra Rizza, *L'agenda rossa di Paolo Borsellino*, Chiarelettere, 2007.

Lucentini, Umberto, *ibid*.

Testimony of Agnese Piraino Leto to Borsellino-ter trial, quoted in Lo Bianco and Rizza, *ibid*.

Author interview with Francesco Lo Voi.

Negotiating with the Mafia

Arlacchi, Pino, *ibid*.

Biondo, Nicola and Sigfrido Ranucci, *Il Patto*, Chiarelettere, 2010.

Ciancimino, Massimo and Francesco La Licata, *Don Vito: The secret life of the mayor of the Corleonesi*, Quercus, 2011.

Ingroia, Antonio, *ibid*.

Lo Bianco, Giuseppe and Sandra Rizza, *L'agenda nera*, Chiarelettere, 2010.

Torrealta, Maurizio, *La trattativa*, BUR Rizzoli, 2010.

'The TNT has come for me.'

Ayala, Giuseppe, *ibid*.

Borsellino bis, Corte d'assise di Caltanissetta, Testimony of Antonio Ingroia on 12.11.97.

Capaci I grado, testimony of Carmelo Canale on 22.02.97.

Capaci I grado, testimony of Liliana Ferraro on 08.01.96.

Ciancimino, Massimo and Francesco La Licata, *ibid.*

Gruppo Abele, *ibid.*

Lampedusa, Giuseppe Tomasi di, *The Leopard*, Harvill, 1992.

Lo Bianco, Giuseppe and Sandra Rizza, *ibid.*

Lo Bianco, Giuseppe and Sandra Rizza, *L'agenda rossa di Paolo Borsellino*, Chiarelettere, 2007.

Lodato, Saverio, *ibid.*

Lucentini, Umberto, *ibid.*

Scafetta, Valeria, *U baruni di Partanna Mondello: Storia di Mutolo Gaspare, mafioso, pentito*, Editori Riuniti, 2003.

Schifani, Rosaria and Felice Cavallaro, *ibid.*

Tescaroli, Luca, *Perchè fu ucciso Giovanni Falcone*, Rubbettino, 2001.

Testimony of Gaspare Mutolo to the anti-Mafia commission of the Rome parliament, February 1993.

Torrealta, Maurizio, *ibid.*

Author interview with Giuseppe Ayala.

Author interview with Francesco Lo Voi.

Sea air and a sleepless siesta

Bongiovanni, Giorgio and Lorenzo Baldo, *ibid.*

Lo Bianco, Giuseppe and Sandra Rizza, *ibid.*

Lucentini, Umberto, *Paolo Borsellino*, *ibid.*

Via d'Amelio

Ayala, Giuseppe, *ibid.*

Caponnetto, Antonino, *ibid.*

Commissione parlamentare di inchiesta sul fenomeno della Mafia e sulle associazioni criminali similari, Audizione del collaboratore di giustizia Antonino Calderone, 11.11.92.

Lodato, Saverio, *ibid.*
Lucentini, Umberto, *ibid.*
Mignosi, Enzo, *Ma i miei colleghi potevano salvarsi,* in
  Corriere della Sera, 18 July 1994.
Schifani, Rosaria and Felice Cavallaro, *ibid.*
Preface by Gian Carlo Caselli, in Nicola Tranfaglia, *Perchè la
  mafia ha vinto,* UTET, 2008.

Author interview with Giuseppe Ayala.

Rita Atria, the Mafiosa in skirts

Ingroia, Antonio, *ibid.*
Madeo, Liliana, *Donne di Mafia,* p. 202, Mondadori, 1994.
Rizza, Sandra, *Una ragazza contro la mafia: Rita Atria,* pp.
  127–8, La Luna, 1993.

3. Hunt: July 1992–2012
Don Vito's 'delicate' mission

Abbate, Lirio and Peter Gomez, *I complici: Tutti gli uomini di
  Bernardo Provenzano da Corleone al parlamento,* Fazi, 2007.
Bianconi, Giovanni and Gaetano Savatteri, *ibid.*
Ciancimino, Massimo and Francesco La Licata, *ibid.*
Lo Bianco, Giuseppe and Sandra Rizza, *L'agenda nera,* pp.
  26–7, Chiarelettere, 2010.
Torrealta, Maurizio, *ibid.*

Giuseppe Marchese betrays the law of silence

Bianconi, Giovanni and Gaetano Savatteri, *ibid.*
Gruppo Abele, *ibid.*
Lodato, Saverio, *ibid.*
Sabella, Alfonso, *ibid.*

Case closed?

Salvatore Cancemi and Mario Santo Di Matteo, quoted
    in Francesco Viviano and Alessandra Ziniti, *I misteri
    dell'agenda rossa*, Aliberti, 2010.
Lo Bianco, Giuseppe and Sandra Rizza, *ibid*.

The hunt for Antonino Gioè's 'den'

Bianconi, Giovanni and Gaetano Savatteri, *ibid*.
Lodato, Saverio, *ibid*.
Torrealta, Maurizio, *ibid*.

The godfather's downfall

Bianconi, Giovanni and Gaetano Savatteri, *ibid*.
Cancemi, Salvatore, *Riina mi fece i nomi di ... : Confessioni di un
    ex boss della Cupola a Giorgio Bongiovanni*, Massari, 2002.
Lodato, Saverio, *ibid*.

The Mafia on tape

Bianconi, Giovanni and Gaetano Savatteri, *ibid*.

Gioè's last letter

Bianconi, Giovanni and Gaetano Savatteri, *ibid*. Also quoted
    by prosecutor Luca Tescaroli in Capaci I grado.
Cancemi, Salvatore, *ibid*. (also requisitoria, Capaci primo
    grado).
Gruppo Abele, *ibid*.
Sabella, Alfonso, *ibid*.

Author interview with Francesco Lo Voi.

A plotter turns collaborator

Capaci I grado, testimony of Mario Santo Di Matteo on
15.04.96 (requisitoria Tescaroli, Part I, Vol I).
*Commissione parlamentare di inchiesta sul fenomeno della
Mafia e sulle associazioni criminali similari, Audizione del
collaboratore di giustizia Gaspare Mutolo*, 09.02.92.
Gomez, Peter and Marco Travaglio, *L'amico degli amici*, RCS,
2005.
Sabella, Alfonso, *ibid.*
Lodato, Saverio, *ibid.*

Author interview with Alfonso Sabella.

On Brusca's trail

Longrigg, Clare, *Boss of Bosses*, John Murray, 2008.
Sabella, Alfonso, *ibid.*

Author interview with Alfonso Sabella.

A Mafia code

Sabella, Alfonso, *ibid.*

Author interview with Alfonso Sabella.

Retribution for 'The Executioner'

Lodato, Saverio, *ibid.*
Sabella, Alfonso, *ibid.*

Author interview with Luigi Li Gotti.
Author interview with Alfonso Sabella.

Brusca's secrets

Capaci I grado, testimony of Calogero Ganci on 20.09.96,
(requisitoria Tescaroli, Part I, Vol II).
Lodato, Saverio, *ibid.*
Sabella, Alfonso, *ibid.*

Author interview with Luigi Li Gotti.
Author interview with Alfonso Sabella.

'Baldy' chooses between God and Coşa Nostra

Interview with Gian Carlo Caselli, in *La Repubblica*,
30.05.10.
Falcone, Giovanni and Marcelle Padovani, *ibid.*
Genchi, Gioacchino, *Il caso Genchi*, Aliberti, 2009.
Lo Bianco, Giuseppe and Sandra Rizza, *L'agenda nera*,
Chiarelettere, 2010.
Testimony of Antonino Giuffrè at trial of Carmelo Umina
and others, Palermo, and arrest warrant in trial of
Bernardo Provenzano and others (Grande Mandamento),
Palermo, quoted in Clare Longrigg, *Boss of Bosses*, John
Murray, 2008.
Testimony of Gaspare Spatuzza to prosecutor Sergio Lari,
quoted in *La Repubblica*, 27.10.11.

Author interview with Luigi Li Gotti.
Author interview with Alfonso Sabella.

Bibliography

Archival sources

General

Sentenza della Corte di Assise di Palermo nei confronti di Francesco Adelfio + 96, Palermo. Appeal court verdict on murders in Palermo 1980s–1990s. 20 November 2003.

Bruno Contrada

Sentenza della Corte di Assise di Appello nei confronti di Bruno Contrada, Palermo. 25 February 2006.

Murder of Salvo Lima

Sentenza di primo grado nei confronti di Salvatore Riina + 31, Palermo. Lower court verdict on murder of Salvo Lima. 15 July 98.

Sentenza della Corte di Cassazione nei confronti di Giuseppe Graviano + 7, Rome. Supreme Court verdict on murder of Salvo Lima. 2 October 2003.

Murder of Giovanni Falcone

Sentenza della Corte di Assise nei confronti di Pietro Aglieri + 40, Caltanissetta. 26 September 1997.

Sentenza della Corte di Assise di Appello, Caltanissetta, 7 April 2000.

Sentenza della Corte di Cassazione nei confronti di Pietro Aglieri + 32, Rome. 18 April 2003.

Murder of Paolo Borsellino

Sentenza della Corte di Assise nei confronti di Vincenzo Scarantino +

3, Caltanissetta. 27 January 1996.

Sentenza della Corte di Assise nei confronti di Salvatore Riina + 17, Caltanissetta. 13 February 1999.

Sentenza della Corte di Assise nei confronti di Mariano Agate + 26, Caltanissetta. 9 December 1999.

Sentenza della Corte di Assise di Appello nei confronti di Mariano Agate + 26, Caltanissetta. 7 February 2002.

Sentenza della Corte di Assise di Appello nei confronti di Salvatore Riina + 16, Caltanissetta. 18 March 2002.

Sentenza della Corte di Cassazione nei confronti di Mariano Agate + 9, Rome. 17 January 2003.

Sentenza della Corte di Cassazione nei confronti di Salvatore Riina + 14, Rome. 12 March 2004.

Baldassare di Maggio

Sentenza della Corte di Assise di Appello nei confronti di Baldassare di Maggio + 18, Palermo. 6 April 2002.

Arrest of Salvatore Riina

Sentenza di primo grado nei confronti di Mario Mori e Sergio de Caprio, Palermo. 20 February 2006.

Bernardo Provenzano

Comunicazione notizia di reato relative all'attività investigative svolta per la cattura del latitante mafioso Bernardo Provenzano, report to prosecutors by the Sezione Catturandi of the Palermo police flying squad. 8 February 2001. (Printed in Enrico Bellavia and Silvana Mazzocchi, *Iddu: La cattura di Bernardo Provenzano*.)

Arresto del latitante Provenzano Bernardo, report to prosecutors by the SCO police unit and the flying squad of the Palermo police. 12 June 2006. (Printed in Bellavia and Mazzocchi, *ibid.*)

Newspapers

Corriere della Sera (Milan)
Giornale di Sicilia (Palermo)
La Repubblica (Rome)

Interviews

Anti-Mafia prosecutors, Palermo:
Antonio Ingroia
Sergio Lari
Guido Lo Forte
Roberto Scarpinato

Anti-Mafia prosecutors, Rome:
Giuseppe Ayala
Pietro Grasso
Alfonso Sabella
Luca Tescaroli

Giovanni Bianconi, *Corriere della Sera*, Rome
Renato Cortese, former member of police Mafia-hunting unit, Rome
Martino Farneti, ballistics expert, Rome
Francesco La Licata, *La Stampa*, Rome
Luigi Li Gotti, lawyer, Rome
Francesco Lo Voi, national member for Italy, Eurojust, The Hague
Valeria Maffei, lawyer, Rome

Testimony by informers

Tommaso Buscetta to Giovanni Falcone and others, July–August 1984, 3 vols. (Copies available at Cambridge University Library.)
Commissione parlamentare di inchiesta sul fenomeno della mafia e sulle associazioni criminali simili, Audizione del collaboratore di giustizia Tommaso Buscetta, 19 November 1992.
Giovanni Brusca, *Deposizione al processo di appello per la strage di Capaci*, Caltanissetta. 16 June 1999, 1 July 1999, 2 July 1999, 3 July 1999.
Salvatore Cancemi, *Deposizione al processo di appello per la strage di Capaci*, Caltanissetta. 22 October 1999.

Books

Abbate, Liro and Peter Gomez, *I complici*. Fazi, 2007.

Alexander, Shana, *The Piazza Connection*. Diana, 1988.

Arlacchi, Pino and Antonino Calderone, *Gli uomini del disonore*. Mondadori, 1992.

Ayala, Giuseppe, *Chi ha paura muore ogni giorno*. Mondadori, 2008.

Bellavia, Enrico and Salvo Palazzolo, *Voglia di mafia*. Carocci, 2004.

Bellavia, Enrico and Silvana Mazzocchi, *Iddu: La cattura di Bernardo Provenzano*. Baldini Castaldi, 2006.

Biagi, Enzo, *Il boss è solo*. Mondadori, 1986.

Bianconi, Giovanni and Gaetano Savatteri, *L'attentatuni: storie di sbirri e mafiosi*. Baldini & Castaldi, 1998.

Biondo, Nicola and Sigfrido Ranucci, *Il patto*. Chiarelettere, 2010.

Bolzoni, Attilio, *Parole d'onore*. Rizzoli, 2008.

Bolzoni, Attilio, and Giuseppe D'Avanzo, *Il capo dei capi*. Mondadori, 1993.

Buongiorno, Pino, *Totò Riina: La sua storia*. Rizzoli, 1993.

Calderoni, Pietro and Gaetano Savatteri, *Voci del verbo mafiare: Aforismi di Cosa Nostra*. Tullio Pironti, 1993.

Camilleri, Andrea, *Voi non sapete*. Mondadori, 2007.

Cancemi, Salvatore, *Riina mi fece i nomi di. . . .* Massari, 2002.

Caponnetto, Antonino. *I miei giorni a Palermo*. Garzanti, 1992.

Caruso, Alfio, *Da cosa nasce cosa*. Longanesi, 2005.

Caruso, Alfio, *Milano ordina, uccidete Borsellino*. Longanesi, 2010.

Caselli, Gian Carlo, *Le due guerre*. Melampo, 2009.

Catania, Enzo and Salvo Sottile, *Totò Riina: Storie segrete, odii e amori del dittatore di Cosa Nostra*. Liber, Milan, 1993.

Cavallaro, Felice and Rosaria Schifani, *Vi perdono, ma inginiocchiatevi*. Tullio Pironti, 1992.

Clare, Horatio, ed., *Sicily: Through Writers' Eyes*. Eland, 2006.

Davis, John H., *Mafia Dynasty: The Rise and Fall of the Gambino Crime Family*. HarperTorch, 1993.

Di Cagno, Giovanni and Gioacchino Natoli, *Cosa nostra ieri, oggi, domani*. Dedalo, 2004.

Dickie, John, *Cosa Nostra: A History of the Sicilian Mafia*. Hodder & Stoughton, 2004.

Dickie, John, *Blood Brotherhoods: The Rise of the Italian Mafias.* Hodder & Stoughton, 2011.

Di Lello, Giuseppe, *Giudici: Cinquant'anni di processi di mafia.* Sellerio, 1994.

Falcone, Giovanni with Marcelle Padovani, *Men of Honour.* Fourth Estate, 1992.

Follain, John, *The Last Godfathers: The Rise and Fall of the Mafia's Most Powerful Family.* Hodder & Stoughton, 2008.

Genchi, Gioacchino, *Il caso Genchi.* Aliberti, 2009.

Giordano, Francesco Paolo and Luca Tescaroli, *Falcone: Inchiesta per una strage.* Rubbettino, 1998.

Gomez, Peter and Marco Travaglio, *L'amico degli amici.* Rizzoli, 2005.

Grasso, Pietro and Francesco La Licata, *Pizzini, veleni e cicoria.* Feltrinelli, 2007.

Grasso, Pietro and Salvatore Lodato, *La mafia invisibile: La nuova strategia di Cosa Nostra.* Mondadori, 2001.

Grasso, Piero and Albero La Volpe, *Per non morire di mafia.* Sperling & Kupfer, 2009.

Gruppo Abele, *Dalla mafia allo stato.* Edizioni Gruppo Abele, 2005.

Hess, Henner, *Mafia.* Laterza, 1973.

IMD, *Catturandi.* Dario Flaccovio, 2009.

IMD, *100% sbirro.* Dario Flaccovio, 2010.

Ingrascì, Ombretta, *Donne d'onore: Storie di mafia al femminile.* Bruno Mondadori, 2007.

La Licata, Francesco, *Storia di Giovanni Falcone.* Feltrinelli, 2002.

Lampedusa, Giuseppe Tommaso di, *The Leopard.* Harvil, 1992.

Lewis, Norman, *The Honoured Society: The Sicilian Mafia Observed.* Eland, 1984.

Lo Bianco, Giuseppe, *L'agenda rossa di Paolo Borsellino.* Chiarelettere, 2007.

Lo Bianco, Giuseppe, *L'agenda nera.* Chiarelettere, 2010.

Lo Bianco, Giuseppe and Sandra Rizza, *Il gioco grande.* Editori Riuniti, 2006.

Lodato, Saverio, *Trent'anni di mafia.* Rizzoli, 2006.

Lodato, Saverio, *La mafia ha vinto: Intervista a Tommaso Buscetta.* Mondadori, 1999.

Lodato, Saverio, *'Ho ucciso Giovanni Falcone': La confessione di Giovanni Brusca.* Mondadori, 1999.

Lodato, Saverio, and Marco Travaglio, *Intoccabili*. Rizzoli, 2005.

Marino, Giuseppe Carlo, *I padrini*. Newton Compton, 2006.

Montanaro, Silvestro and Sandro Ruotolo, eds., *La vera storia d'Italia*. Tullio Pironti, 1995.

Monti, Giommaria, *Falcone e Borsellino*. Editori Riuniti, 2006.

Monticciolo, Giuseppe and Vincenzo Vasile, *Era il figlio di un pentito*. Bompiani, 2007.

Mori, Cesare, *Con la mafia ai ferri corti: Le memorie del prefetto di ferro*. Flavio Pagano, 1993.

Mori, Cesare, *Tra le zagare oltre la foschia*. La Zisa, 1988.

Oliva, Ernesto and Salvo Palazzolo, *Bernardo Provenzano: Il ragioniere di Cosa Nostra*. Rubbettino, 2006.

Olla, Roberto, *Padrini*. Mondadori, 2003.

Padovani, Marcelle, *Les dernières années de la Mafia*. Gallimard, 1987.

Palazzolo, Salvatore, *I pezzi mancanti*. Laterza, 2010.

Palazzolo, Salvatore and Michele Prestipino, *Il codice Provenzano*. Laterza, 2007.

Paoli, Letizia, *Mafia Brotherhoods: Organised Crime, Italian-style*. Oxford University Press US, 2003.

Paternostro, Dino, *I corleonesi: Storia dei golpisti di Cosa Nostra*. Published with *L'Unità*, 2005.

Pironti, Tullio, ed., *La vera storia d'Italia*. Tullio Pironti, 1995.

Rabb, Selwyn, *Five Families: The Rise, Decline and Resurgence of American's Most Powerful Mafia Empires*. Thomas Dunne Books, 2005.

Rizza, Sandra, *Una ragazza contro la mafia: La storia di Rita Atria*. La Luna, 1993.

Sabella, Alfonso, *Cacciatore di mafiosi*. Mondadori, 2008.

Scafetta, Valeria, *U baruni di Partanna Mondello: Storia di Mutolo Gaspare, mafioso, pentito*. Editori Riuniti, 2003.

Sciascia, Leonardo, *A ciascuno il suo*. Einaudi, 1988.

Sciascia, Leonardo, *Candido: Ovvero un sogno fatto in Sicilia*. Einaudi, 1977.

Sciascia, Leonardo, *Il giorno della civetta*. Einaudi, 1972.

Sterling, Claire, *The Mafia: The Long Reach of the International Sicilian Mafia*. Grafton, 1991.

Stille, Alexander, *Excellent Cadavers: The Mafia and the Death of the First Italian Republic*. Vintage, 1996.

Tescaroli, Luca, *I misteri dell'Addaura: ... ma fu solo Cosa Nostra?* Rubbettino, 2001.

Tescaroli, Luca, *Perchè fu ucciso Giovanni Falcone*. Rubbettino, 2001.

Tescaroli, Luca, *Le faide mafiose tra i misteri di Sicilia*. Rubbettino, 2003.

Torrealta, Maurizio, *La trattativa*. Rizzoli, 2010.

Torrealta, Maurizio, *Ultimo, il capitano che arrestò Totò Riina*. Feltrinelli, 1999.

Tranfaglia, Nicola, *La sentenza Andreotti*. Garzanti, 2001.

Ultimo, *La lotta anticrimine: Intelligence e azione*. Laurus Robuffo, 2006.

Violante, Luciano, *Mafia & potere*. L'Unità, 1993.

Vitale, Giusy with Camilla Costanzo, *Ero cosa loro*. Mondadori, 2009.

Zingales, Leone, *Giovanni Falcone, un uomo normale: Conversazione con Anna e Maria Falcone*. Aliberti. 2007.

Zingales, Leone, *Il padrino ultimo atto: Dalla cattura di Provenzano alla nuova mafia*. Aliberti, 2006.

Zingales, Leone, *Provenzano: Il re di Cosa Nostra*. Luigi Pellegrini, 2001.

Zingales, Leone, *Rocco Chinnici: L'inventore del pool antimafia*. Limina, 2006.

Index